EATYMOLOGIES

EATYMOLOGIES

Historical Notes on Culinary Terms

WILLIAM SAYERS

with illustrations by
Clara Jane Timme

ᑭℬ

2015

First published in 2015 by Prospect Books,
26 Parke Road, London SW13 9NG.

BRITISH LIBRARY CATALOGUING IN PUBLICATION DATA:
A catalogue entry of this book is available from the British Library.

Typeset by Tom Jaine.

ISBN 978-1-909248-38-0

Printed and bound by the Gutenberg Press, Malta.

Table of Contents

Starters

A surprising number of English words are still without satisfactory explanations of origin or full accounts of their early history, despite a lively interest, both academic and more general, in that branch of historical linguistics called etymology. To feed the interest and fill the gaps we have, at one end of the spectrum, weighty printed etymological dictionaries for most of the languages of western Europe and the British Isles, and at the other, lively online discussion groups and blogs, where rigorous scholarship is matched by insightful or fanciful speculation on the birth and growth of English and other vocabulary. The several dialects of early English, as well as the emerging literary standard, drew on a wide variety of more or less closely related languages: other Germanic languages and dialects such as Dutch, Low German, Flemish, Old Norse; the Romance languages, particularly French and Italian, and both classical and later Latin; the insular Celtic languages, Welsh, Cornish, Irish, Manx, Scots Gaelic; and a host of others with which English speakers came into contact through trade, pilgrimage, war, and, of course, reading. The search for a word's ultimate origin must never lose sight of this dynamism.

Loans from one language to another are the product of cultures in contact and the resultant hybrid lexical offspring often have unpredictable features. This is the case not least in the sphere of food and food preparation, as when the *Jerusalem artichoke* (*Helianthus tuberosus*) takes it name from an auditory appreciation of the French or Italian word *girasol(e)* ('sunflower, turning with the sun') combined with an implicit comparison of its taste to that of the artichoke, with which the tuberous plant, an import to Europe from North America, has no relation. Yet, as a counter-example, *yogurt* faithfully replicates Turkish *yōghurt*.

Several of the articles and notes of *Eatymologies* have been previously published in academic journals and special-interest publications such as *Petits Propos Culinaires*. With the exception of references to the circumstance of composition of Walter of Bibbesworth's *Treatise*, they are reproduced as originally written, with some few updates in the notes. The project of a retrospective collection was launched by the kind invitation of Tom Jaine of Prospect Books. The book's organization is roughly that of a menu but there are some unconventional or now outdated dishes – *great auk* and *salmagundi* – and there is naturally no effort at comprehensiveness. May the reader take potluck! The book is dedicated to my wife, Edna Edith Sayers, who shares my interests in cultural history, language, lexis, and good cooking – but not always my opinions.

WILLIAM SAYERS

Scullions & drudges

The *Oxford English Dictionary*'s basic definition of the now all but obsolete word *scullion* is 'a domestic servant of the lowest rank in a household who performed the menial offices of the kitchen'.[1] The first written attestation is from the 1480s, which may account for the tentative tone of the proposed etymology: 'Perh. an alteration of F[rench] *souillon* scullion, due to assimilation to scullery'.[2] Before pursuing this tentative French source, we may note that the cross-reference to *scullery* leads to such further interesting words as *squiller*, 'a maker or seller of dishes' and 'a servant having charge of the scullery'. Yet there is no explicit association in the dictionary of *squiller* and *scullion*. We might imagine, from this juxtaposition, that in a large household the former supervised the latter.

The semantics of French *souillon* link it to the verb *souillir* 'to soil, befoul'. It is not found in continental French with the meaning 'kitchen servant', more specifically 'one who washes dishes', until 1530.[3] Early use of *souillon* and related forms such as *souillart, -ard* point more towards slovenliness of personal habit than to kitchen duties that might entail dirty objects or getting dirty oneself. Yet *souillard* (but not *souillon*) is represented in the French of Britain, as documented in one of the French translations of the early thirteenth-century *Ancrene Riwle*: 'si vous soffrez danger de [S]uillard le quistron, le garsçoun le qu qe lave les esqueles en la cusyne'.[4] The antecedent phrasing in the English manuscript tradition that the translator is judged to have followed would have been close to '3ef 3e þolieð danger of Sluri þe cokes cneaue, þe wescheð ant wipeð disches i cuchene'.[5] The future anchoresses are encouraged to suffer gladly the annoyances of the cook's boy, for whom we have three descriptors:

a nickname, *Sluri* in English, *Suillard* in French (perhaps *Grubby* in modern English); the synthetic French term *quistron* and its more analytic English counterpart, *cokes cneaue*; and explanatory phrases in both languages identifying his duties as dish-washing. I return to both *quistron* and *cook's knave* below.

Let us turn from the purported influence of French *souillon* in the formation of *scullion* and pursue the dictionary's other etymological lead, *scullery* and related. Here we find ample Anglo-Norman evidence in the forms *escuieler, esquieler, esquilier, esquillier*, derived from a Late Latin *scutellarius*, which in turn has an origin in *scutela* 'salver'.[6] The term was apparently used of two related household offices: (1) the official in charge of the scullery, as referenced in '… ewer, qi receivera le vesselle de la dit cuissine par endenture de l'esquillere' ('the ewerer [officer in charge of water for washing hands] who will receive the dishware of the above-mentioned kitchen according to the inventory of the squiller')[7] and (2), much lower on the scale of rank, the scullion, as illustrated in the story of Havelock the Dane, early in Geiffrei Gaimar's *Estoire des Engleis*. 'Il iert issi en la meisun Escuieler a un quistrun; Dous vadlez ot qu'il nurriseit' ('There were then in the household a scullion and a cook's boy, two young servants that he [Havelock, here under the name Cuaran] had and of whom he took good care').[8] This Anglo-Norman terminology, *escuieler* and related, then seems the likely antecedent of early Modern English *scullion*, although there remains the problem of explaining the variant suffix, the element that the *OED* sought to link to French *souillon*.

I suggest that Gaimar provides the clue, in his linking of *escuieler* and *quistrun*. We have seen the latter above as *quistron* and the more etymological spelling *cuistron* is also found. The word derives from Late Latin **coquistro* 'cook's boy' (also 'illegitimate child').[9] We have another snapshot of such a lad at work in Walter of Bibbesworth's domestic treatise from about 1275, which gives mock orders to the cook's boy, 'Va t'en, quistroun, ou toun havez Estrere le hagis del postnez'.[10] *Havez* is glossed *fleyschhock* in one manuscript of the work and the verses translate as, 'Off you go, cook's lad, and remove the haggis from the cooking pot with your meat hook'. We then have two menial but essential functions in the medieval British kitchen, the cook's helper, the *cuistron*, and the squiller's assistant, the **sculion*, a form, I contend, that represents Anglo-Norman *(e)scuieler* recast with the diminutive suffix *-on* – a marker of both age and rank – seen in *cuistron*. This said, there does seem to have been semantic interaction between the 'dish' words, *escuel*, etc. and dirtiness, *souille*, in both France and England.[11] Lastly, English *cook's knave* would appear an analytic calque on French *cuistron*, in the absence of any diminutive or derivative of Old English *cōc* (< Latin *coquus*) that would have been formed with native morphological resources.

In a listing from the late sixteenth century, we find a figurative use of *scullion*, now in the company of a new term:

> But after that the Gabaonites had yelded them, the Jewes perceyuinge that they were restrayned by their othe to slee them or cruelly entreate them, they made of the Gabaonites, beinge their confederates, their skullions and drudges; wherwith all mighty god was no thinge contented.[12]

Although Dr Johnson's equation of the lexicographer and drudge is well known,[13] this word too has resisted easy etymological explanation. The *OED* offers as definition 'one employed in mean, servile, or distasteful work; a slave, a hack; a hard toiler' and claims that 'the derivation of this and the associated vb. is obscure … The forms [which include *drugge*, *drug*] and sense would both be satisfied by an OE. n. **drycȝea* "labourer" … or by an OE. vb. **drycȝean* … but of these no actual trace has been found either in OE. or ME.' There is no explicit consideration of a possible French source. Palsgrave's dictionary from 1530 offers a French reflex of *drudge*: 'Drudge, a woman servaunt, *druge, meschine*'.[14] Earlier French does have *druge* with several different meanings (all seemingly derivative of *dru* 'favourite, esteemed, intimate') but none suggestive of menial household duties.[15] Here, as elsewhere, the bilingual Palsgrave may have been none too careful, presenting a word as represented in both English and French.

The Anglo-Norman dialect of French included *drage* (variants *drache, dragge, drake, drasce, drasche, drasge, draise, drasie*) with the meanings 'solid residue, refuse of grapes, herbs etc. after straining; swill, hog's-wash; dredge, mixed grain; mixture' but even though lowly kitchen servants might be considered the 'dregs' of the household, such a figurative use seems unlikely, since the semantic nucleus of *drudge* as noun and verb seems to lie in arduous labour not in the underclass origins of the labourers. To take another tack, the most thorough dictionary of early modern and modern Irish, Dinneen's *Foclóir Gaedhlige agus Béarle – An Irish–English Dictionary*, has an entry for *drugaire*, glossed 'a drudge or slave', citing O'Reilly's *Irish–English Dictionary* from 1874.[16] In the absence of a convincing antecedent in Old or Middle Irish, this might well be a loan from English, plausibly originating in the great houses of Ireland.[17]

An explanation more satisfying than any of the above, one with the added attraction of staying squarely in the context of well-to-do medieval households, is found in the common early medieval Germanic terminology for household officers, where we find *truhtsôzo, truhtsezzo*. This compound designates the seneschal or steward, literally the 'seater of the host' (at dinner in a royal or ducal hall) and is variously glossed *archimagirus, dapifer, discophorus, discum ferens*.[18] It is also found in Latinate form as *drossatus, drossardus*.[19] If, as is plausible, there were a reflex of this term in Old Saxon, it could have been brought to Britain with the invasion. If it was also present in Frankish, it could have entered Gallo-Romance, including the Norman dialect, and thence have moved to Britain and English.[20] The absence of evidence for intermediate stages between a Germanic **truhtsezzo* and the *drudge* of late fifteenth-century English means that this derivation be judged highly speculative. It would entail, in phonological terms, the voicing of the consonants and some compression and, in semantic terms, a process of pejoration, reference shifting from senior to menial servant, a downward movement on the scale on which *squiller* and *scullion* have been situated. We have seen that the terms for senior household officials tend to be neutral, while those at the bottom of a given scale have affective values. In this case the devaluation may have been the result of the introduction or coexistence of other terminology, such as the Germanic antecedent of the very common *seneschal* 'steward, major domo', etymologized as 'old = senior + servant'. More generally, a loan word from another language may be thought to be more susceptible to semantic shift, as it loses its moorings in a cluster of related words, its etymology becomes opaque, folk-etymologizing forces come to bear on it in a new linguistic environment, and so on.

As the ordinances for royal English households indicate, there was an extremely rich terminology for functions and ranks, as well as large numbers of servants – senior officials (household knights), their sergeants, and menials (valets).[21] We have only to think of the personnel resources that would have been associated with the cellar, larder, pantry, buttery, wardrobe, to name only functional areas whose names, like the scullery and kitchen, have continued into modern English. It is noteworthy that this terminology is almost exclusively of medieval French origin. We may tend to associate these functions with real architectural spaces in a royal residence but they also had a more notional identity as areas of responsibility to be managed under the contingent circumstances of royal travel. At the risk of too elaborate a mental exercise, we may imagine a grid: one coordinate would detail various functional areas of a large household, the duties of steward, squiller, and the like; a second would pass through the various ranks, from senior officer to the least of servants engaged in a given area (squiller to scullion, hall steward to kitchen drudge). Far from static, the grid and its terminology would reflect pressures and priorities within the household and the interplay among functional areas, as when *steward* supplants *seneschal* in English or *marshal* moves from the horses and stables to more general military administration.[22]

NOTES

1. This note was originally published as 'Scullions, Cook's Knaves, and Drudges', *Notes & Queries* 56: 4 (2009), 499–502, and is reproduced with the permission of the publisher.
2. *Oxford English Dictionary, s.v. scullion.* Nor does the *Middle English Dictionary* have any entry for a form approximating *scullion* that might clarify the picture offered by the *OED*.
3. *Trésor de la langue française, s.v. souillon.*
4. *The French Text of the Ancrene Riwle,* 276.
5. *Ancrene Wisse,* 143, 6.448–49 and n. See the Hubert edition of the French translation, xiv, for the affiliation of the manuscripts.
6. *Anglo-Norman Dictionary, s.v. escuiler.*
7. *The Ordinances of York,* 'Appendix I, The Household Ordinances of Edward II', in Tout, *The Place of the Reign of Edward II in English History,* 262.
8. Geoffroi Gaimar, *L'Estoire des Engleis,* vv. 151–53.
9. *Französisches etymologisches Wörterbuch,* 2.1160a, *s.v. *coquistro.*
10. Walter of Bibbesworth, *Le Tretiz* (1990), vv. 1035–36. See, for this and subsequent mention of Walter, Andrew Dalby's translation, 2012. On haggis, see further in this volume.
11. *Scullion* is found glossed with Late Latin *calixa* and *lixa* 'dishwasher' (< *calix*).
12. Elyot, *The boke named the governour,* Book 3, Part 4, 151.
13. 'Lexicographer, a writer of dictionaries; a harmless drudge, that busies himself in tracing the original, and detailing the signification of words'; Samuel Johnson, *A Dictionary of the English Language.* On this entry, see William Sayers, 'A Source for Dr. Johnson's Self-Referential Entry *lexicographer*'.
14. Palsgrave, *Lesclarcissement de la langue francoyse,* 215/2.
15. *Dictionnaire de l'ancienne langue française* and *Altfranzösisches Wörterbuch, s.v. druge.*
16. *Foclóir Gaedhlige agus Béarla – An Irish–English Dictionary* and *An Irish–English Dictionary.*
17. The Irish adjective *droch* 'bad' occurs in compounds indicating people of low estate, e.g., *drochduine,* but none points toward kitchen duties. Note, however, Old Irish *drochta* 'vessel, tub', which is, however, not found with an agent suffix; *Dictionary of the Irish Language.*
18. *Althochdeutsches Wörterbuch.*
19. *Mediae latinitatis lexicon minus,* 360; the editor also notes the form *drost* in Belgium, without other specifics.
20. Yet no forms are attested in Old Saxon or Frankish; *Altsächsisches Wörterbuch, Französisches etymologisches Wörterbuch.*
21. See, in addition to Tout, n. 7, Woolgar, *The Great Household in Late Medieval England.* Among more recent studies may be noted Carpenter, 'The Household Rolls of King Henry III of England (1216–72)'; Egan, 'Le mobilier et le décor de la maison médiévale à Londres'; and Tebbit, 'Household Knights and Military Service under the Direction of Edward II'.
22. On a possible source for *steward,* see Sayers, '*Stew, sty* and *steward*' (2013).

Ale

The early medieval literatures of Britain, in English, Anglo-Norman French, Welsh, and Latin, make frequent references to the necessities of life, prime among which food, but always in passing.[1] Something as common as brewing seldom rises to the level of narrative motif or an element of theme. Figurative use of household essentials such as food and clothing is often made in Christian homiletic works, but this offers little insight into process. Utilitarian writings, such as account books, do provide a basic vocabulary for mashing and brewing but these are often paratactic entries, unconnected among themselves. Nonetheless, such documentation often offers the first recorded instance of large blocks of medieval technical vocabulary. But well before the first true cookbooks in vernacular languages of the fourteenth century, British literature does offer a little-utilized source for the vocabulary in French and English of several domestic activities.

In the 1230s the Hertfordshire knight Walter of Bibbesworth composed a *Tretiz* or treatise at the invitation of his acquaintance, Dionisie de Munchensi, mistress of estates stretching across southern England from Kent to Herefordshire. Editor William Rothwell states that the work 'was written in order to provide anglophone landowners in the late thirteenth century with French vocabulary appertaining to the management of their estates in a society where French and Latin, but not yet English, were the accepted languages of record'.[2] The fictional addressee of the tract is, however, not the male landowner but rather the mistress of the house, *mesuer* in Anglo-Norman French, *housewif* as glossed in Middle English. The assumption of the work is that she will be prepared to pass along accurate French vocabulary to her offspring.[3] Walter passes in review such specialized vocabularies as the terminology for the human body, clothing, collective terms for various domesticated and wild animals and their vocalizations, fields and their crops. He then addresses the brewing of ale. His objective is not so much lively description or an explanation of techniques and processes as a simple communication of pertinent vocabulary. In one of the best preserved of the many manuscripts, the columns of rough-and-ready French verse have interlinear English glosses in red ink.[4]

In this essay, the vocabulary of mashing and brewing in the French text and English glosses is the object of a detailed examination. The passage may be considered a lightly narrativized catalogue. One of the rules of this popular medieval sub-genre was that no term be mentioned more than once or twice. Context and the better-known terms then assist us in addressing those more difficult from our often imperfect knowledge of medieval technology. Given Walter's objectives, terminology rather than techniques will have to be our chief concern, although the bilingual nature of the treatise will permit some degree of cross-illumination of the two cultural traditions. The possibility of lexical and/or technical borrowing will be explored, and the origins of the two fairly discrete mashing and brewing vocabularies, Anglo-Norman French and Middle English, will be examined. For example, do all the French terms simply derive from Latin or Late Latin, or did the Franks introduce some Germanic words into Gallo-Romance? Similarly, are the Middle English terms all to be traced to Old English or do some come from Norman French and, at a greater remove, the Old Danish that the Northmen brought to the future Normandy and also to the Danelaw of early medieval Britain? Here, it should be noted that etymology is no sure guide to later meaning. Similarly, new technologies may generate or introduce appropriate new terminology, especially in the event of a technical transfer between cultures. Conversely, an established technical term may persist, even when its original referent has been superseded by new techniques and artifacts, so that the old word wins a new signification. What is the historical depth of medieval British brewing as recoverable from simple lexical evidence?[5]

In the following, the Anglo-Norman text is first given in full, with the interlinear English glosses moved to the right margin (and rendered, for clarity, in italics). Each of Walter's terms will be examined for its meaning, history, and origin.[6] The interface between French terms and English glosses will be addressed. Here, we must recognize that we have no assurance that the glosses are the work of the author of the verses. The verbal component of this vocabulary will be seen to have both general and narrower meanings, specific to brewing. With the exception of the names for the ingredients, the nominal component also tends to reflect the general Anglo-Norman vocabulary. This detailed examination will yield a full English translation of the passage, appended to this article. First, then, Walter's text, which begins with the subheading, 'Now the French for mashing malt and brewing ale'.

Ore le fraunceis pur breser brece e bracer cerveise:
Puis ki desore suffist
Le fraunceis qe vous ai dist,
Ore ferreit bien a saver

Cum l'en deit breser e bracer	*breser*
5 A la manere ke hom fest serveise	
Pur fere nos noces bien a ese.	*kisses*
Allumés, auncele, une frenole.	*a keiex*
Quant averas mangé de kakenole,	*a cake of spices*
En une cuve large e leez	*fat*
10 Cel orge la enfondrez,	*stepe*
E quant il est bien enfondré,	
E le eauwe seit descouelé,	*laden outh*
Mountez dune cele haut soler,	
Si le facez bien baler,	*swepen*
15 E la coucherez vostre blé	
Taunt cum seit bien germee;	*spired*
E de cele houre apeleras	
Breez qe einz blé nomaz,	*malt*
Le breez de vostre mein movez	

20	En mounceus ou est rengez,	*rouwes*
	E puis le portés en une corbail	*lepe*
	Pur enseccher au torrail,	*kulne*
	Car corbail ou corbailloun	
	Vos servirunt tut a foisoun.	
25	Puis serra le brez molu	*grounden*
	E de eauwe chaude bien enbu.	
	Si le lessez descoure ataunt	
	Hors de keverel meintenaunt	*mahissing fate*
	Taunt cum la bresceresce entent	
30	Ki ele eit bersil a talent,	*wort*
	E puis le berzize prendra	*grout*
	De forment ou orge ki ele a,	
	E par le geeste e le berzille berme	*worte*
	Dunt home plus se sutille,	
35	Par dreit dever de bracerye.	
	Mes tut diviser ne sai jeo mie,	
	Mes tut issint de art en art	
	Attirez chescune part	
	Deskes vous eez bone serveise,	
40	Dount home devient si ben a eise	
	Ki les uns en pernent taunt	
	Ke il enyverent meintenant.	
	Serveise fet miracles e merveilles:	
	De une chaundaile deus chaundailes:	
45	Yveresce tent lais home a clerke;	
	Home mesconnu fet aver merke;	
	Yveresce fet hom fort chatoner;	
	Home aroé fet haut juper;	*hose houten*
	Yveresce fet coyfe de bricoun	
50	Rouge teint saunz vermeilloun,	
	E dunt dist home ki par seint Jorge	
	Trop ad il bu grece de orge.	
	A teles li auctour se repose,	
	Car parler veut de autre chose.[7]	

Walter's title for this section plunges us into the problems of polyvalence, homophony and homonymity, contextualized signification, and orthographical variation (from word to word, and from continental French to Anglo-Norman French). Elsewhere in the treatise Walter disambiguates homonyms, e.g., various meanings of *litter* in the context of heating a baking-oven, and even coins pairs of words undocumented elsewhere, in this same instance *pail* for 'chaff' and *paille* for 'straw'.[8] Here *brece* refers to malt and *cerveise* to ale. *Bracer* (Mod. Fr. *brasser*) is the standard term for 'to brew' but Walter appears to create a parallel term *breser* to cover the prior activities of grinding and infusing the malt produced from the germinated barley. Iconic for the multiple origins of brewing terminology is the origin of the very object of such domestic work: *cerveise* or ale. It is unglossed by the author and, unless this is an oversight, we may assume the word to have been well known. It is traced to Gaulish, the Celtic language spoken in pre-Roman Gaul, where a reflex of Celtic *curmi* 'ale' appears in Gallo-Latin as *ceruesia*, whence Old French *cerveise* with other Romance cognates.[9] See below for other key terms from the section title.

Walter provides a few bridging verses back to his previous topic, the dressing of flax and spinning of linen thread, then states that the housewife would do well to master the techniques of *breser* and *bracer* for the brewing of ale. The latter is found in such modern French terms as *brasser* 'to brew' and *brasserie*, originally the site of production, subsequently of consumption. This terminology focuses on the processing of the barley and malt, rather than on the end product, ale. The early French word for malt was *brais* (seen later in Walter's text as *breez*), derived from Latin *braces,* a term taken from Gaulish for a local grain, perhaps some kind of spelt.[10] Walter's *breser* 'to process malt' then reflects *breez* 'malt', while *bracer* points ahead to later forms of the more common term for 'to brew'. The author even glosses Anglo-Norman *breser* with *breser* in Middle English, although the word is not elsewhere attested, *breuen* and variants being the common terms.[11] Walter states that one of the objectives of brewing is to produce ale to enliven wedding feasts. The French term, *noces*, also referred to the wedding ceremony but this is unlikely to have featured food and drink. In Rothwell's edition this is glossed *kisses*. This could prompt thoughts of the kiss exchanged between bride and bridegroom, or of the *osculum*, the symbolic gift to the bride, but the manuscript reading has now been corrected to *ristes, rites* in Modern English.[12] Walter's next couplet (vv. 7–8) presents some problems but, as these are not relevant to brewing, they will not occupy us long. The context here still seems to be that of the wedding feast. *Allumés* are some kind of lighting, whether torches or lamps; *frenole* is similarly a term for a rush-light, as the English gloss *keiex* attests. *Auncele*, and forms we might associate with it, is known only as a term for a young woman (cf. Eng. *ancillary*), a set of scales, and a font or stoup. Let us provisionally accept some large serving vessel filled with fresh ale among the torches and lights as part of the festive atmosphere. The next verse, 'when you will have eaten a spice-cake' is plain enough, and might be associated with both wedding feasts and a thirst for ale.

We then come to the brewing process proper, which begins with malting the grain (vv. 8–20). The barley that will be used for ale-making is to be steeped in water in a large, deep vat. Old French *orge* 'barley' derives in linear fashion from Latin *hordeum*.[13] Its Middle English equivalent, *barli*, is not given. The vat, *cuve*, is not a utensil specific to brewing (< Latin *cupa* 'vat'; Middle English *fat*). Or we should perhaps say that the term is not restricted to malt processing, as is also the case for the verb *enfondrer* 'to sink, submerge', less analytic since less discrete in its meanings than the English gloss *stepe* 'steep'. When the barley has been well steeped, the water is to be removed. Here there may be some tension between French terminology and English gloss. Walter says the water is to be *descouelé*, which we might translate as 'drained off', that is, removed by a natural flow, probably from the bottom. The gloss *laden outh* suggests removal from the top, although such a process cannot have been as effective as drainage. The brewster is then to go to a sunny upper room (*soller*) or loft, the floor of which is to be swept clean. The barley, here called *blé*, which originated as a general term for grain and then came to be used preferentially of wheat,[14] is to be spread (*coucher*) on the floor and left until it germinates (*germee, spired*).[15] As we shall see, the grain was probably laid down in rows or piles, in order to permit access for further treatment. From this point on, the grain is no longer called barley but rather malt (*breez*, see above). Like the other Middle English terminology met to date, *malt* is of native English origin.[16] The mounds of malt should be stirred (*mover*) by hand from time to time. *Mounceus* means 'mounds' but the French verb *rengez* suggests that they were laid out in a grid pattern, hence English *rouwes*, 'rows'.

When the germination process, aided by light and ventilation, is complete, the malt is moved to the next stage of processing (vv. 21–28). It should be carried in a basket, small or large according to circumstances, to be dried. Again, the French and English terms, *corbaill / corbailloun* and *lepe,* are not specific to brewing. Nor is a special term used of curing or drying (*enseccher*). This is effected in an oast or grain-drying kiln. Walter's French term is *torrail.* This term is unrelated to Latin *furnus* or *fornax*, or Old French *four* in the general sense of oven. Nor does it mirror the English gloss *kulne*, which points ahead to Modern English *kiln.*[17] It is to be derived from Latin *torrere* 'to roast' and is then the most specific piece of equipment met thus far.[18] The term was, however, also used of lime-kilns. Walter's account is telescoped, with little reference to time intervals between the processing stages. The optimal time between the drying and use of malt is about three weeks.

The malt is then to be ground (*molu, grounden*).[19] How this may have differed from the regular milling of grain is left unexplained and Walter passes to the next stage, the addition of hot water. This infusion or mashing process is reflected in the French verb *enbeverer* 'to steep, soak', here seen in its reduced past participial form *enbu*. No equivalent English verb is named. Again the malt, now better called mash, is to be drained (*descoure* 'to run off', this too unglossed).

Up to this point, Walter is relatively easy to follow. Yet, the remainder of the passage offers both discontinuities in the brewing process and between the 'French' and 'English' steps, with the English terminology somewhat more specific than the French. A case in point is the *keverel* from which the mash is to be removed. This is a small *cuve* or vat (see above) and the terminology seems not process-specific, but the English gloss is *mahissing fate*, 'mashing vat' (the common modern term is *mash tun*). Mashing in this sense is a common Germanic brewing word and we can only regret the absence of its Anglo-Norman equivalent.[20] The brewster (*bresceresce*) must then determine whether she has sufficient wort.[21] We have seen how barley became malt. Now, just before the boiling and fermentation processes get under way, a new term is introduced. This is designated *bersil* in French and glossed *wort* in English. One verse later, *berzize* seems also used of the wort or *grout*, as it is here glossed.[22] Thus we have two pairs, *bersil/berzize* in Anglo-Norman and *wort/grout* in Middle English.

Bersil and congeners have not attracted the attention of ety-mologists. The word is found only in Walter's treatise and in some medical recipes, also of Anglo-Norman provenance. The explicit glossing in Walter and the pairing with ale in other texts leave no doubt as to meaning. This restricted distribution would argue against an origin in Gaulish, along with *cerveise* and *brais*, ale and malt, while raising the possibility of a loan from Old Norse, the Germanic languages of the Rhineland, even Old English. Its varied phonological contours do not hide its resemblance to known 'barley' words, although even these have a curious distribution, *far* in Latin, *barr* in Old Norse, *bere* in Old English, with no representation in other continental Germanic. A form such as Old Norse *barlog* 'sweet wort' suggests a possible Scandinavian source for *bersil* but the more likely case is of a derivative, with typical Romance suffixation, of French and Norman *brais* 'malt', with the signification 'infused malt'.[23]

Walter's gloss *grout* is of interest since this term (now often written *gruit, grut*) was also used of herb mixtures added to the wort in order to bitter and flavor it, before the widespread use of hops. Here *grout* may reference both the malt and the additive, similarly coarsely ground, the basic meaning of the term.[24] Only at this point (v. 32) does Walter inform us that ale may be brewed of wheat or barley. Old French *forment* (Mod.Fr. *frument*) is used of the former,[25] *orge* of the latter (see the earlier note on *blé*, first grain generally, then wheat). But he offers no specifics as concerns the actual boiling of the wort or brewing. Walter then matches up two more pairs of specialized terms, *geeste* and *berzille* in French, glossed *berme* and *worte* in English. *Geeste* is the yeast that is added to the boiled wort (*berzille*) to initiate the fermentation process. The word *geeste* also appears to have deep historical roots and has been linked with Gaulish **jesta* 'yeast'.[26] Middle English *berme*, as a term for the froth or scum on the surface of fermenting ale and for brewer's yeast, is the development of Old English *beorma*.[27] It is evident that this would have been a yeast that floated on the top of the wort during fermentation and not a bottom yeast. At this point, Walter retreats to a more general statement about brewing that suggests, as does his remark 'But I can't comment on it all' (v. 36), that he had exhausted his technical vocabulary and was not concerned with the end stages of the process, e.g., clarifying the ale, putting it in casks, delivering it to consumers. Instead, Walter admonishes the brewster to complete successfully each of these final steps until she has a good ale.

He concludes with remarks on the effects of excessive drinking – miracles and marvels – none of which has lost its pertinence: sharpened wits, double vision, enhanced appreciation of one's own knowledge, social boldness, quadruped locomotion, loud speech, and finally a red face. Punning on *orge* 'barley' and St George, he concludes by saying that people will say of the drunken man that 'By St George he has drunk too much of the fat (or cream) of the barley'.

This section of Walter's treatise has yielded a modest vocabulary for the processing of malt and the brewing of beer. The Anglo-Norman French lexis is preponderantly of Gallo-Romance origin but some essential terms are traceable to Gaulish. The more limited English vocabulary, on the other hand, is entirely of 'native' origin, supporting conclusions drawn from other evidence that brewing had a long history in Britain before the Conquest. In comparison with Walter's disquisitions on baking and on flax and linen (where he stops short of the actual weaving process), his section on brewing gives a less full appreciation of the processes involved and also a less comfortable fit between French verse and English gloss.[28]

The easy glossing of French by English suggests that brewing in the fourth decade of the thirteenth century did not differ significantly on the two sides of the Channel, although the two vocabularies were discrete. Walter's lightly narrativized catalogue offers the first attestations in continuous prose (as distinct from simple interlinear glossing) of many of the French terms reviewed above. Written Middle English emerged from the shadow of Anglo-French in rather different fashion than did Old French from medieval Latin, but Walter's treatise also offers the first attested use of many of the Middle English words seen here.[29] The *Tretiz*, while scarcely a masterpiece of medieval didactic literature, is nonetheless a worthy, if understudied, forerunner to such later household manuals as the *Mesnagier de Paris* and, as concerns culinary arts, to such cookbooks of the next century as *The Forme of Cury* from cooks at the English royal court and Taillevent's *Viandier*.[30] Taken as a whole, Walter's work also poses important questions, little addressed here, on child-rearing and the social and supervisory networks of the English-speaking mistresses of rural estates in Britain in the last quarter of the thirteenth century.[31] From our perspective, there is also an underlying tension in the work, since, bilingual vocabulary aside, Walter doubtless knew less about the household matters on which he expounds, in particular the final stages of brewing ale, than his nominal addressee.[32]

APPENDIX

Now the French for mashing malt and brewing ale

Since the French that I have told you about will henceforth be sufficient [for dressing flax and spinning linen thread], now it would be good to know how to mash and brew in the process of making ale, as we do to make our wedding feasts enjoyable – with torches, serving bowls, and rush lights – and when you have eaten a spice-cake. In a deep and wide vat steep your barley and when it is well steeped and the water has been drawn off, go up then to that high loft and have it well swept out, and leave your grain spread out on the floor, until it has fully germinated. From that moment on you will call malt what was formerly called grain. Stir the malt in the piles where it is laid out with your hand, and then carry it in a basket in order to dry it in the oast (kiln), for the basket, big or little, will serve you amply. Then the malt is to be ground and well infused with hot water. Then let it drain a while, now outside the mashing vat, until the brewster sees that she has the wort as she wants it. Then she will take this grout, of wheat or barley, that she has, and with the barm and wort (by which people sharpen their wits) [she will carry out] the true duties of brewing. But I am not able to give you a full account. But thus, with one process after the other, complete each stage until you have good ale, which makes people feel so good that some drink so much that they become drunk. Ale produces miracles and marvels, makes two candles out of one. Drunkenness turns a layman into a clerk; it gives an insignificant man a high profile. Drunkenness makes a man crawl; it makes a hoarse man cry aloud. Drunkenness gives you a fool's face, a red complexion without rouge. And this leads people to say that, by Saint George, he has drunk too much of the cream of the barley. With this, the author rests, for he will speak of other matters.

NOTES

1. Originally published as 'Brewing Ale in Walter of Bibbesworth's 13 c. French Treatise for English Housewives', *Studia Etymologica Cracoviensia* 14 (2009), 255–67, and reproduced with the kind permission of the editor.

2. Walter of Bibbesworth, *Tretiz* (1990). This edition, however welcome, is without lexical notes or glossary. In all, sixteen manuscripts of Walter's work have been preserved. Earlier editions include Wright (1909), which reproduces the text from British Library, Arundel 220, ff. 299–305, and Owen (1929), which publishes Cambridge University Library MS Gg.1.1. The Owen edition, with its many shortcomings, is now superseded by Rothwell's edition of the same manuscript.

3. Editors and scholars have questioned Dionisie's competence in French, given her modest origins in a minor landed family. But the two step-children who entered her life after her marriage had illustrious antecedents and were destined to act on a much grander stage than she, so that their need for fluent French was

greater than hers. On these and other matters of the circumstances and date of composition of Walter's *Tretiz*, see the thorough discussion that introduces Andre Dalby's 2012 translation of the work.

4. We must allow for the possibility that the English glosses were not part of Walter's original conception and, however interesting, may reflect a second mind at work. The apparent equivalences must then not necessarily be seen as due to the author.

5. See Unger.

6. Lexicographical notes for Anglo-Norman French words are organized on this pattern: the head-word from *Anglo-Norman Dictionary* (*AND*), where other exemplification is usually found, followed by the Modern French (Mod.Fr.) form; proposed origin in classical Latin (Lat.), Late Latin (LLat.), or other languages, with hypothetical reconstructed forms marked *; reference to other French attestations in Tobler and Lommatzsch's *Altfranzösisches Wörterbuch* (TL); finally, the reference for discussion in *Französisches etymologisches Wörterbuch* (*FEW*). Some few words have also been treated by a work still in progress, *Dictionnaire étymologique de l'ancien français* (*DEAF*). For Walter's Middle English glosses, the pattern is: headword from *Middle English Dictionary* (*MED*), proposed origin in Old English (OE) or Old French (OFr.); finally, Modern English entry in *Oxford English Dictionary* (*OED*), with special reference to the etymological notes attached to entries.

7. Vv. 459–512 in Rothwell's edition (1990).

8. This aspect of Walter's style is studied in Rothwell (1994).

9. *AND, cerveise*; Mod. Fr. *cervoise*; < LLat. *ceruesia* < Gaul. *curmi*; *Dictionnaire de la langue gauloise*, 133; TL, 2.139, *cervoise*, *FEW*, 2.612, *cervesia*.

10. *AND, brais*; Mod. Fr. *brai* ; < LLat. *braces* < Gaul. *bracis*; *Dictionnaire de la langue gauloise*, 85; TL, 1.1115, *brais*; *FEW*, 1.483, *brace*.

11. *MED, breuen* ; < OE *breowan*; *OED, brew.*

12. I am grateful to an anonymous editorial reader of a draft note devoted to this crux for information on the most recent examination of the manuscript.

13. *AND, orge*; Mod.Fr. *orge*; < Lat. *hordeum*, TL, 6.1254, *orge*; *FEW*, 4.234, *hordeum*.

14. *AND, blé*; Mod.Fr. *blé*; < LLat. **blatum*; TL, 1.996, *blé*; *FEW*, 15.1.126, **blad*. Cf. Gaulish *blato-*, *Dictionnaire de la langue gauloise*, 78.

15. Neither verb, *germer* in French, *spiren* in English, is specific to mashing and brewing, and they have clear Latin and Old English antecedents, respectively. On the former, see *DEAF*, G. 5

16. *MED, malt*; < OE *malt*; *OED, malt.*

17. *MED, kilen*; < OE *cylen*; *OED, kiln.*

18. *AND, toraille*; Mod.Fr. *four* (substitution); < Lat. *torrere* 'to roast'; TL, 10.397; *FEW*, 13.2.107, *torrere*.

19. *AND, moudre*; Mod.Fr. *moudre*; < Lat. *molere*; TL, 6.355, *moudre*; *FEW*, 6.3.29, *molere*; *MED, grinden*; < OE *grindan*; *OED, grind.*

20. The terminology seems to have originated in the verbal notion *mashen* 'to mix ground malt and water', yielding the present phrase *mahissing fate* 'mashing vat'.

Mash as a noun is a later development; *MED, mashinge* ; < OE *mascan*; *OED, mash.*

21. *AND, braceresse*; ModFr. *brasseuse*; *MED wort*; < OE *wyrt*; *OED, wort.*

22. *MED, grout*; < OE *grut*; *OED, grout.*

23. *AND bersil* (see also *bersise*); Mod.Fr. *moût* (substitution); < Norman *brais*; TL, 1.935, *bertiz*; *MED, wort*; < OE *wyrt*; *OED, wort.*

24. Richard Unger (pers. comm.).

25. *AND, frument*; Mod.Fr. *froment*; < Lat. *frumentum*; TL, 3.2111, *forment*; *FEW*, 3.828, *frumentum.*

26. *AND, gest*; Mod.Fr. *levure* (substitution); < Gaul. **jesta*; TL, 4.296, *geste*; *FEW*, 5.35, ** jesta*; *DEAF*, G.655. The last-named work would distinguish between a masculine form, loaned from Old English, and feminine forms, loaned from continental Germanic. The former transfer is the less probable.

27. *MED, berme*; < OE *beorma*; *OED, barm.* If there is a distinction between the two Anglo-Norman terms, *bersil* and *bersize* it might be that the latter is used of the wort after the yeast has been added, that is, when the fermentation process has begun. But the English glosses do not follow suit.

28. See the companion pieces to the present article, Sayers, 'Learning French in a Late Thirteenth-Century English Bake-House', and 'Flax and Linen in Walter of Bibbesworth's 13 c. French Treatise for English Housewives'.

29. There is considerable variation among the Bibbesworth manuscripts, so that some few additional brewing terms in both French and English might be gleaned from the study of this largely unpublished material.

30. Walter of Bibbesworth's *Tretiz* was also incorporated in a larger work that is known under the title *Femina.* Here his interlinear English glosses are expanded to full translation or paraphrase of the various French texts. Rothwell (1998) provides a general assessment of this composite and largely unstudied text. He has since published an excellent annotated online edition of one manuscript, *Femina* (2005), which also casts useful light back on Walter's text.

31. While the point is made in this essay that Walter's interest for the history of the French and English terminology of the crafts and trades has largely been ignored, other scholars have seen the treatise as principally a pedagogical work. This prompted Rothwell's squib, 'A Mis-Judged Author and His Mis-Used Text: Walter de Bibbesworth and His "Tretiz"'. For a more recent assessment of Walter's work in the sphere of second-language acquisitions, see Kennedy. The British author's relevance to the history of writing on food preparation is assessed in Hieatt.

32. On medieval didactic poetry generally, see the recent collective volume, *Calliope's Classroom.*

Pigs & whistles

The *Oxford English Dictionary* defines *pigs and whistles* as 'fragments, pieces; odds and ends, trivial things' but goes on to list an idiom with a subtly different shading: *to go to pigs and whistles* 'to fall into ruin or disrepair'. The dictionary adds the qualifier 'now *rare*' and this would seem to apply equally to both usages. The disparity between the domestic animal and the instrument or sound (pigs never being whistled for like dogs) would seem to shore up the meaning of 'odds and ends'. Yet an earlier generation of lexicographers and word enthusiasts, scrutinizing English dialect and technical use, identified the *pig* of the expression as 'a pot, pitcher, jar, or other vessel, usually made of earthenware; a crock'.[1] This, in turn, would provide a justification for the 'fragments' of the definition, always assuming that earthenware had been shattered. Unsurprisingly, *pigs and whistles* has been the object of fanciful etymological speculation. *Pegs* in the sides of a common tankard to mark each drinker's share plus the toast *Wassail!* exemplify such enthusiastic ingenuity.

Joseph Wright's *English Dialect Dictionary*, from almost a century before the *OED* entry, provides a parallel understanding of *to go to pigs and whistles*: 'to go to wrack and ruin'. Yet this example is not to be found in the entry for *whistle* but rather in that for the now-archaic word *wissel*.[2] Judged a cognate with German *Wechsel* 'change, exchange', *wissel* was common as a term meaning 'change' in the form of coins from a monetary transaction. In a figurative use, *to get the wissel of one's groat* meant 'to get retribution'. Wright cites Alexander John Ellis's *On Early English Pronunciation* from 1889 for the period's best understanding of the interplay of ideas: '*Gone to pigs and whistles* means gone to potsherds and small change, pig being the common word for an earthen pot'.[3]

From domestic animals and wind instruments we have now moved to earthen pots and small coins, but has any clarity been gained? The key to understanding the origin of the phrase *pigs and whistles*, and the succession of meanings assigned to it, lies in additional meanings of the word *wissel*. *To wissel words* was 'to talk, exchange words of anger, quarrel'. With time the unfamiliar *wissel* may have been reinterpreted, yielding in North America to the quite new phrasing *weasel word*, 'an equivocating or ambiguous word which takes away the force or meaning of the concept being expressed' (*OED*). More important for present purposes, the meaning 'an office taken in succession' is established for *wrixl*, the Old English antecedent of *wissel*.[4] The word is also related to *vicissitude*, both word and concept, and this may have influenced the later turn toward 'wrack and ruin'. *To wissel* also meant 'to join in paying for drinks'. While we might imagine a tavern bill divided among a number of drinkers, a better sense of *wissel* is perhaps had in the modern expression *to stand a round*.

Attestations of both the expression *pigs and whistles* and the word *wissel* as both verb and noun are found in early Scottish letters, raising the possibility that an original formation, *pigs and wissels*, originated in the north.[5] Since *pig* as 'earthenware pot' seems to have an equivalent in Scots Gaelic *pige, pigean*, it may be wondered whether *pigs and wissels* was not a loan translation from Scots Gaelic. Yet Dwelly, in the laborious fieldwork associated with the compilation of his *Illustrated Gaelic-English Dictionary*, did not recover the phrase. The *OED* would trace *pigean* to English *piggin*, variously 'a small pail, a (wooden) drinking vessel; a scoop or ladle' and thought to be derived in its turn from *pig* (via an earlier *pig-kin*?) in the sense here under consideration.[6] Still the Celtic-looking diminutives of *piggin* and *pigean* give pause.

It is then proposed that *pigs and wissels* were originally the succession of jugs or pitchers of beer or wine paid for in turn by a members of a party of drinkers. *To go to pigs and wissels* would then have been to dissipate one's assets in drink and tavern life. Over time, *wissel* lost its currency and transparency, and folk etymology provided the substitute *whistle*. *Pig* was very nearly lost in the same way and is perhaps so lost to most speakers still using the phrase today.

After *pigs and whistles* had surrendered its original references to tavern life, the two elements of the phrase could be interpreted in their most common meanings, as the name of a domestic animal and a term for a high-pitched sound or the means to its generation. Yet this resolution interacts with elements of a larger word cluster: *whister* was a local variant of *whisper*; at the other end of the sonar spectrum from *whistle* is *whisper*; pigs have *whiskers*, of a sort; something *whisked* away is moved quickly. These and doubtless other associations provided a matrix for a new phrasing: *in a pig's whisper*. It does not figure in the *English Dialect Dictionary* but the *OED* accords it a separate entry, with a first meaning 'a very short space of time, an instant', attested in familiar language from 1780 and used by Dickens in *The Pickwick Papers* in 1837, and a second 'a whisper; a confidential tone of voice', from 1846.[7] The dictionary takes the components of the phrase at face value (*pig* + *whisper*) and, aside perhaps from the tacit assumption that a pig's whisper is a most unlikely acoustic event and thus is as short in duration as rare in occurrence, offers no explanation of the formation. In North American English, however, we instead find, from the mid-nineteenth century, a possibly earlier phrasing, *in a pig's whistle*, meaning not only 'in a very short space of time' but, minus the preposition, also 'a thing of little value or significance'.[8]

While *pigs and whistles* now appears a much less far-fetched collocation than earlier thought, it is of interest that as the name for a public house, *The Pig and Whistle* was never common in England. Dunkling and Wright's *Wordsworth Dictionary of Pub Names* counted only ten pubs by this name in the United Kingdom in the 1980s.[9] More striking, a survey of 17,000 London pub signs from the nineteenth century found not a single instance of *The Pig and Whistle*.[10] Today there is a proliferation of *Pigs 'n Whistles*, the majority a commercial export of Merrie Olde Englande to cultures struggling under the lack of bitter.

The expressions reviewed here show that words and phrases whose origins and early history become obscured by phonetic change, while not being shored up by membership in a word cluster, lose their semantic anchors and thus become *disponibles* for the assignment of new meaning. Animals have always been a ready source of metaphor in popular speech. The combined efforts of folk etymology and references to the natural world then provide clarity in an evolving linguistic situation, often adding a familiar affect. Since *pig* as 'earthen pot' had a variant or homonym in *prig*, it is apposite to cite the development of other meanings of this word, also divorced from its roots: from 'highway robber' it passed to 'dandy' then to a 'fastidious person' and eventually (via familiar terminology for a style of cleric) to a bit of a 'prude'.[11] In the case of *pigs and whistles*, the surreal association of domestic animal and wind instrument resulted, even in the reassignment of meaning, that the phrase and its derivatives were situated at the end of various spectra: low in internal congruity, of little worth, hushed in volume, quick in passing. In conclusion, a modern equivalent of the original *pigs and wissels / whistles* may be proposed: *pints and rounds* – still a programme for wrack and ruin.

NOTES

1. *Oxford English Dictionary*, *s.v. pig*, n.², A.1.b. An earlier form, *piggin*, has been proposed. The terms *sow* and *pig* are also used in the casting of metal. This note was first published as '*Pigs and Whistles*', *American Notes & Queries* 25:2 (2012), 75–77, and is reproduced with the permission of the publisher.
2. *English Dialect Dictionary*, 5.518, *s.v. wissel*.
3. Ellis, *On Early English Pronunciation*, 5.738.
4. *An Anglo-Saxon Dictionary*, *s.v. wrixl*, Llewellyn would trace *wissel* to Dutch. Instances of the metathesized intermediate form *wirstle* (before the loss of *-r-*) are however found in English (*OED*, *s.v. wissel*).
5. For *pigs and whistles*, see Colvil, 'Discoursing of their Pigs and Whistles, And strange experiments of Mussels', II.66, and Keith's harvest poem, *Har'st Rig*: 'For he to pygs and whistles went, And left the land', st. 48; for *wissel*, see the numerous examples in *Dictionary of the Scottish Language*, *s.v. wissel*.
6. *Illustrated Gaelic-English Dictionary*, 721, *s.vv. pige, pigean*.
7. *OED*, *s.v. pig's whisper*. *In a pig's whisker* has also been reported with the same meaning.
8. *OED*, *s.v. pig*, n.².
9. *The Wordsworth Dictionary of Pub Names*.
10. Lillywhite, *London Signs*.
11. Sayers, 'The Etymologies of Some Terms of Disparagement'.

Bread

The medieval literatures of Britain, in English, Anglo-Norman French, Welsh, and Latin, make frequent references to the necessities of life, prime among which food, but always in passing. Something as common as bread seldom rises to the level of narrative motif or an element of theme. Figurative use of household essentials such as food and clothing is often made in Christian homiletic works, but this offers little insight into process. Utilitarian writings, such as account books, do provide a basic vocabulary for milling and baking, but these are often paratactic entries, unconnected among themselves. Nonetheless, such documentation often offers the first recorded instance of large blocks of medieval technical vocabulary. But well before the first true cookery books in vernacular languages of the fourteenth century, British literature does offer a little-utilized source for the vocabulary in French and English of several domestic activities.

In 1234 or 1235, Walter of Bibbesworth composed a treatise at the instigation of his Hertfordshire friend and possibly neighbour Dionisie de Munchensi, whose marriage had brought numerous estates across southern England under her domestic sway. Editor William Rothwell states that the work 'was written in order to provide anglophone landowners in the late thirteenth-century with French vocabulary appertaining to the management of their estates in a society where French and Latin, but not yet English, were the accepted languages of record.'[1] The fictional addressee of the tract is, however, not the male landowner but rather the mistress of the house, *mesuer* in Anglo-Norman French, *housewif* as glossed in Middle English. The assumption of the work is that she will be prepared to pass along accurate French vocabulary to her offspring. Walter passes in review such specialized vocabularies as the terminology for the human body, clothing, collective terms for various domesticated and wild animals and their vocalizations, fields and their crops. He then addresses the milling of grain and baking of bread. His objective is not so much lively description or an explanation of techniques and processes as a simple communication of pertinent vocabulary. In one of the best-preserved of the many manuscripts, the columns of French verse have interlinear English glosses in red ink.

In this essay, the vocabulary of milling and baking in the French text and English glosses is the object of a detailed examination. The passage may be considered a lightly narrativized catalogue, with digressions to discuss homonyms.[2] One of the rules of this popular medieval sub-genre was that no term be mentioned more than once or twice. Context and the better-known terms then assist us in addressing those more difficult from our often imperfect knowledge of medieval technology. Given Walter's objectives, terminology rather than techniques will have to be our chief concern, although the bilingual nature of the treatise will permit some degree of cross-illumination of the two cultural traditions. The possibility of lexical and/or technical borrowing will be explored, and the origins of the two fairly discrete milling and baking vocabularies, Anglo-Norman French and Middle English, will be examined. For example, do all the French terms simply derive from Latin or Late Latin, or did the Franks introduce some Germanic words into Gallo-Romance? Similarly, are the Middle English terms all to be traced to Old English or do some come from Norman French and, at a greater remove, the Old Danish that the Northmen brought to the future Normandy and also to the Danelaw of early medieval Britain? Here, it should be noted that etymology is no sure guide to later meaning. Similarly, new technologies may generate or introduce appropriate new terminology, especially in the event of a technical transfer between cultures. Conversely, an established technical term may persist, even when its original referent has been superseded by new techniques and artifacts, so that the old word wins a new signification. What is the historical depth of medieval British bread production as recoverable from simple lexical evidence?

In the following, the Anglo-Norman text is first given in full, with the interlinear English glosses moved to the right margin. This is immediately followed by an English translation, for ready comparison. The translator's choices are defended in the following paragraphs in which each of Walter's terms is examined for its meaning, history, and origin.[3] The interface between French terms and English glosses is addressed. The verbal component of this vocabulary will be seen generally to have both general and narrower meanings, specific to harvesting, milling, and baking, e.g. *knead*. The nominal component tends rather to have parallel meanings, e.g. French *rastel* designating rakes of different kinds, here an oven-rake. First, then, Walter's text, which begins with the subheading 'Now the French for baking your bread in the oven'.

	Ore pur pestre vostre pain au fourn le fraunceis:		
	Quant vostre ble est ben batu,		
	Puis ventez e puis molu,	*windewith*	*grounden*
	Mes pur plus parfitement		
	Parler devaunt bone gent		
5	Il ad suffler, venter e corneer		
	Dunt la resoun fet a saver:		
	Le fu suffle li quistroun		
	E le vent vente parmi le busschoun,		
	Mes venour proprement corneie		
10	Quant chace prent de pure preihe.		
	Mes par le moudre devint farin	*grist*	*mele*
	Ceo qi en greine fust huy matyn		
	E de farine ja deveint flour		
	Par le bulenge le pestour;		
15	Car par le bulenge est severe	*bolting cloth*	
	La flour en fourfre einz demoré.	*branne*	
	A vos chivaus le fourfre donez.		
	Eauwe teve a la flour medlez		

	E vostre paste ensint pestrez		
20	E de un rastuer la auge moundez.	*ribbe*	*trohw*
	Mes il i ad raster e rastuer	*rake*	*ribbe*
	Ki servent de diverse mester.		
	Li pestour ad en mein la rastel,		
	Mes li rastuer fest li auge bel;	*ribbe*	*trohw*
25	Car quant le paste a auge aerd,		
	Li rastuer de ceo lur cert,		
	E tant cum feins sunt en prés		
	Est li rastel sovent manez.		
	Eschauffez le fourn de feugere		*feron*
30	Pur defaute de littere.		
	Littere e littere sunt divers,		
	Discordaunt dient ces clers.		
	Li faucheour littere fauche;	*the mouwer*	*mouweth*
	Pur eise en littere hom chivauche.		
35	Littere proprement sanz faille		
	En pure fauncés dist hom 'paile'.		
	Pail e paille sunt nomez		*chaf stre*
	Quant du greine sunt severez,		
	E si paile ne seit pas,		
40	Pernez dunc le pesaz.		*pese stre*
	E quant le forn est bien chauffé,		
	Du pel seit le past entré.[4]		

Now the French for baking your bread in the oven:
When your wheat is well threshed, then winnowed (*ventez*) and then ground – but to speak more correctly before fine folk there are [the verbs] *suffler*, *venter* and *corneer* whose signification should be known. The kitchen boy blows on (*suffle*) the fire and the wind blows (*vente*) in the bushes, but the huntsman properly blows his horn (*corneie*), when he gives chase to his true prey. But, through grinding, what was grain this morning becomes meal, and from meal is turned into fine flour by the baker's bolting cloth. For the flour that would otherwise be left mixed in with the bran is separated by means of the bolting

cloth. Give the bran to your horses. Mix warm water into the flour and then knead your dough, and clean out the kneading trough with a scraper. But there is both an oven rake (*raster*) and a scraper (*rastuer*), which serve different purposes. The baker has the rake in his hand but the scraper cleans out the kneading-trough, for when the dough sticks to the trough, the scraper serves to remedy this. And the rake is often handled just as with hay in the meadows. Heat the oven with fern, if litter (straw) is lacking. But one litter differs from another; having 'discrete meanings' as the schoolmen say. The mower cuts litter with his sickle and for comfort some people travel in litters. In good French, however, the real 'litter' is called *paile* (straw). They are called chaff (*pail*) and straw (*paille*), when they are separated from the grain. And if there isn't any straw handy, then take some pease straw. And when the oven is well heated, the dough is slid in with the peel.

Walter's title for this section plunges us into the problems of polyvalence, homophony and homonymity, contextualized signification, and orthographical variation (from word to word, and from continental French to Anglo-Norman French). *Pestre* here would seem unquestionably to mean 'to bake' but a later use will suggest a somewhat different, or alternate semantic focus. Fuller discussion is deferred to that point. The Old French *pain* of the section title is a direct descendant of Latin *panis* 'bread'.[5] *Fourn* 'oven' is similarly a direct reflection of Latin *furnus* 'oven, bakehouse'.[6]

Walter's first concern is the terminology of harvesting (vv. 1–10). *Ble* was a generic term for cereals but came to be used preferentially for 'wheat', the most prized grain for bread-making. It is traced to a hypothetical Late Latin **blatum* with the same meanings.[7] The wheat is first threshed (*batu* < *batre* 'to beat'), the common French verb here taking on a narrower meaning. The grain must then be winnowed. Tossing the threshed wheat in the air permits the wind to carry off the chaff. The verb *venter* is related to *vent* 'wind' and is the occasion of the first English gloss, *windewith* and is also Walter's first digression to warn against the incorrect use of homonyms, which would mar the quality of one's French spoken in the company of fine folk (*bone gent*). *Venter* is the evolved form of a Late Latin **ventare*, just as English *windewith* is the past participle of the Middle English verb *windwen* 'to expose to the wind, winnow' (< Old English *windwian*). Walter isolates three kinds of blowing. The scullion or kitchen-boy blows (*sufle*) on the fire; the wind blows (*vente*) among the bushes; and the hunter blows his horn (*corneie*) when he sights and gives chase to his prey. Here, we may pause only over *quistroun* (var. *cuistron*), another word with a Late rather than Classical Latin origin, **coquistro* 'cook's boy'.

Now to milling (vv. 11–17). Through grinding (*le moudre*, the infinitive used as a noun), the grist or, as Walter has it, 'that which was grain in the morning' becomes meal (*farin*, glossed *mele* in English < OE *melu, meolo*).[8] The grist is identified by this very word in English (< OE *grist*)[9] but Old French appears not to have had a discrete term for 'grain to be ground'. Anglo-Norman *greine* is traced to Latin *granum*.[10] *Moudre* is derived from Latin *molere* 'to grind'.[11] In a common kind of figurative use, the French word for 'flower' or 'bloom' (*flor, flur*) was used of the finest quality meal.[12] The image, perhaps with attenuated valence, was borrowed into English as *flour*, while Modern French retains *farine*, while also having such expressions as *fleur de farine* 'fine wheaten flour'. But for the best flour to be recovered from the coarser meal, it must be sifted.

This is effected 'par le bulenge le pestour' (v. 23). Here we enter a complicated and disputed area. *Pestour* derives from Lat. *pistor*, which originally referenced the grinder of meal and then, in an instance of semantic progression, the tradesman who further processed the product, i.e. the baker.[13] The separation of the meal is carried out with the bolting cloth, an open-meshed fabric that permitted the finer ground matter to pass through, while the bran was retained. Walter's term is *bulenge* and it is pointedly identified (in one and the same verse) as part of the equipment of the baker (*le pestour*, v. 14).[14] The Modern French term for a baker of bread is *boulanger*, which displaced *pestour* (among other terms).[15] Is the *boulanger* being characterized by a piece of equipment, just as the *pistor* of late Antiquity was characterized by the grinding process, in a kind of metonym where one part of the process stands for the whole? Although not a term employed by Walter of Bibbesworth, *boulanger* is a word so fundamental to French lexis that a slight expansion of our discussion is warranted. The word is attested in Latinized form (*bolengarius*) from north-western France as early as about 1100. Other Picard texts display similar forms and the vernacular reflex *bolengier* is first noted from about 1170. Authoritative lexicographical works derive the term from Old Picard *boulenc* 'one who makes round loaves of bread'. The agent suffix *-enc* would here derive from the Germanic ending *-ing*. The proposed source is an Old Low Franconian or Frankish **bolla* 'round loaf'. The baker is then a 'round-loaf-ing-er'. Cognates of the root element in Germanic languages are Middle Dutch *bolle* 'round loaf', Old High German *bolla*, glossed as fine cereal flour, Middle High German *bolle* 'rests of flour' and bakery products made of it, and, at somewhat greater remove, Latin *pollen* 'fine flour'.[16] These same authorities reject any connection with Walter's term *bulenge* (elsewhere *bolenge*), chiefly on the grounds of geographical and chronological incompatibility.[17] Several observations are in order. First, as a general consideration, we cannot rule out the possible role of folk etymology, whereby the sounds of a word in one language or dialect are replaced, in the course of a cultural transfer, with the closest match in the host language, so that French *girasol* for a species of sun-flower with a tasty root appears in English as *Jerusalem artichoke*, the latter half of the compound based on similarity of taste, just as the first was based on similarity of sound. Second, sharpening the focus to *boul-* as a round loaf excludes consideration of related words that reference not the finished loaf and its shape but rather earlier stages in the process, in particular both fine flour and flour of inferior quality. Third, there is no evidence in northern French that *boule* or something similar signified a *round* loaf of bread. This notion was first proposed by the lexicographer of medieval Latin, Du Cange, and latter shored up only by references to Netherlandic forms.[18] But, for the sake of argument, let us assume that *boule* at some point did reference a round loaf. We might then envisage the following development: a term for fine flour (the *boll-*

word) becomes attached to its end product, which is then seen to be characterized not its its ingredients but by its shape (influenced by *bull-* words, cf. Eng. *ball*). As we have seen with Latin *pistor*, initially the miller, latterly the baker, such shifts were not uncommon. A last observation: the multi-element compound, with a Germanic root (*boul-*), Germanic agent suffix (*ing* < *-enc*), then, at a later stage, a further agent suffix, now Romance, (*-ier*), is not a very convincing assembly.

We momentarily leave *boulanger* for Modern French *bluteau* (var. *blutoir*) 'sieve, bolting cloth', the term whose medieval reflexes are more frequently found than Walter's *bolenge*. As early as 1105 *buretel* is found as an Old French gloss in Rashi's commentaries on the *Talmud*, that is, a word familiar to the Jewish community of northern France is used to explain a difficult Hebrew word.[19] From the second half of the thirteenth century we have the form *buletiel* and, from a period well after Walter, *blucteau*, *buletau*, and *blutteau*. The variant orthographies in reality reflect the effects of dissimilation and metathesis in the spoken language.

We have seen that Germanic-speaking communities also distinguished between fine and second-grade flour. Let us for a moment imagine that the metaphor of the 'flower of the flour' did not originate in Romance but rather in Germanic. A Frankish term cognate with Gothic *bloma* 'flower', Middle High German *bluot* 'blooming, blossom', and Old English *bled* 'sprout, flower' could have generated a Frankish verb rather similar to Modern English 'to bolt', by which is meant 'to sift ground meal in order to recover the finest flour, the "flower".' But the figurative use of the flower to designate the choice part of something is found in classical Latin and is unlikely to have been borrowed into a Germanic language along the borders of the Empire. It is rather to such words as Old High German *butil*, Middle High German *biutel* that we should look.[20] They were used of sacks, bags, and pockets generally but, since the bolting cloth was in the nature of a sack, also generated the Middle High German verb *biuteln*. The Modern German reflex *beuteln* means 'to shake', but originally referencing bolting, the shaking of the sack-like bolting cloth. In early northern French, where Frankish influence was greatest, this 'bag-shaking, sifting word', was variously configured. The liquid consonant alternates between *-l-* and *-r-* and metathesis occurs, to generate nominal end forms such as *buretel* and *buletiel* 'bolting cloth' and the verbs *bureter* and *buleter*, the latter the source of English *bolt*.[21] To return to earlier observations, I propose that, while *boule* may well have entered both Norman and mainstream French from the Picard dialect with the secondary meaning 'round loaf', influenced by Netherlandic usage, its origin lay in Germanic with bolted flour. *Boulanger* and its antecedents would then have referenced one who worked with fine flour, with a subsequent shift in semantics toward the end product, the baked loaf. In Walter of Bibbesworth, whose Anglo-Norman French would have had affinities with Picard, we have what appears a substitution. To designate the bolting cloth he has employed not a term with its origins in the bag-shaking process, e.g., *buletel*, but rather has turned to the image of the end product of such action, the fine flour. His *bulenge* 'bolting cloth' may then be judged a back formation from *boulanger* 'meal-bolter, flour-sifter'.

To return to Walter's text, the bolting cloth is referred to a second time (and so identified in English) and its purpose is stated as to separate (*severer*) the bran (*fourfre*) from the flour (*flour*). Here we should note that the English term *bolting cloth* is based on a verb more often seen in Middle English as *bulten*. Unlike the English words seen to date, this is traced to Norman French, where the comparable verb for 'to sift' was *buleter* from an earlier *bureter*, reflexes of which are seen above in *buletiel and buretel*. This is our first example of an English term loaned from French. The French term *fourfre* (var. *furfre*) 'bran' is derived from Latin *furfur* but has been replaced by *son* in Modern French.[22] Rather surprisingly, Middle English *bran* is also derived by some lexicographers from Old French and this French term is, in turn, traced to the Celtic substratum of early French, i.e. the Gaulish language.[23] We have evidence in Gaulish for a root *brauon-* 'mill', with cognates in other Celtic languages such as Irish, Welsh, Cornish, and Breton.[24] This raises the possibility of a word for bran having percolated up from Brittonic or Late British, the language spoken in regions invaded by the Anglo-Saxons, on the model of the Gaulish word in French. Yet the absence of *bran* from the Old English vocabulary rules against this derivation. Thus we seem to have two Middle English terms associated with the sifting of coarse flour (*bolting, bran*) that appear loans from French. Although the Romans would also have sifted their flour, a particular kind of bolting cloth then appears to have been a Germanic innovation, first introduced into Francia and Gallo-Romance, and from there to Britain. It may have replaced wickerwork sieves or riddles. But back to Walter: the bran is best fed to the horses.

Walter now passes to the preparation of the dough for baking (vv. 18–28). Warm water is to be mixed with the flour. There is no explicit mention of the use of a leavening agent, although we may assume that some dough has been saved from an earlier day's baking. The resulting mixture is called *paste* or dough. This is cognate with such words as Mod.Fr. *pâte* 'dough', *pâté* 'pastry', and Eng. *paste, pastry*, derived from LLat. *pasta* with these same meanings and ultimately traceable to the Greek name (*pasta*) for a dish prepared with flour and cheese.[25] The dough must be worked or kneaded, and Walter uses the verb *pestrer* to identify this process.[26] This is plausibly traced to Latin *pistrire* 'to knead'. Yet we had earlier met *pestre* in Walter's title, in a context that implied that it was the basic work for 'to bake' or at least the identification of what was seen as the key process in the production of bread. But English 'to bake' does precisely the same thing, albeit focussing on what we perceive as the final, perfective stage of the process.[27] When the dough has been thoroughly kneaded, the kneading trough, *auge* in Norman French, *trowh* in Middle English, must be scraped clean. *Auge* is the French reflex of Latin *alveum* with the same meaning, while *trowh* is represented in Old English as *trog, troh*.[28] The tool to be used is called *rastuer* in Anglo-Norman French, which highlights its function. The English gloss, *ribbe,* might seem to point to an origin in an animal's rib (OE *ribb),* a derivation advanced by *MED*.[29] *OED*, on the other hand, more correctly recognizes a verb *to rib* 'to rub or scrape (flax or hemp) with a flat iron tool in order to remove the particle of core adhering to it after the process of breaking'. This is best seen as a loan from Flemish, where we find the verb *ribben* (cf. Middle Low German *ribbeisern* 'scraping iron').[30] The term seems to have been loaned for comparable scraping operations such as cleaning the kneading troughs. *Rastuer* is related to such English words as *eraser* and *razor* and is derived from a Late Latin **rasitoria* 'scraper'.[31] Comparable simple pieces of equipment were used in the preparation of leather and parchment.

This prompts Walter to another discussion of near-homonyms, although we remain in the bakery. The oven-rake (*raster*, best seen as a variant of *rastel*, if not a slip on Walter's part) has a name rather similar to the scraper (*rastuer*) but they serve different purposes. *Rastel* goes back to a Late Latin *rastellus* with the same meaning.[32] These terms are glossed in English with *rake* (< OE *raca*) and *ribbe*.[33] Walter has then created two pairs, *rastuer / ribbe* and *rastel / rake*, all on initial *r-*. The baker handles the rake (to remove the baked loaves from the oven), while the scraper is used in the preceding cleaning of the trough after kneading. Walter is rather long-winded at this point, as if his discussion of near-homonyms had muddled rather than clarified matters, again returning to the need for a scraper when the dough sticks to the trough but saying that the baker's rake is not dissimilar from the hay-rakes used in the meadows. Thus, the tools in the bakehouse have phonological similarities, without quite qualifying as homonyms, but also have homologues outside the bakehouse, in the leather-worker's hut and in the fields.

The next stage is to heat the oven (vv. 29–40). Walter recommends the use of ferns (*feugeure, feron* in Middle English < OE *fearn*) if straw, here called *littere* in French, is not available. *Litter* may mean more than one thing, according to Walter. The mower (Middle English *mouwer*) cuts litter in the field, while some people also travel in a litter. Walter observes that the proper name in 'pure French' for litter is *paille* or 'straw'. He makes a distinction between *pail* and *paille*, glossing the one chaff (*chaf*) in English and the other straw (*stre*), but there is no other textual evidence for *pail* in French and *paille* is from Latin *palea*, however reasonable we may find the distinction between the useless chaff and more valuable straw that results from threshing. If straw is not on hand, the housewife may also use pease straw (*pesaz* in French, *pease stre* in English). The former has parallels in French *avenaz* 'oat straw', *favaz* 'bean straw'.

The last stage (vv. 41–42), after which Walter abruptly ends his discussion, here as in other sections, is to slide the loaves into the well-heated oven. Only the word *past* is used to designate the dough, not a term indicative of the size or shape of loaves. The tool used here, *pel*, the *peel* of modern pizza-bakers, was a shovel-like instrument with a long handle. Reflected in Modern French *pelle* 'shovel', it derives from Latin *patella*.[34] Despite Modern English *peel*, *pel* is not attested with this meaning in Middle English. In these 42 verses and their glosses, Walter has used the French word *pain* 'bread' only in his title and Middle English *bred* (from the rarely attested OE *bread*) does not appear at all.

The author employs three techniques, in addition to verse, to clarify and add emphasis to his exposés in French. 1) He offers interlinear glosses in English. Only a few French terms that we would judge important to the baking operation are left unglossed and they may be thought to have been well known. 2) He disambiguates homonyms, on average once or twice in the course of a specific passage. These often seem more like bad puns. 3) He further adds emphasis through apostrophe and paraphrase, as when he identifies the addressee as Dame Hude or Dame Murel and, in a light narrativization, walks her through the steps of the process. This third rhetorical device is not represented in the section on baking, further circumstantial evidence that it is not the mistress of the house who is charged with the heavy work of the baker, especially the kneading.

This section of Walter's treatise has yielded a modest vocabulary for the processing of grain and the baking of bread. Only a few terms are specific to the bakery, scrapers, rakes, and shovels having many other applications in medieval households. The Anglo-Norman French lexis is preponderantly of Gallo-Romance origin but with at least one term, process, and object traceable to Frankish. Some features of the sack-like bolting cloth would appear to have been a Germanic invention. The English vocabulary is, in comparable fashion, almost all Germanic, save in this same area of sifting flour and naming its byproduct, bran. The semantic fluidity of living languages is apparent in several of the terms reviewed, with grist-grinders, flour-sifters, and dough-kneaders becoming bakers, bag-shaking becoming meal-sifting, and fine flour perhaps turning into round loaves. These examples suggest a linear teleology, significations moving forward in steps from referencing raw materials and their attendant processes to end products. This may be illusory. What we may be seeing is a succession of figurative metonyms, one or another stage of bread production being singled out to characterize the whole, perhaps by reason of perceived labour-intensivity, material resources such as ovens, etc. The true picture is doubtless even more complex, since we cannot recover the geographical and temporal distribution of what appear quasi-homonyms, French bakers being variously, in time and space, called *pestours*, *boulangers*, *talemeliers*, *fourniers*, that is (according to the argument presented here), grinders, bolters, kneaders, and oven-men but never **painiers* 'bread-makers'.[35]

The easy glossing of French by English might suggest that bread-baking in the late thirteenth century did not differ significantly on the two sides of the Channel. Yet we should recall that both Walter's English and his French vocabulary are anchored in the realities of thirteenth-century Britain. But, with words such as *pastry* in English, we doubtless move to a higher culinary level, where the effects of French cuisine on English cooking are a good deal more evident. On balance, Walter's treatise yields little in the way of new information, although it has prompted a more detailed consideration of semantic substitutions, the origins of the bolting cloth, and the etymology of French *boulanger*. But at the same time, his lightly narrativized catalogue offers the first attestations in continuous prose (as distinct from simple interlinear glossing) of many of the French terms reviewed above. Written Middle English emerged from the shadow of Anglo-French in rather different fashion than did Old French from medieval Latin, but Walter's treatise also offers the first attested use of many of the Middle English words seen above.[36]

Walter of Bibbesworth's concerns were largely lexical, so that readers are treated to a discussion of homonyms when we might have preferred more lively detail from the bakehouse.[37] The *Tretiz*, while scarcely a masterpiece of medieval didactic literature, is nonetheless a worthy, if understudied, forerunner to such later household manuals as the *Mesnagier de Paris* and, as concerns culinary arts, to such cookbooks of the next century as *The Forme of Cury* from cooks at the English royal court and Taillevent's *Viandier*.[38] Taken as a whole, Walter's work poses important questions, thus far little addressed, on bilingualism, linguistic code-switching, awareness of intra- and inter-lingual tensions, child-rearing, the social networks, supervisory hierarchies, and more, of landholders and their households in Britain in the second quarter of the thirteenth century.[39]

NOTES

1. Walter of Bibbesworth (1990), 1. This edition, however welcome, is without lexical notes or glossary. In all, sixteen manuscripts of Walter's work have been preserved. Earlier editions include Wright (1909), which reproduces the text from British Library, Arundel 220, ff. 299–305s, and Owen (1929), which publishes Cambridge University Library MS Gg.1.1. The Owen edition, with its many shortcomings, is now superseded by Rothwell's edition of the same manuscript. Some few glosses from the Wright edition that are not found in Rothwell's will be noted. This article was first published as 'Learning French in a Late Thirteenth-Century Bake-House', *Petits Propos Culinaires* 88 (2009), 35–53.
2. This feature of Walter's treatise is studied in Rothwell (1994).
3. Lexicographical notes for Anglo-Norman French words are organized on this pattern: the head-word from *Anglo-Norman Dictionary* (*AND*), where other exemplification is usually found, followed by the Modern French (Mod.Fr.) form; proposed origin in classical Latin (Lat.), Late Latin (LLat.), or Frankish (Frank.), with hypothetical reconstructed forms marked *; reference to other French attestations in Tobler and Lommatzsch's *Altfranzösisches Wörterbuch* (TL); finally, the reference for discussion in *Französisches etymologisches Wörterbuch* (*FEW*). For Walter's Middle English glosses, the pattern is: headword from *Middle English Dictionary* (*MED*), proposed origin in Old English (OE) or Old French (OFr.); finally, Modern English entry in *Oxford English Dictionary* (*OED*), with special reference to the etymological notes attached to entries.
4. The passage represents verses 368–409 in Rothwell's edition, here renumbered 1 through 42 for more convenient reference.

5. *AND, pain*; Mod.Fr. *pain*; < Lat. *panis*; TL, 7.39, *pain*; *FEW,* 7.543, *panis*.

6. *AND, forn*; Mod.Fr. *four*; < Lat. *furnus*; TL, 3.2049, *for*; *FEW,* 3.902, *furnus*.

7. *AND, blé*; Mod.Fr. *blé*; < LLat. **blatum*; TL, 1.996, *blé*; *FEW,* 15.1.126, **blad*.

8. *AND, farine*; Mod.Fr. *farine*; < Lat. *farina*; TL, 3.1637, *farine*; *FEW,* 3.419, *farina*; *MED, mele*; < OE *melu, meolo*; *OED, meal.* The manuscript edited by Wright (155) has *movele* instead of the verb *moudre*, a term glossed with *mille-stoon*; see *AND, s.v. moele* 'mill-stone'.

9. *MED, grist*; < OE *grist*; *OED, grist*.

10. *AND, grain*; Mod.Fr. *graine*; < Lat. *granum*; TL, 4.520, *graine*; *FEW,* 4.227, *granum*; *Dictionnaire étymologique de l'ancien français*, Fasc. G, 1157–78, *grein*. This is the only word from Walter's baking vocabulary to have been dealt with by this last-named work in progress.

11. *AND, moudre*; Mod.Fr. *moudre*; < Lat. *molere*; TL, 6.355, *moudre*; *FEW,* 6.3.29, *molere*.

12. *AND, flur*; Mod.Fr. *fleur* and *farine*; < Lat. *flos*; TL, 3.1934, *flor*; *FEW,* 3.630, *flos*. Classical Latin employed *flos, floris* 'flower' for 'the choice part of something' and there is an instance of its application to grains and flour in Pliny's *Natural History,* 18.89.

13. *AND, pestour*; Mod.Fr. *boulanger* (substitution); < Lat. *pistor*; TL, 7.846, *pestor*; *FEW,* 8.602, *pistor*.

14. *AND, bolenge*; Mod.Fr. *bluteau*; see the following discussion as concerns etymology and origin.

15. At least two other terms for baker were also in use during this period, qualified perhaps by geography, period, techniques, and the difficulty to assess notion of economic centre of gravity: *fournier* ('oven-man') and *talemelier* ('kneader-mixer'). Generally speaking, the etymology of obsolete words receives little attention and the last-named term is a good instance. It may reflect the medieval French verbs *taler* 'to beat' and *meler* 'to mix'. Creating an agent noun from this particular stage of the bread-making process is certainly consonant with the other evidence reviewed here.

16. *Bolle* and congeners are treated in *Indogermanisches etymologisches Wörterbuch*, I.802, *pel-* 2 b, 'dust, meal'.

17. The foregoing summarizes the discussion of etymology in *Trésor de la langue française, boulanger*, and *FEW,* 15.1.176, **bolla*. The object of this criticism is the argument brought to full flower in Marchot (1921) in subsections entitled, 'La famille du franc **bolla* 'fleur de farine' en français' and 'Ancien picard *boulenc*, boulanger (Amiens, XIIe s.),' at 207–17. Marchot's line of reasoning is close to that laid out here, although his treatment of bolting is less developed as is his understanding of Walter's choice of words.

18. Du Cange (1883–87), *s.v. bolendegarii*.

19. Levy (1964), 154.

20. *Mittelhochdeutsches Handwörterbuch, biutel*; *IEW,* I. 99, *b(e)-, bh(e)u-* 'blow up, swell'.

21. *AND, boleter*; Mod.Fr. *bluteau, blutoir*; TL, 1.1205, *bluter, bureter* (the proposed derivation from LLat. **burattare* is to be rejected); *FEW,* 1.123, *biuteln*; *MED,*

bulten; OED, *bolt*.

22. *AND, furfre*; Mod.Fr. *son* (substitution); < Lat. *furfur*; TL, 3.2094, *forfre*; FEW, 3.895, *furfur*.

23. *AND, bren*; TL, 1.1133, *bren*; FEW, 1.513, *brenno; MED, *bran*; < OFr. *bran*; OED, *bran*. The multiplicity of words in early French for bran may be due to terms originally specific to one grain or another – wheat, spelt, barley, oats, rye – being successively used more generally. The topic merits further investigation.

24. *Dictionnaire de la langue gauloise* (2003), 86, *brauon-*.

25. *AND, paste*; Mod.Fr. *pâte*; < LLat. *pasta*; TL, 7.460, *paste*; FEW, 7.744, *pasta*.

26. There is no gloss in the manuscript here followed, although *kned* appears in Wright's edition (155).

27. *AND, pestre* (the dictionary allows two senses: 'to knead' and 'to bake'); Mod. Fr. *pétrir;* < Lat. *pistrire*; TL, 7.847, *pestrer*; FEW, 8.603, *pistrire*.

28. *AND, auge*; Mod.Fr. *auge*; < Lat. *alveus*; TL, 1.668, *auge*; FEW, 24.379, *alveus*; MED, *trough*; < OE *trog, troh*; OED, *trough*.

29. *MED, ribbe* 3; < OE *ribb*; OED, *rib*.

30. Flemish weavers were encouraged to settle in Britain in the twelfth century by Henry I. See further Pokorny, *Indogermanisches etymologisches Wörterbuch*, I. 858, *s.v. reib-*.

31. *AND, rastuer*; Mod.Fr. *racloir* (substitution); < LLat. *rasitoria; TL, 8.328, *rastoire*; FEW, 10.89, *rastoria.

32. *AND, rastel*; Mod.Fr. *râteau*; < LLat. *rastellus*; TL, 8.325, *rastel*; FEW, 10.94, *rastellus*.

33. *MED rake* 1; < OE *raca*; OED, *rake*.

34. *AND, pele*; Mod.Fr. *pelle*; < Lat. *patella*; TL, 7.9, *päelle*; FEW, 8.1, *patella*.

35. Even *pâtissier* refers to a specific kind of enriched dough.

36. Some of Walter's early interlinear English glosses have escaped the attention of the editors of *Middle English Dictionary* – bran, bulten, mele, pese – although the words are exemplified by citations from other writings. There is considerable variation among the Bibbesworth manuscripts, so that some few additional milling and baking terms in both French and English might be gleaned from the study of this largely unpublished material.

37. A companion piece to the present article is Sayers, 'Flax and Linen in Walter of Bibbesworth's 13 c. French Treatise for English Housewives'.

38. Walter of Bibbesworth's *Tretiz* was also incorporated in a larger work that is known under the title *Femina*. Here his interlinear English glosses are expanded to a full translation or paraphrase of the various French texts. Rothwell (1998) provides a general assessment of this composite and largely unstudied text. He has since published an excellent annotated online edition of one manuscript, *Femina* (2005), which also casts useful light back on Walter's text.

39. While the point is made in this essay that Walter's interest for the history of the French and English terminology of the crafts and trades has largely been ignored, other scholars have seen the treatise as principally a pedagogical work. This prompted Rothwell's squib, 'A Mis-Judged Author and His Mis-Used Text: Walter de Bibbesworth and His "Tretiz"' (1982). For a more recent assessment of

Walter's work in the sphere of second language acquisitions, see Kennedy (1998). The British author's relevance to the history of writing on food preparation is assessed in Hieatt (1982). On medieval didactic poetry generally, see the recent collective volume, *Calliope's Classroom* (2007).

Court-bouillon & chowder

The vocabulary of technology, the trades, and crafts is often conservative but, historically, has also been very receptive to loans and calques from other languages, especially when such lexical transfer is accompanied by the introduction of a new tool, process, style, or taste. This is particularly true of the culinary arts and of English as a host language for the terminology of a variety of international cuisines, not least French. The French connection dates from at least the eleventh century and may precede it in some respects. Not only did Anglo-Norman French impose itself in all spheres of British life and exert a determining influence on the future of English, French cooking was early viewed as having an enviable cachet.

Some of this culinary terminology is adopted into mainstream language, as *beef, veal, pork,* and *mutton* illustrate in relation to *cow/ox, calf, pig,* and *sheep,* while other foreignisms stay largely within the specialist vocabulary of professionals, although well known among devoted amateurs. This note explores such an early reference to *court-bouillon*, conceivably the first mention of the term in either written French or English. By *court-bouillon* we understand a combination of water and one or more of the following: milk, wine, vinegar, vegetables, salt, seasoning with pepper, herbs, and spices. The note argues that the term is reflected in a passage from the *Liber Cure Cocorum*, a work thought to detail culinary practice at the court of, or at least in the time of, Henry VI (*ca.* 1430). The dish in question is haggis.

> *For hagese*
> Þe hert of schepe, þe nere þou take,
> Þo bowel nogt þou shalle forsake,

On þe turbilen made, and boyled wele,
Hacke alle togeder with gode persole,
Isop, saveray, þou schalle take þen,
And suet of schepe take in, I ken,
With powder of peper and egges gode wonne,
And sethe hit wele and serve hit þenne,
Loke hit be saltyd for gode menne.
In wyntur tyme when erbs ben gode,
Take powder of hom I wot in dede,
As saveray, mynt and tyme, fulle gode,
Isop and sauge I wot by þe rode.[1]

Leaving a key term for later discussion, we may translate as follows:

[The recipe] for haggis
Take a sheep's heart and kidneys, and do not discard the intestines. After being cooked in *turbilen* and boiled well, chop them up with fresh parsley, and hyssop, savory – all of these – and work in mutton suet, I say, along with ground pepper and eggs, as is customary. Boil it well and then serve; see that it is well salted, as good folk like. In wintertime, when herbs are good [additions to dishes], I recommend you use, in ground form, savory, mint and thyme, in goodly amounts, and hyssop and sage too, as I well know, by the Cross.

The haggis consists of chopped sheep's heart, kidney, intestine (and perhaps other offal), and suet, seasoned with salt, pepper, and a variety of herbs (parsley, hyssop, savory, mint, thyme, sage). There is no mention of oatmeal or other grain or pulse additives. Perhaps the eggs served to bind the mixture together. Similarly unmentioned is the casing in which the haggis was cooked, traditionally a sheep's stomach. The offal is first to be cooked, then chopped, and finally combined with other ingredients, before the assembled haggis is boiled ('sethe hit wele'). At least this seems what is meant by the verse 'On þe turbilen made, and boyled wele'. The key word here is *turbilen*.

The *Middle English Dictionary* tentatively identifies *turbilen* as 'a broth or stock made by boiling vegetables, herbs, etc. in water.'[2] The likely derivation, it contends, is from Anglo-Norman *turbeillun*, a variant of Old French *torbillon* 'whirlwind'. The figurative use of this word would reference the seething liquid in which the haggis and like dishes were boiled. This is the single occurrence of *turbilen* in Middle English. Rather than see a metaphorical use of 'whirlwind', I propose to identify *turbilen* as an orally transmitted, slightly garbled Anglo-Norman **curtbuillun,* or *court-bouillon* to give the term its modern French spelling.[3] Indeed, *MED* goes on to add 'court-bouillon' to the definition quoted above, although, strictly speaking, court-bouillon is not a broth or stock in the sense of a likely component of a subsequent sauce. If such an identification obtains, what are the French antecedents of the term?

Bouillon is a derivative of the Old French verb that yielded Modern French *bouillir* 'to boil'. Medieval meanings for the nominal form included the action of boiling, the bubbles that formed on the surface of a boiling liquid, bubbles in glass, even bubble-like ornaments on clothing.[4] The first attestation of *bollon* as a liquid in which food was cooked is from the thirteenth century. The satirical *Le Romans des franceis* mocks French cooking habits and cautions that attention must be paid to the *bollon* or the food that is cooking in it will be cast from the pot by the seething liquid, offering a chance meal for the cat.[5] The narrower culinary term, *court-bouillon*, is not attested until several centuries later (1654), raising doubts that our example from *ca.* 1430 is a true reflex of the same notion and formation.[6] Middle English offers no early derivative of French *bouillon* save in *bullion* (vars. *bolion, billon*) as a bar or ingot of precious metal (metal that had previously been molten and thus productive of bubbles). Only in 1656 does *bouillon* appear in an English context in its purely culinary application (although the *Oxford English Dictionary* identifies the term as meaning 'broth, soup').[7] Lastly, *court-bouillon* is first noted in Modern English in 1723, in a context strongly marked by French culinary lexis (*Cook's and Confectioner's Dictionary*), in a recipe for preparing perch.[8] Here the *OED* definition is quite accurate ('A stock in which fish is boiled, consisting of water, wine, vegetables, seasoning, etc.') but does not include a reference to cooking offal.

Since the 'royal cooks' provide a recipe for haggis in connection with the mention of *turbilen*, it is worth returning to the first attestation of the former term in order to note the accompanying culinary vocabulary. In about 1275 Walter of Bibbesworth sought to provide a working vocabulary in French for the English-speaking mistresses of rural estates – or so the authorial conceit would have it.[9] Walter provides invaluable insight into the late thirteenth-century vocabulary in French and English (here in the form of interlinear glosses) for such household operations as brewing, baking, dressing flax, and spinning.[10] In a section entitled 'Ore pur attirer bel la mesoun' ('Now [the French] for decorating the house [for a feast]'), Walter has a great deal to say about spreading layers of tablecloths – the cleanest on top – washing out drinking cups and bowls,[11] and cutting fingernails with scissors, perhaps those of the servants! He enlivens the imagined scene with an apostrophe to the cook's boy: 'Va t'en, quistroun, ou toun havez \ Estrere le hagis del postnez' (vv. 1035–36). *Havez*, elsewhere found as *havet*, means 'meat-hook' and the English gloss is appropriately *fleyschhock*. *Estrere* is readily seen as allied to *extract*, and *postnez* is identified as a cooking pot. The verse then translates as 'Off you go, scullion, and lift the haggis out of the cooking pot with your meat hook.' However interesting for haggis studies – and this is the first attested use of the word – this does not tell us just what else was in the *postnet* or cooking pot.[12] But clearly some boiling liquid was envisaged. Walter's text was adapted in *Femina*, a hybrid Anglo-Norman or Anglo-French text in several senses, that reproduces didactic material from various French sources, now with full English verse paraphrases rather than simple glosses. It is dated to about 1400. The French verse that matches up with Walter's is 'estreiez le hagyz du posnet' and the English equivalent is 'Draweþ out þe hagys of þe posnet'.[13] But, again, there is no mention of the liquid in which the haggis cooked, perhaps because it was so common as to be taken for granted.

The chief objection to identifying the *turbilen* of *Liber Cure*

Cocorum with an Anglo-Norman **curtbuillun* and later *court-bouillon* is the 300-year interval between this and the next attestation, or the shorter interval before we find *bouillon* in a comparable sense. We should also admit that the European culinary vocabulary would have been elaborated over time, and that *court-bouillon* might be thought a terminological refinement on a simplex, *bouillon*. On the other hand, in favour of the argument here advanced is that offal, intended for further processing and combining with other ingredients, would be very unlikely to have been boiled in anything other than a simple salted, acidified and/or seasoned liquid, for reasons of simple (medieval) economics. Second, we find Anglo-Norman *cort* used to describe a strong, full-bodied wine, with a robustness comparable to heavily spiced court-bouillon.[14] Third, the French whirlpool word, *turbillon*, advanced by the *Middle English Dictionary*, is not otherwise attested as a figurative term for a boiling, seething liquid. In fact, the standard Old French reflex is *torbeil, torbil* and the regular figurative meaning is 'combat, mêlée'.

The instructions to the cook, 'Þe hert of schepe, þe nere þou take, Þo bowel nogt þou shalle forsake, On þe turbilen made, and boyled wele, Hacke alle togeder with gode persole', are then best understood as simple first steps in processing offal for incorporation in a haggis: 'Take a sheep's heart and kidneys, and do not discard the intestines. After being put in court-bouillon and boiled well, chop it all up with good parsley …'[15] If this conclusion is accepted, the *turbilen* of *Liber Cure Cocorum,* a term for the traditional medium for cooking offal, must be seen not as imagistic language – whirlpools – inserting itself into the practical and pragmatic environment of the kitchen but as the representative of a richer and more nuanced early medieval vocabulary for boiling techniques.

******

The *Oxford English Dictionary* locates and defines *chowder* as follows: 'In Newfoundland, New England, etc.: A dish made of fresh fish (esp. cod) or clams, stewed with slices of pork or bacon, onions, and biscuit'. [16] The accompanying etymological note is anecdotal, originates in nineteenth-century commentary, and pursues the origin of the word only to the putative source of a lexical loan:

> App[arently] of French origin, from *chaudière* pot. In the fishing villages of Brittany ... *faire la chaudière* means to supply a cauldron in which is cooked a mess of fish and biscuit with some savoury condiments, a hodge-podge contributed by the fishermen themselves, each of whom in return receives his share of the prepared dish. The Breton fishermen probably carried the custom to Newfoundland, long famous for its chowder, whence it has spread to Nova Scotia, New Brunswick, and New England.

The first attestations of the soup or stew name *chowder* in English are no earlier than the second half of the eighteenth century. In America, the *Boston Evening Post* of 23 September, 1751, offers a recipe, while in Britain Tobias Smollett, in 1762, has a character claim 'My head sings and simmers like a pot of chowder'.[17] In another work, Smollett has a dog named *Chowder*; perhaps an animal of mixed breed is intended.[18]

This note attempts to provide a deeper historical perspective on the name and on the composition of the dish, as exemplified above. But first, some observations. The Grand Banks off Newfoundland were fished by Europeans from the late fifteenth century onwards, if not earlier, perhaps as a not-too-well kept trade secret among Norman, Breton, English, Basque, or Portuguese fishermen, all of whom could have sailed due west, 'on a latitude' as the limited navigational aids of era encouraged, in order to reach the teeming shoals of the New World. At this time Breton fishermen would have been Breton-speaking, although doubtlessly not exclusively so. Thus, *faire la chaudière* ('make up the cooking pot') may be a calque (loan translation) from Breton to French or, if originating in French, have been similarly transferred into Breton. Second, modern French *chaudière* is so evidently a derivative of Late Latin *calidaria/caldaria* 'cooking kettle' (literally 'heating utensil' < *calidus* 'warm'), whence

English *cauldron*, via Anglo-Norman *cauderon,* and Breton *kaoter*, that it holds little interest for the etymologist.[19] But this will not be true of the culinary historian.

The French counterpart of the *OED*, *Le Trésor de la langue française*, shows the term, as *jaldiere*, in use as early as the first decades of the twelfth century as Talmudic scholar Rashi's French gloss on, or explanation of, a difficult Hebrew word.[20] Interestingly, perhaps only some few years later, the large cooking vessel (*caldere*) is found on the leather-hulled, curragh-style ship that carried St Brendan and his Irish monks from one marvellous island to another in the North Atlantic in the Anglo-Norman version of *The Voyage of St Brendan*.[21] Naturally, its use was not restricted to cooking fish or soups and we find medieval mention of the boiling of millet, chickpeas, lentils, and meat.[22]

Closer in time to the appearance of *chowder* in English letters, the French explorer Jean-François de La Pérouse wrote in 1797 of the practice on board French ships of cooking up a portion of the day's catch in a common cooking vessel: *À chaque repas, la chaudière de l'équipage en était remplie* ('At every meal the crew's cooking pot was filled with it').[23]

The kind of semantic transfer that we see in a term shifting reference from container to contents, e.g., *faire la chaudière* 'make up the pot' > *faire la chaudière* 'make the fish soup', is a common feature in the history of many languages and can even more easily occur in a loan from one language to another, viz., French *chaudière* 'kettle' > English *chowder* 'fish soup (in a kettle)'. This shift in meaning does not appear to have happened within the parameters of Middle English *caudron* (this, too, a loan from French), which never comes to signify its contents.[24] We may then accept in principle the *OED*'s explanation of the origin of *chowder*, while remaining a bit wary of its proposed simple historical scenario. Yet, since words form sets and clusters on their own – it almost seems – the historical situation may be a trifle more complex.

Caldumen is a hypothetical Late Latin reconstruction (again derived from *calidus*) based on linguistic evidence from both Balkan and western Romance languages.[25] Its core meaning would have been the edible viscera of animals, while more specific meanings emerged under local circumstances, so that we find Romanian *calmoniu* 'liverwurst', Albanian *gardump* 'stuffed intestine', Sicilian *quadumi* and Catalan *escaldums* 'fricasée', and, in Gallo-Romance, Middle French *chaudun* 'pork viscera', Old Walloon *caudain* 'soup made from the bouillon in which sausages were cooked', Picard *chaudun* 'blood sausage', and so on across many French dialects. The term was also loaned into northern German as *kaldaunen* and Swedish as *kallun* with the meaning 'tripe, chitterlings'.

Further derivations, via suffixing, in Middle French include *chaudumel* 'fricasée of pork intestine' and *chaudumé*, the name of a kind of sauce. In late-fourteenth-century *Le Ménagier de Paris*, now skilfully translated as *The Good Wife's Guide*, *chaudumée* is the name given a fish soup, more exactly pike soup: *chaudumée d'un brochet*.[26] The pike is roasted whole or, if large, cut crosswise into pieces. The broth includes saffron, long pepper, clove, grain of paradise, mixed with verjuice, wine, and a dash of vinegar. Toasted bread is soaked in pea water or fish stock, then ground, passed through a strainer, and added to the spices. Boiled, the sauce is poured over the pike. We can easily imagine a shipboard variant with other firm fish (cod or flounder), salt pork (a shipboard staple), water, and ship's biscuit, which would have had the same general makeup as ordinary bread. Yet, the association of *caldumen* with a variety of of animal body parts – blood, organs, viscera – also appears to have been in the nature of a pre-condition for the shipboard kettle to accept a variety of contents.

Other English-language usage may have been operative in shaping the future *chowder*. If not all true derivatives from a single source, a number of *chew*-words form a set in English. First, the verb *to chew* itself. Second, *to chaw*, *to chow* as regional or dialect variants on *to chew* and also as the unit chewed, e.g., a quid or bite from a twist of tobacco (a practice that may just have first been picked up by seamen; see early examples in the *OED*).[27] *Chow*, a popular term for 'food', is now viewed as an Australianism, although the *OED*'s association with *chow* as a vulgarism for Chinese or a Chinese breed of dog is not convincing. Yet chowder is not especially chewy and, at most, these *chew*-words throw only a slight colouration over *chowder*, perhaps mostly in the sense of food served to a small collectivity or community (e.g., a ship's crew; cf. Army slang *chow*).

Chowder is then in the nature of a hybrid construct. It (1) combines, in semantic terms, French *chaudière* 'kettle' and *chaudumée* '(fish) soup', while (2) retaining the external, phonological form of the former and (3) absorbing some aspects of register and situation from other English words for mastication. Retired Admiral William Smyth, in *The Sailor's Word-Book* from 1897, describes *chowder* as 'the principal food in the Newfoundland bankers, or stationary trading vessels'.[28] It is the *ad hoc* international community formed by the semi-permanent bankers and their crews that would have facilitated the transfer of *chowder* from French to English, and from ship to shore.[29] Here it should be recalled that there were long French-speaking communities in south-western Newfoundland, the material circumstances of which would not have differed that greatly from those of their English-speaking counterparts. *Chowder* continued only as a term for the edible contents of a kettle at sea and did not displace the word *kettle* itself. Kettles were otherwise extremely important in the exploitation of the New World, used in rendering blubber in the whaling industry.

In conclusion, we return to three early mentions of this North American dish: 'A large pot of victuals was prepared. They called it Chouder. Chouder may be made of any good fish, but the ingredients of our mess were as follows: 1, fat pork; 2, flounders; 3, onions; 4, codfish; 5, biscuit'.[30] From the early nineteenth century: '*Chowder* ... is made in the following manner: a fish ... skinned, cut up ... and put into a kettle, under which is laid some rashers of salt pork or beef, and some broken pieces of biscuit; then the whole is ... covered with water, and boiled about ten minutes'.[31] Lastly: 'To tell her how to make a chowder ... a layer of fish, then one of pilot-bread, and potatoes and onions; another of fish; a little dash of lard; milk; pepper and salt; a dish for a prince'.[32]

NOTES

1. *Liber Cure Cocorum*, edited by Richard Morris (London: A. Asher. 1862), 52–53. Since this edition, the manuscript has been re-dated to *ca.* 1475. This chapter consists of two notes published in *Petits Propos Culinaires*: 'Court-Bouillon: An Early Attestation in Anglo-Norman French.' *PPC* 89 (2010), 77–83; 'Chowder: Origin and Early History of the Name', *PPC* 91 (2010), 88–93.

2. *Middle English Dictionary*, edited by Hans Kurath et al. (Ann Arbor, Michigan: University of Michigan Press, 1952–2001), <http://quod.lib.umich.edu.proxy. library.cornell.edu/m/med/'.

3. Both elements of the compound are found in a variety of spelling; see *Anglo-Norman Dictionary*, edited by William Rothwell et al. (London : Modern Humanities Research Association, 1992), Anglo-Norman On-Line Hub, <http:// www.anglo-norman.net/'; *s.v.v. cort²*, *buillun*.

4. Examples in *Altfranzösisches Wörterbuch*, compiled by Adolf Tobler and Erhard Lommatzsch (Stuttgart: F. Steiner, 1925–2001); *Anglo-Norman Dictionary*; *Französisches etymologisches Wörterbuch*, edited by Walther von Wartburg et al. (Bonn, F. Klopp Verlag, 1928–). *Dictionnaire étymologique de l'ancien français*, edited by Kurt Baldinger, Jean-Denis Gendron and Georges Straka (Québec: Presses de l'Université Laval; Tübingen: Niemeyer; Paris: Klincksieck, 1974–), has not yet addressed the letter B.

5. *Le romans des franceis, Nouveau recueil de contes, dits, fabliaux, et autres pièces inédites du XIIIe siècle*, edited by Achille Jubinal (Paris. É. Pannier, 1839–42), II.13.

6. François Pierre de la Varenne, *Le Cuisinier François* (La Haye: A. Vlacq, 1654), 221, cited, with other contemporary examples, in Frank-E. Rouvier's study of early attestations of culinary terms, 'Datations nouvelles', *Français Moderne*, 24 (1956), 220–22, at 221, *s.v. court-bouillon*. The beginning of the section on cooking fish, most easily consulted in the modernized edition, *Le Cuisiner françois*, edited and translated by Jean-Louis Flandrin, and Philip and Mary Hyman, Bibliothèque bleue (Paris: Montalba, 1983), 260, makes it clear that the term was well known. In the first recipe, for cooking turbot, the ingredients of a *court-bouillon* are given, but not its name. This figures in the second recipe, for *barbues* 'brill', in which it is stated that the *court-bouillon* should have a less rich taste than in the foregoing recipe. *Le Mesnagier de Paris*, from 1393, recommends fish being cooked in what to all practical purposes is *court-bouillon*: 'A cuire poisson convient premierement mectre l'eaue fremir, et du sel, et puis mectre … ('to cook fish, first put water to boil with salt, then put in …' (the fish, cooking the head and tail first, then the fish as a whole). However, *court-bouillon* does not figure as a technical term in the work; *Mesnagier de Paris*, edited and translated into Modern French by Georgina E. Brereton, Janet M. Ferrier, and Karin Ueltschi (Paris: Livre de Poche, 1994), 684, par. 167, ll. 1630–31.

7. Thomas Blount, in *Glossographia, or a dictionary interpreting such hard words … as are now used* (London: Thomas Newcomb, 1656; repr. Menton, Yorks.: Scolar Press, 1969), identifies *bouillon* as a loan from French.

8. *The Cook's and Confectioner's Dictionary or, the accomplish'd housewife's companion*

..., revised edition by John Nott (London: C. Rivington, 1723).

9. Walter of Bibbesworth, *Le Tretiz*, edited by William Rothwell (London: Anglo-Norman Texts Society, 1990), 1.

10. See, as a representative study of a specialized vocabulary, William Sayers, 'Brewing Ale in Walter of Bibbesworth's 13 c. French Treatise for English Housewives', *Studia Etymologica Cracoviensia* 14 (2009), 255–67.

11. Walter's term for bowl is *queles* (v. 1033). *Anglo-Norman Dictionary* has an entry under the head-word *escuele* but seems not to have noticed this variant form.

12. See William Sayers, 'The Genealogy of the Haggis', *Miscelánea* 39 (2009), 103–10.

13. *Femina: Trinity College, Cambridge MS B 14.40*, edited by William Rothwell (The Anglo-Norman On-Line Hub, 2005), <http://www.anglo-norman.net/texts/femina.pdf>, 74.

14. See *AND*, *s.v. cort²*, citing Paul Meyer 'Le Dit du bon vin', *Romania* 11 (1882), 574–5, at 574.

15. The early history of the comparable English term *parboil* is instructive in this respect. Its present meaning is restricted to the process of partial cooking by boiling the ingredients for only a limited time. Yet, during the medieval period, *parboiler, parbuler, perboillir*, to quote Anglo-Norman forms, also meant 'to boil thoroughly', with the prefix *par-/per-* here understood in a perfective sense; see Constance B. Hieatt and Robin F. Jones, 'Two Anglo-Norman Culinary Collections Edited from British Library Manuscripts Additional 32085 and Royal 12.C.xii', *Speculum*, 61 (1986), 859–882, note on ll. 869–70, which offer a recipe for *luces en supes* 'pickerel soup' (young northern pike). One is tempted to posit an original form **pre-bouillir* (< Late Latin **prae-bollire*) 'to pre-boil', which then experienced metathesis of the *-r-*, yielding a form that allowed, for a limited time, the perfective meaning. The verb has not survived into modern French, and the English signification, in this scenario, would show that the original meaning was reasserted. Yet, we have no textual evidence to authorize such a reconstruction.

16. *The Oxford English Dictionary*, 2nd ed (Oxford: Oxford University Press, 1989), *s.v. chowder*.

17. The *Boston Evening Post* is quoted from the *OED*; Tobias Smollett, *The Adventures of Sir Launcelot Greaves* (London: J.Coote, 1762), xvii. (D.)

18. See Beverly Scafidel, 'Smollett's *Humphry Clinker*', *Explicator* 30 (1972), p. Item 54.

19. *Französisches etymologisches Wörterbuch*, edited by Walther von Wartburg (Bonn: F. Klopp, 1928–), 2.75–78, *s.v. calidaria*.

20. *Le Trésor de la langue française*, edited by Paul Imbs (Paris: Centre national de la recherche scientifique, 1971), and web, *s.v. chaudière*.

21. Benedeit, *The Anglo-Norman Voyage of St. Brendan*, edited by Ian Short and Brian Merrilees (Manchester: Manchester University Press, 1979), v. 873. Compare the phrasing in the Middle English version of the *Voyage* from about 1300: 'Hi makede fur & soden hem fisch in a caudroun' ('they kindled a fire and boiled fish for themselves in a kettle'); *The South English Legendary ... from Corpus Christi College Cambridge MS. 145 and British Museum MS. Harley 2277 ...*, edited by C.D'Evelyn

and A.J. Mill, 3 vols. (London: Oxford University Press, 1956–59), 1.161.

22. *Anglo-Norman Dictionary*, edited by William Rothwell et al., 2nd ed. (London: Manley Publishing for the Modern Humanities Research Association, 2005–) and web, *s.v. chaudere*.

23. Jean-François de La Pérouse, *Voyage de La Pérouse autour du monde,* 4 vols (Paris: Imprimerie de la république, 1797), II.188.

24. *Middle English Dictionary*, edited by Hans Kurath et al. (Ann Arbor, Michigan, 1952–2001), *s.v. caudroun*. The *-l-* of the modern spelling is a learned Renaissance addition in imitation of Latin.

25. *FEW*, 2.78, *s.v. caldumen*.

26. *The Good Wife's Guide: Le Ménagier de Paris, A Medieval Household Book*, translated by Gina L. Greco and Christine M. Rose (Ithaca: Cornell University Press, 2009), 295. A comparable recipe is found in Taillevent; *The* Viandier *of Taillevent: An Edition of All Extant Manuscripts*, edited by Terence Scully (Ottawa: University of Ottawa Press, 1988). Spanish *cardumen* as a 'shoal of similar fish' (not necessarily all of the same species), if related, combines the notions of fish and variety like Latin *caldumen* 'viscera of various kinds'.

27. *English Dialect Dictionary*, compiled by Joseph Wright (London and New York: Putnam, 1898–1905), 1.557, *s.v. chew*.

28. William Smyth, *The Sailor's Word-Book* (London: Blacke and Son,1897), *s.v. chowder*.

29. On the possibility of the nautical word *hoist* and its Atlantic seaboard congeners (early modern English *hysse*, Portuguese *içar*, Spanish *izar*, French *hisser*, Breton *hiñsen*, Dutch *hijschen*, and German *hissen*) all deriving from Basque *jaso* 'to lift, raise', see William Sayers, '*Capstan, Windlass* and *Winch, Hoist, Haul* and *Tow*', *Notes and Queries* 57 (2010), 465–73.

30. *Philadelphia Weekly Magazine*, 18 August, 1798.

31 *The Naval Chronicle* 21 (1809), 22.

32. Horace Bushnell, *Sermons for the New Life* (New York: Scribner, Armstrong and Co., 1858), xx, 430.

Fishponds

In 1995 and in the pages of *Archaeologia Cantiana* Neil R. Aldridge summarized the history of a large moated enclosure at the Trinitarian priory of Motynden at Headcorn in Kent.[1] Evidence for fishponds was found among traces of moat and field systems, and a rabbit warren. Naturally the specific features of a fishpond, whether man-made or natural, leave relatively little in the archaeological record. As recently as 1988 Brian K. Roberts could write of the 'rediscovery of fishponds'.[2] Yet additional information on early fish farming may be available from an unexpected source with Kentish affinities. First, some general considerations.

The early medieval literatures of Britain, in English, Anglo-Norman French, Welsh, and Latin, make frequent references to the necessities of life, prime among which food, but always in passing. Something as common as fishing or brewing seldom rises to the level of narrative motif or an element of theme. Figurative use of household essentials such as food and clothing is often made in Christian homiletic works, but this offers little insight into process. Utilitarian writings, such as account books, do provide a basic vocabulary for many techniques but these are often paratactic entries, unconnected among themselves. Nonetheless, such documentation often offers the first recorded instance of large blocks of medieval technical vocabulary. But well before the first household manuals in vernacular languages of the late fourteenth century, British literature does offer a little utilized source for the vocabulary in French and English of several domestic activities.

One of the estates of Dionisie de Munchensi, at whose suggestion Walter of Bibbesworth composed his *Tretiz* on domestic management in the first decades of the thirteenth century, was Swanscombe in Kent, although she would also have known nearby parts of England, as well as her childhood home, Anesty Castle in Hertfordshire.[3] Editor William Rothwell states that the work 'was written in order to provide anglophone landowners in late thirteenth-century with French vocabulary appertaining to the management of their estates in a society where French and Latin, but not yet English, were the accepted languages of record.'[4] The fictional addressee of the tract is, however, not the male landowner but rather the mistress of the house, *mesuer* in Anglo-Norman French, *housewif* as glossed in Middle English. The assumption of the work is that she will be prepared to pass along accurate French vocabulary to her offspring. Walter passes in review such specialized vocabularies as the terminology for the human body, clothing, collective terms for various domesticated and wild animals and their vocalizations, fields and their crops. He then addresses fishing and fish ponds. His objective is not so much an explanation of techniques as a simple communication of pertinent vocabulary. In one of the best preserved of the many manuscripts, the columns of rough-and-ready French verse have interlinear English glosses in red ink.

In this essay, the vocabulary of fish farming in the French text and English glosses is the object of a detailed examination. This and similar passages may be considered lightly narrativized catalogues. One of the rules of this popular medieval sub-genre was that no term be mentioned more than once or twice. Context and the better-known terms then assist us in addressing those more difficult from our often imperfect knowledge of medieval technology. Given Walter's objectives, terminology rather than technique will have to be our chief concern, although the bilingual nature of the treatise will permit some degree of cross-illumination of the two cultural traditions. The possibility of lexical and/or technical borrowing will be explored, and the origins of the two fairly discrete fish pond vocabularies, Anglo-Norman French and Middle English, will be examined. Here, it should be noted that etymology is no sure guide to later meaning. Similarly, new technologies may generate or introduce appropriate new terminology, especially in the event of a technical transfer between cultures. Conversely, an established technical term may persist, even when its original referent has been superseded by new techniques and artifacts, so that the old word wins a new signification. What is the historical depth of medieval British fish farming as recoverable from simple lexical evidence?

In the following, the Anglo-Norman text is first given in full, with the interlinear English glosses moved to the right margin. Walter's key terms are examined for their meaning, history, and origin.[5] The interface between French terms and English glosses will be addressed. This detailed examination will yield a full English translation of the passage, appended to this article. First, then, Walter's text, which begins with the subheading 'Now the French for the fisher in fish ponds or pools'.

	Ore pur peschour en viver ou en estauncke le fraunceis:		
	Si saver voillez la manere		
	Cum pescher devez en vivere,		*fische*
	Vivere est proprement nome		
5	Ou ewe vif est trove,		
	E euwe de servour primes espuchez,		*laden houte*
	Car du peissoun la ne faudrez,		
	E si vous faudrez a cel estauncke		*pole*
	Ou le eauwe est ades coraunt,		*alwei*
10	Alez dounc saunz delai		*abidinge*
	Ou espleiteromes tut dreit au lay,		*grete pole*
	Car c'est eauwe en butemay.		*muire*
	La coveint pescher de nace		*szyne*
	Ou petite rei ne trove grace.		*neth*
15	Il I ad nace e crivere ausi,	*szine*	*ridel*
	Commune fraunceis a chescuni.		
	La nace est menuement overez,		*smale*
	Mes plus large partuz assez		
	Ad le crivere pur quei le di.		
20	Car autre difference n'ad ici.		
	Mes returnoms a la matire		
	Ki de pescher vous voille dire.		
	Le gurget de nace revercez,	*þe boþem*	*torn hep*

L'ordure leins engettez;		*fulþe*
25 Crapaude e lezart ne esparniez,	*tode*	*hevete*
Serpent e colure ausi tuez;	*neddre*	*snake*
Gravele e cailloun eruez,	*greet*	*flint*
E lymaçoun ausint destruez.		*snayl*
Si du pesschun i trovez,		
30 Par les vemberges le pernez.		*gilles*
Ci il seit mulewel de mer,		*kelinge*
Overer le devez e espander,		
Le no tantost en oustez,		
Bouwele e eschine ensi le frez.		
35 Si returnez ver mesoun		
Du gardin par cele crevessoun		*gappe*
Tant cum venes au vert terail	*grene*	*balke*
Ou le pastour est ou le aumail,		
Puis par ceo bois en cel umbrail		*szadewe*
40 Passerez desouz le hourail.	*wode*	*hevese*
Mes dounc servent atant des peres		
Ki sunt appelez passueres		*stepinstones*
Pur passer secke le russeles		*stremes*
Il i ad ourail par .h. escrit,		
45 Orail ausi saunz .h. est dist.		
Desouz le hourail se kevere laroun,	*lindes*	*huides*
E par le orail oil meint hom.		
Mes einz ki passez plus avaunt,		
De terail vous ert plus disaunt,		*balke*
50 Pur ceo qu'il ad plus de sens.		
Dunt tel i ad il difference.		
Il ad tenoun e terail,		
E tenailles ki n'est merveille.		
Li tenoun tent li cotyver,	*handel*	*tilier*
55 E par le terail passe meinte ber,		
Mes tenailles servent des carbuns	*tonges*	*colles*
En yver quant au fu seoms,		
E au fevre servent de custume		*smith*
Quant du martel fert sur l'enclume.[6]		

Walter's title for this section refers to the French terminology needed by the fisherman (*peschour*) and appears to make a distinction between *viver* and *estauncke*. The former derives from Latin *vivarium* 'a place where living creatures are kept' and suggests both that the pool is artificially constructed, or at least adapted from its natural state, e.g., a stream with a weir, and that its stock of fish may have been introduced rather than being native. *Estauncke*, later glossed *pole,* is a natural formation such as a pond or small lake, with no significant inlet or outlet (*estauncke*, var. *estanc*, Modern French *étang*, < *estanchier* 'to block off' [cf. English *staunch*] < Late Latin **stanticare*, ultimately < Latin *stare* 'to stand', and thus related to English *stagnant*). In the ensuing verses, however, Walter states that *vivere* is properly used of a site on a stream. This is likely a bit of a folk etymology, with the 'liveliness', the quality of being *vif*, transferred from the fish to the water. Thus, Walter establishes a different distinction than we recognize between vivarium or fish pond and pool, one based on whether or not there is running water. A third term, *servour*, is now introduced. Other usage suggests that this is also a term for a reservoir or vivarium (< Latin *servare* 'to keep, retain'; cf. Eng. *reservoir*). The water, most likely after being dammed up with a weir, is to be scooped out of the reservoir to facilitate taking up the fish – or so Walter's text and its English gloss *laden hout* would seem to suggest.

If the fish farmer is unsuccessful at a site by a stream or, more likely, does not have this option, he should go to a body of water such as lake (French *lay* < Latin *lacus* 'reservoir'; English gloss, *grete pole*) or large pool that is fed with water draining from higher land or the heath. The author's phrase is *eauwe en butemay*; 'bog water' we might say. The latter part of the phrase is derived from Latin *bitumen* 'pitch' but has been extended from the 'tar' to the 'pit' where it is found. The Middle English gloss *muire* 'moor, heath' assists in this identification. On balance, we must judge Walter's text relatively uninformative as concerns the actual creation of a vivarium, whether it be in a partially blocked stream or in a pool on the heath.

The treatise now turns to fishing methods. In lakes and large pools Walter recommends a seine (*nace* < Latin *nassa* 'seine', *szyne* in

English) rather than a smaller net (*petite rei, neth*). Nets are also to be distinguished from the *crivere* (< Latin *criblum* < *cribrum* 'sieve'; Modern French *crible*). This is glossed *ridel* in English and would designate a riddle or sieve, although Modern English would not use this terminology of a fishing basket or cage. If not a true net, the riddle may have been some kind of wickerwork construct that would trap the fish but permit the release of the water. Walter states that the seine is small-meshed (*menuement overez* 'small-worked'), while the openings (*partuz*) in the 'riddle' are larger. But they have the same function.

The author then passes to the actual handling of the seine when it is taken up. The 'neck' (*gurget* < Late Latin *gurga* < Latin *gurges* 'gulf, abyss'; English gloss, *bothem* 'bottom') of the seine, where the fish are trapped, is to be turned out and cleaned of debris, stones, and any toads, lizards, snails, or other vermin that has found its way into the net. Any fish in the net, a mulwel for instance (glossed *kelinge* in English), is to be lifted out by the gills (*vemberges*, English *gilles*), split and spread out.[7] Fins, guts, and back-bone are to be removed. Walter's account then takes a very curious and perhaps personal turn.

The addressee of the treatise, Walter's patroness or a more general 'reader', is imagined as leaving the pool and its fish, and returning to the house from the garden (*gardin*), which we must imagine as rather large, by an otherwise unspecified 'gap' (*crevessoun*), perhaps an opening in a hedge or fence surrounding the pond. The gap gives on to a green band of uncultivated land, *terail* in French, *balke* in English. Here will be found the herd and his flocks (*aumail* 'domesticated animals'). Then the housewife continues either through the woods or along their shadowy edge (French *hourail*, glossed *hevese* 'eaves' in Middle English). She comes to a stream with stepping-stones, called *passueres* in French ('passers') and so can cross the beautiful, clear stream without getting her feet wet.

In trying to plot this walk back to the manor, we may propose two spatial models. The first is concentric, with the manor on the floor of a valley, a garden on one side, then pasture land surrounding the estate, with a further concentric ring of woods, and finally the distant heath. The other model would be based on altitude or height differentials. The high heath, then woods, meadows, stream, garden, and manor house. But neither of these seems a useful backdrop onto which to project the housewife's itinerary, which begins in the garden, then proceeds to the gap, strip of green pasture, the edge of the woods, and on to the stream with its stepping stones.[8] Of course, a linear trajectory need not be envisaged. This puzzle need not occupy us further but it does raise the question of just what, in terms of extent and content, was understood by *gardin* in the late thirteenth century.

One could speculate that this scene was addressed to his friend Dionisie and reflected the actual circumstances, however common, of one of her estates. Of Dionisie's holdings, Swanscombe in northern Kent is a plausible candidate for the setting of this imagined walk.[9] Certainly the higher ground on three sides of the settlement could easily be imagined behind Walter's description. We may chose to call this scene a semi-pastoral *locus amoenus* but what we should note is that it is the husbandry exercised on the farm land and woods that is highlighted. Its focus is domesticated nature, tilled and tended, rather than the mystic charm of the wilderness. Such glimpses are relatively rare in medieval literature and may go some way to alleviating our disappointment at not learning more about medieval fish farming.

After the stepping stones, Walter abruptly shifts and begins a little disquisition on homophones, taking *hourail* 'edge' as point of departure. This discussion of changes rung on *horail* 'edge' and *terail* 'strip of land' occupies a further sixteen verses, and give snapshots of thieves lurking under eaves, the ploughman holding the cross-piece of the plough handles, tongs used to rearrange the coals in a fireplace in winter, and the smith's tongs used to hold firm the piece being forged on the anvil. None of this terminology is of special interest and the shifting topics mean that we do not have the same concentration of technical terms that even the brief disquisition on fishing provides.

Compared to other sections of Walter's *Tretiz*, in particular those dealing with dressing flax, spinning linen thread, baking bread, and brewing ale, the author's treatment of fish ponds and fishing is less informative.[10] While these other vocabularies are basically of Latin origin, there are also terms from Celtic and Germanic, pointing to

processes and instruments inherited from the Gauls or introduced by
the Franks. Some even suggest cultural loans from Scandinavia via
the settlement of the Northmen in the future Normandy. In these
sections, the glosses provide early attestations in Middle English of
a technical vocabulary also open to external influences. But here,
in the section on fish ponds, these dimensions are unrepresented,
perhaps because operations were at a greater remove from the manor
house and less visible to a member of the minor gentry. Instead,
the author indulges his taste for disambiguating homophones and,
as compensation, treats the reader to a vividly imagined walk back
to the house from the fish pond or lake, perhaps one with pleasant
memories for his friend and dedicatee.

APPENDIX

Now the French for the fisher in fish ponds or pools
If you wish to know the way in which you should take up fish from
a vivarium, *vivere* is the correct term where running water is found.
First, then, draw off the water from the reservoir, for you will not be
lacking in fish there. And if you don't succeed with a pool where there
is running water, go, then, without delay to where we can directly
access a lake or large pool, for this is water that will have gathered on
the heath. There it is suitable to fish with a seine, since you won't do
well with a fine-meshed net. There is the seine and also the fishing
basket or cage, each with its standard French name. The seine is
worked with small meshes but the [wickerwork?] cage has rather
larger openings, which is why I mention it, for there is no other real
difference [in function]. But let us get back to our subject, which is
fishing that I want to tell you about. Turn out the neck of the seine
and clean out any filth in it. Don't spare the toads and lizards. Kill,
too, any adders or snakes; throw away pebbles or stones, and also
destroy any snails. If you find any fish in the seine, take it by the gills.
Whether it is a mulwel from the sea [or another fish] you ought to
split it and spread it out. First remove the fins, and do the same with
the innards and backbone. Then you will go back toward the house
from the garden by way of the opening until you come to the green

strip of unploughed land, where the herd is with his flock. Then through the woods in the shade you will pass under the edges [of the overhanging trees]. But there you will then be served by stones that are called 'passers' (stepping stones), in order to pass dry-shod across the streams that are so clear and fine. There is a word *ourail* written with an *h-*, but there is also an *orail* without *h-*. Under the *horail* (eave or forest edge) hides the thief and with his *orail* (hearing) many a person hears the horn. But before you go any farther, I wanted to tell you more about *terail,* because there is more than one meaning and there are differences among them. There is *tenoun* and *terail,* and *tenailles,* which is hardly surprising. The ploughman holds the *tenon* (the cross-bar between the handles) and many a coffin passes into the *terail* (ground), but *tenailles* (tongs) serve to handle coals in winter when we sit before the fire, and they commonly serve the smith, when he strikes with the hammer on the anvil.

NOTES

1. Aldridge, 'The Trinitarian Priory of Motynden at Headcorn'. This article was originally published as 'Walking Home from the Fishpond: Local Allusion in Walter of Bibbesworth's 13 c. Treatise for English Housewives', Kent Archaeology Society Online Research 2008, web, and is reproduced with permission.

2. Brian K. Roberts, 'The Rediscovery of Fishponds'; see also Delderfield, 'The Origins of Ancient Woodland and a Fishpond in Pound Wood, Thundersley, Essex', and Currie, 'Southwick Priory Fishponds: Excavations 1987'.

3. As a corrective to myths about Kentish land-holding conditions, see Smith, 'The Swanscombe Legend'.

4. Walter of Bibbesworth, *Le Tretiz*, ed. Rothwell (1990), 1. This edition, however welcome, is without lexical notes or glossary. In all, sixteen manuscripts of Walter's work have been preserved. Earlier editions include Wright's in *Femina*, which reproduces the text from British Library, Arundel 220, ff. 299–305, and *Le Traité de Walter de Bibbesworth sur la langue française*, ed. Owen, which publishes Cambridge University Library MS Gg.1.1. The Owen edition, with its many shortcomings, is now superseded by Rothwell's edition of the same manuscript.

5. Walter's vocabulary in this section is rather less demanding than elsewhere in the *Tretiz* and most terms are readily identified. Principal lexicographical resources for addressing his Anglo-Norman and Middle English lexis are *Altfranzösiches Wörterbuch*; *Anglo-Norman Dictionary*; *Dictionnaire étymologique de l'ancien français*; *Französiches etymologisches Wörterbuch*; *Middle English Dictionary*; and *The Oxford English Dictionary*, in the last-named work with special reference to the etymological notes attached to entries.

6. Vv. 513–571.

7. This is the only species named here by Walter. Other sections of the *Tretiz* address the collective names for domestic and wild animals, and their vocalizations but fish are not among them. There is a brief reference to herring at vv. 316–17. Another section of the treatise, on animals generally, has the line 'Li peschour en viver pesche' linked with the verse 'Le prestre en le eglise preche' ('The fisherman fishes in a fish pond – The priest preaches in the church', vv. 292–93). Here Walter mentions both net and hook (*rey/hesche, nette/hock*). *Vemberges* 'gills', with widely varying orthography, is elsewhere used only of the flashing on roofs, e.g., to seal off a gable. A Dutch compound such as **windbrek-* 'wind-break' seems the most plausible origin (**windbrek > *guimbreg > guimberge*) and Walter's use must be figurative and possibly idiosyncratic.

8. The garden could be brought closer to the manor, if we amended Walter's verses to read 'Si returnez ver mesoun / *Au* gardin par cele crevessoun'.

9. Walter names his muse in his introduction (3, P1–2) but does not specify her land holdings.

10. The author addresses these several topics in studies elsewhere in this volume or listed in the bibliography.

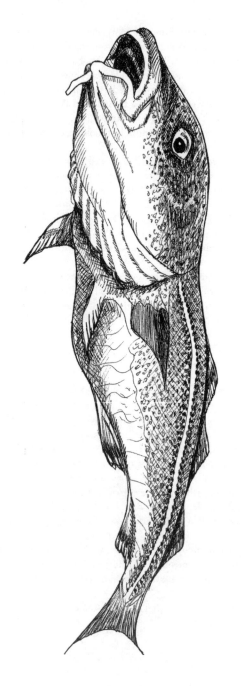

Cod

The cod (*gadus morhua*) makes a relatively late appearance in English documents, the first attestation dating from 1357: 'les trois sortz de lob bynge [read: ling] & cod,' preceded by the somewhat earlier personal name *Thomas cotfich* (1273). The *OED*, from which these examples are cited, states that the origin is uncertain and that 'the name is known only in English'.[1] The Greek term behind modern zoological Latin *gadus* cannot be claimed as a source. The *OED* continues that the ichthyonym may be related to Eng. *cod* 'bag', although there is no ready justification for the cod to be called a 'bag-fish'. Flemish *kodde* 'club' has been adduced, perhaps because of the preliminary culinary treatment given dried cod or stockfish, but Flemish does not so designate the cod.

Lists of the names for fishes are a regular feature of Old English glossaries but none of those edited by Wright and Wülcker has an entry in either Latin or Old English pointing to the cod.[2] Does this evidence suggest that the Atlantic cod, a cold-water fish that generally remains near the bottom, was not accessible to Anglo-Saxon fishing techniques? Yet the cod is found in inshore regions as well as in somewhat deeper waters and line-fishing must surely have been possible with early English boats and ships as we know them.

A very different picture is found in linguistic sources from farther north on the Atlantic coast.[3] Old Norse *þorskr* appears in early Icelandic literary and legal sources and it is evident that the cod was regularly fished.[4] The original meaning of *þorskr* is 'fish that is dried'. Derivatives and cognates of *þorskr* are found south and east of Scandinavia in Middle Low German (*dosch*), High German (*Dorsch*), Finnish (*turska*), Estonian (*tursk*), Livonian (*turska*), Russian (*treska*), and in the west in Faroese (*torskur*), Shetland Norn (*tusk*), Scots Gaelic (*trosg*) and Irish (*trosg, trosc*).[5] This attests to a wide European market for Atlantic stockfish, as it is likely that the word entered most of these languages attached to a preservation technique, however simple, or a trade commodity, although medieval fishermen resident on the eastern Baltic shore must surely have fished for local species of the cod. Given the Norse settlement of the future Normandy, we might expect some reflex of *þorskr* in Norman French but none has been found (see below).[6]

A rather similar situation is met farther south on the Atlantic seaboard, with one or two terms having reflexes in a number of languages. Many first attestations are from the sixteenth century when the Grand Banks off Newfoundland began to be regularly exploited. In the south are found Spanish *bacalao*, Basque *bakallao, bakailo, makailo*, Portuguese *bacalhau*, Catalan *bacalla*, Provençal *bacalau*, Italian *baccala*, Arabic *baqlah*, to cite modern forms, and in the north, in what has been seen as metathesized form, Gascon *cabilhau*, French *cabillaud*, Dutch *kabeljauw*, Middle Low German *Kabelaw*, German *Kabeljau*, Danish *kabeliau*, Swedish *kabeljo*. It would be attractive to assume that all these reflected cod preserved with the aid of salt, rather than the simple air-drying that was practicable in the north and reflected in the etymology of *þorskr*, or that none referenced fresh fish, but this is not the neat case. French *cabillaud*, for example, denotes fresh cod.

A convincing case has been made for the origin of Iberian forms such as *bacalao* in Latin *baculus* 'staff, stick' via the diminutive **bacallanus*; reference would be to the cod in its split, salted and dried form. Jan de Vries accepts this derivation and also the metathesis of *bacalao* into *kabeljauw*, suggesting that it may have occurred under the influence of the French ichthyonym *cabot, chabot*, a fish name derived from Latin *caput* that would have the connotation 'thick-headed' (cf. its English equivalent *bullhead*).[7] But an equally celebrated etymologist, Joan Corominas, proposes just the opposite. Latin *baculus* 'staff, stick' is rejected as a possible origin of the Spanish term *bacalao* (although he does not explore the notion of derivative Latin forms). French *cabillaud*, perhaps more precisely Gascon *cabilhau,* is seen as the source from which both Germanic and Iberian forms derive. In this view it is *bacalao* that is the metathesized form, and Basque a likely locus for this transformation.[8]

Several previously unnoticed bits of evidence may now be adduced in the pursuit of a more fully satisfactory explanation of the two continental European terms, always with the intention to return to English *cod.*[9] One historical source has Basque fishermen reaching North American waters as early as 1372,[10] although current scholarship would put the Portuguese there somewhat before the Basques and Bretons.[11] Here, it is opportune to observe that the Basques were unusually well positioned to exploit cod on the Grand Banks, having ready access to both iron for ship-building and salt for curing, and being among the geographically most proximate sailors. Less controversial is the fact that from 1520 to 1580 their presence was so considerable and is so evident in the toponymical evidence, where *bakailo* is a frequent element, that the trade pidgins that developed in the sixteenth century between the Micmacs, Montagnais, and Europeans have a substantial Basque component.[12] Included in the pidgin are *bacailos* and *makia.*

Even at an early date there was a question as to the origin of the term *bacalao.* Pietro Martire d'Anghiera wrote in 1516 concerning Cabot's second voyage:

Is ea littora percurrens quae Bacalaos appelauit ... Bacallaos Cabottus ipse terras illas appellauit: eo quas in earum pelago tantam reperit magnorum quorundam piscium: tinnos emulantium: sic vocatorum ab indigenis.

[He, in following those coasts which he called Bacalaos ... Cabot himself called these lands Bacallaos, for he found such an abundance of certain great fish in their sea, which rival tuna, so called (bacallaos) by the local people.]

A little over a century later (1643), Fournier writes:

... ces terres sont appellées du nom d'Isles de Bacaleo, comme d'un nom assez connu. Or on ne peut douter que ce nom leur esté donné par les Basques, qui seuls en toute l'Europe appellent ce poisson *Bacaleos* ou *Bacallos* et les Originaires le nomment *Apagé*.[13]

But there is no evidence for an origin of *bacalao* in an Amerindian language and a very early loan from a European language seems evident. Without being sidetracked, we may note that the supposed indigenous term *apagé* bears a strong resemblance to Iberian *abadejo*, yet another term for cured cod.[14] As for the pidgin term *makia*, the early seventeenth-century historian Lescarbot glosses it with *bois* and later in his listing of Indian terminology with *batons*.[15] This reflects Basque *makila*, always an artifact, generally a walking stick or cudgel but also various kinds of support. Although a stick or staff as mark of office would not be foreign to these circumstances, pidgins generally have a very practical base and it is tempting to see in *makia* an early trade item, saplings cut by native Americans and supplied to the Basque fishermen to construct the flakes or drying racks from which the split fish was suspended. Basque *makila* is derived from Latin *bacillum,* a derivative of *baculus.* This is not in itself evidence that Basque *bakailol/makailo,* Spanish *bacalao,* Portuguese *bacalhau* are similarly derived, albeit from a different diminutive, but is certainly suggestive that the name for salt cod was based on a curing process that shared a drying apparatus with *stokvisch,* to cite the Dutch form. Although the Iberian terminology for the drying racks has not been recovered, there is evidence that they were known as *échafaud* ('scaffolding') in French and as *flakes* in English,[16]

Early mapmakers employed terms such as *Tierra de Bacalaos* or *Stokfischia* to designate the Grand Banks off Newfoundland. The form *Bacalnaos* with *-n-* that appears on an anonymous map from 1520 is a slight but significant bit of evidence of the ultimate origin of the term in a Late Latin **baccallanus.*[17] Basque mapmakers also designated portions of the New World with the Iberian term for salt cod, and it is tempting to think that they may have felt the ending of *Bacalao* to be coincident with that of *Bilbao* (originally ending in *-aha),* that is, a river mouth, in this case the St Lawrence.

Interestingly, Portuguese has an extended meaning of *bacalhaus* as an item of dress: long, wide, heavily decorated collars which extend down over the chest. This seems an image based on the fish split, tied in pairs, and hung over poles to dry. This practice cannot be dated for present purposes but is colorfully suggestive of the traditional early method for drying the salted cod.

To return to Europe, now the northern Atlantic seaboard, *kabeljauw* and its congeners have a distinctly ungermanic look (chiefly because of the palatalized consonant if we so see it) and no Germanic etymology has been proposed. The earliest attestation is a Latinized *cabellauwus* in a 1133 reference from Flanders.[18] From an economic rather than philological perspective, it is questionable whether an Iberian term for salted codfish could have caught on in such thoroughgoing fashion but metathesized form in the Low Countries, Germany, and farther north (de Vries's hypothesis) before the large-scale European exploitation of North American waters in the early sixteenth century. Secondly, metathesis may be thought more likely across pronounced language frontiers, e.g. Romance-German, than within a single family such as Romance, with its northward-moving continuum of Spanish, Portuguese, Galician, Gascon, and French, in the last two of which we have the ichthyonym *cabillaud.*[19]

I then conclude that we have two basic forms. The first, *bacalhau* (to select, arbitrarily, the Portuguese form), derived from the Latin *bacallanus,* with a primary meaning of 'salt-cured cod'. Whether the Portuguese or the Basque were the first to take a traditional method of salting fresh fish to the New World is moot, but I would suggest that the wider currency of words like *bacalhau, bacalao, bakailo* is due to the great quantities of salt cod that the Basques brought to the western European and Mediterranean markets, beginning in the sixteenth century, the period when, for example, *bacalao* is first attested in a Spanish document. The second term *cabillaud* (< Latin *caput* plus a derivative of *latus,* with the meaning 'broad-headed'), on the other hand, was initially only the regional name of a fish of the cod family. It would originally have been used of newly caught fish, as it still does in French; but as the designation of a cured commodity, perhaps with a locally specific degree of salting, it lost this immediate reference to fresh fish of a specific sub-species when sold farther afield. We should recall that cured cod differed considerably in quality and in the relative degrees of drying and salting that went into its curing, from salt-heavy in the warmer south to air-dried in the cooler north, where salt was not readily available from seawater through evaporation. This in part explains the number of terms in use as designations for a considerable variety of cured cod. In this northward extension, *cabillaud/kabeljauw* parallels the extension of *þorskr* beyond Scandinavia and achieves a status in the language of trade fully comparable with *bacalao.*

Cabillaud seems not to have accompanied speakers of French dialects from along the Atlantic coast of France, who made up most sixteenth- and seventeenth-century immigrants to New France. *Morue* not *cabillaud* is found in North American French. If an origin for *cabillaud* is sought in southern Gallo-Romance, it may be that it was already acquiring the meaning 'salt fish' as it progressed northward. The ready access to fresh fish in New France may also explain the absence of a discrete term for cured cod.

Morue deserves some comment in passing. Predictably, one is tempted to say, origins are unclear (a possible Celtic root meaning 'sea' has been advanced) and the first written instance, from 1260, dates to the same general period by which fish had become a long-distance trading commodity. A variety of suggestive terms – *moruel, muluel, moluel* – are found somewhat earlier in Anglo-Norman and Picard.[20] But none of these forms put down roots in Britain as Middle English evolved.[21]

To close this long circle back toward English *cod,* both *kabeljauw* and *bacalao* were known to the English. Palsgrave glosses *codde a fysshe* with *cableau* in 1530.[22] And in an account of the New World from the same century deriving from Pietro Martire d'Anghiera (see above), we read: 'Cabot him selfe names those landes Baccallaos, bycause that in the seas ther about he found so great multitudes of certeyne bigge fysshes … which the inhabitantes caule Baccallaos'.[23]

Other terms for large cod, especially salted, such as *haberdine,* possibly reflecting the name of a Basque district (Labourd, cf. Dutch *labberdaan*)²⁴ near Bayonne, were also known in England before the North American fishing industry was established, but are not pursued in the present context, since they do not bear on English *cod* but present only problems analogous to those explored above.

A less exotic appearing name for cod in its dried but unsalted form is known from late thirteenth-century England: *stock fish*.²⁵ The accepted derivation is from Middle Dutch *stokvisch*, with related forms in other Germanic languages. As Dutch *stok* is a good approximation of Latin *baculus* in this context, it seems plausible that the term refers to the drying racks, rather than to the appearance of the split and dried fish or the housewife's tool for softening up the dried fish before cooking. In English, this explanation also offers a neater parallel with *saltfish*, representing the other principal early means of conservation ('green' was often used of fresh fish). Since the climate of the British Isles was less favorable to salt production than elsewhere, domestic consumption of fresh and cured fish would seem to account for the bulk of the catch and no English term for salt or dried cod ever established itself on foreign markets.

It was earlier noted that no derivative of *þorskr* is attested in Norman nor in post-Conquest Anglo-Norman. If we put this down to the vagaries of written transmission, two cases, the second quite hypothetical, may be reviewed. *Scrod* is defined by the *OED* as a young cod, especially when cut and fried or boiled. Cognate Dutch and Old English words for 'shred' have been adduced as possible sources, an etymology perhaps encouraged by the presence in American English of a verb *scrod* 'to shred prior to cooking', also used of preparing fish for the table. But from the perspective of socio-linguistics a fisherman describing part of his catch by the housewife's vocabulary for food preparation seems as unlikely as a stockman referring to calves as 'ground veal'. The *OED* goes on to state that 'the variant *escrod* is difficult to explain'. This form suggests a presence, perhaps only temporary, of the term in Romance, in this instance likely Norman French, where an epenthetic *e-* was regularly prefixed to Germanic words with initial *sk-*. It is then plausible that *scrod* has a distant ancestry in Norse *þorskr*. *Torsc* would represent regular development in the Gallo-Romance of the future Normandy, *trosc* a more modified form (cf. Irish *trosc*). But it must be admitted that the further metathesis *of trosc* to *scrot/scrod* is a radical adjustment to the phonology of the word.

This said, a second, perhaps even more fanciful case will be explored, beginning with a hypothetical early Norman **tosc* (the -*r*- was already unstable in Norse, as evidenced by the form *þoskr*). Perhaps influenced by Flemish and other terms for stockfish that could have been heard in Norman ports, metathesis could have generated the form **scot/escot*. This would have been coincident with Old French *escot* 'money assessed or paid' and *escot* 'stump, trunk', and some degree of dissimulation would be expected. Perceived word boundaries were occasionally unstable in Gallo-Romance and initial *l-* might be perceived as a form of the definite article or, conversely, a definite article *l'* perceived as part of the base word (agglutination). This possibility could well have been greater when a foreign word or name was being accommodated. Thus the English toponym *Lincoln* appears in Anglo-Norman French as *Nichole,* when the initial sound was interpreted as a definite article and the remainder of the word aligned with better-known names. If somewhat similar processes were operative in the case of a Norman term for the cod, **l'escot* could have been reconfigured in the plural as **les scots,* **les cots. Cot, cod* could have ultimately emerged as the simplex form in late Anglo-Norman and Middle English. Such a proposed evolution, with its repeated call on expedient irregularities, would command little conviction were it not for the presence in English of the word *scrod*.

After this discussion of more and less likely patterns in the diffusion of ichthyonyms, English *cod* then appears all the more isolated in the light of 1) the absence of a name for this fish in the Old English corpus, 2) the dominance on the Atlantic seaboard of derivatives of *þorskr, baculus,* compounds with *caput, stok,* etc., and 3) the tardy appearance of the word in documents from the reign of Edward III. Does a late introduction of this name represent new fishing waters and methods, a fish new to English tables, greater sales of fresh fish, a new or at least locally preferred preservation technique?

During the later medieval period, Scarborough and Grimsby were the centers of the English cod-fishing industry, while the herring fleets had their bases farther south in Yarmouth.[26] While this clearly had a practical explanation, it may serve as our clue now to look to northern Britain for another possible origin for the name *cod*. Gaelic-speaking northern Ireland and Scotland used the terms *cudan* and *cudainn* for the coalfish or saithe, a member of the family Gadidae, generally smaller than the cod but still growing to 35 pounds in weight.[27] The root of *cudan* is not immediately transparent but it may well be related to *cud-* in the sense of 'low', i.e. the cod as a fish of deep waters.[28] In northern Britain *cudainn* was Englished as *cuddy*.[29]

I propose that *cod* is a back formation from *cuddy*, this latter then perceived in English as a diminutive. *Cod* would then be an un-marked, 'non-diminutive' form, appropriate to the larger fish found farther from shore and safely accessible only with larger, more sea-worthy vessels. Such a distinction is found in Irish and Scots Gaelic in other fish names.[30] *Cod* may have made its appearance when British fishermen began long-line fishing on a larger scale and a term was needed to distinguish larger fish of the cod family from smaller, inshore varieties and perhaps distinguish fresh fish from the largely imported stockfish of the same species. The explanatory form *codfish*, with its generic qualifier *-fish*, seen also in *stockfish* and *saltfish*, may also reflect the introduction of a new, non-traditional name for the fresh catch. *Cod*, once established in English, could then generate its own diminutive form for smaller species and *codling* is attested from 1314 onwards (cf. *Thomas cotfich*, 1273, *cod*, 1357). All this is admittedly quite speculative, since the past fishing and trading patterns of coastal communities are likely beyond our grasp, as is the historical distribution of various cod populations in northern European waters.

Richard C. Hoffmann, writing primarily of freshwater fishing, states: 'Historical information about fishing is gathered, summarized, or even listed absolutely nowhere' (xiii). While I suspect that the last words on *cod, bacalao*, and *kabeljauw* remain to be said, this review may leave future etymological fishing expeditions somewhat better prepared.

NOTES

1. *The Oxford English Dictionary, s.v. cod* ; 1357, *Act 32 Edw. III,* Stat. 3, c. 2. See also *Middle English Dictionary* for additional early references. This article was first published as 'Some Fishy Etymologies: Eng. *cod,* Norse *þorskr,* Sp. *bacalao,* Du. *kabeljauw'*, *NOWELE* 41 (2002), 17–30, and is reproduced with the permission of the publisher.

2. *Anglo-Saxon and Old English Vocabularies*; glossaries from the fifteenth century do have *morus* glossed with *haddock* and *mullus* with *codlyng,* cols. 704 and 642, respectively. Although not directly relevant to present concerns, an interesting list of medieval French names for the freshwater fish found in the Meuse is analysed in Schmitt.

3. A recent general study is Kurlansky (1997) but many of the statements made there must be taken *cum grano salis.*

4. Snorri Sturluson concludes his work on poetic diction, *Skáldskaparmál,* with lists of *heiti,* specific names for things which stand metonymically for a generic term. Here *þorskr* figures among fish names (1.126, st. 488). The cod is also found in one manuscript of the Icelandic law compilation *Grágás* (1829 II.359; version in modern Icelandic (1992), 353, par. 55, and 363, par. 69.

5. *Altnordisches etymologisches Wörterbuch, s.v. þorskr.* This simple listing obscures the fact that each of the derivative terms had its own semantic shading and would reward individual scrutiny. In Shetland *tusk,* for example, the term has been transferred to another fish of the cod family (*Brosmius brosme)* and has collided with a homophone meaning 'tuft, tangle'. The larger cod was designated by a number of compounds indicative of age, size, condition, etc., where the second element was often *codling,* which must have entered Norn from Lowland Scots and English (see below). There also existed a simplex, although this was a sea-term and tabu-name in fisherman's language: *knabbi* < Norse *knapi* 'fellow, man', a familiar, apotropaic name clearly indicative of the central position of the fish in the islands' economy. But the central terms for *cod* (*gronge, grodningar*) are drawn from Norse *grunnr* 'shallow' and are indicative of the habitat and conditions under which the fish were caught. See *An Etymological Dictionary of the Norn Language in Shetland* and Rendboe.

6. Anglo-Norman *codnet,* English in origin, refers to a net shaped like or carrying a bag; *Anglo-Norman Dictionary.*

7. In *Nederlands etymologisch woordenboek* de Vries calls the etymology uncertain, possibly from Gascon *cap* 'cape'. It has also been suggested that the term may derive from French *caboter* 'to coast', *cabotage* 'coastal shipping' (from a Provençal or Italian word for 'cape'?). Here it is apposite to cite the entry *kabeljauw* in *Französisches etymologisches Wörterbuch* (2:1.13, with a somewhat fuller entry some years later in vol. 17), *s.v. kabeljauw.* For *cabot, chabot* in the same work, see, 2:1.336b, *s.v. caput.*

8. *Diccionario crítico etimológico castellano e hispánico, s.v. bacalao. Grande Dicionário etimológico-prosódico da lingua portuguesa* also accepts derivation of *bacalhau* from *kabeljauw.* Other standard reference works that address these questions align themselves with these two main positions to a greater or lesser degree. For

example, *Deutsches Wörterbuch* cites only a medieval Latin *dursus* in the entry for German *Dorsch,* with no exploration of related terms. *Etymologisches Wörterbuch der deutschen Sprache* reviews the full set of terms, favoring a derivation of *Kabeljau* from Spanish, but calls the etymology uncertain. *Reallexikon der deutschen Altertumskunde* (Vol. 6, p. 119f., 1986) also provides a good overview of the European terminology but suggests that *Kabeljau* may derive from Late Lat. *capulum* with the meaning 'Fangseil' or 'fishing line'. The notion of 'fish to be dried' seems a plausible original source for the antecedent of Norse *þorskr* but extending a derivative of *capulum* meaning 'fish caught with a line' to the dried and cured fish rather taxes our credulity.

9. *Dictionnaire de l 'ancienne langue française* has an entry for *bacule,* found in a fourteenth-century list of rents from the city of Orleans: 'Chacun perce soit gran soit petit menent poisson .II. d. et de la bacule aussi' (*Rentes d'Orliens,* Arch. Loiret). The compiler Godefroy offers no explanation for *bacule,* although from the perspective of present concerns we might see a relatively early reflex of Iberian *bacalao,* here in contrast to fresh fish. Unfortunately, the original manuscript was lost in the fire of 1940 at the Archives départementales du Loiret but a copy made in the latter part of the eighteenth century (document No. 7598) authorizes this amended reading of the tax on freshwater fish: 'Chalan petit soit grand soit petit menant poisson 11d. et de la barile aussi 2 d.' Thus, no early French attestation of *bacalao.* My thanks to M. Philippe Georges Richard, Directeur des Archives Départementales.

10. Egaña Goya, 54.

11. de Zulueta.

12. Bakker; the quotation in his title ('The Language of the Coast Tribes is Half Basque') is from Lescarbot's *Histoire de la Nouvelle France,* in which a number of Micmac and pidgin terms are found. See the brief summary in Zuazo (8f.). Basque *gatz* 'salt' occurs in a number of compounds describing the curdling of milk or curing of beef and we might be tempted to look for a term for salt fish where *gatz* might have been reduced to *cod* in English, but there is no such evidence.

13. Both citations from Egaña Goya (55). The first observation may have originated with the sixteenth-century Portuguese traveller Corterreal.

14. Corominas (*Diccionario crítico etimológico castellano e hispánico*) offers a lengthy, interesting but in the end unresolved discussion: 1) *abadejo* is derived from *abad* in the sense 'priest' and reference is to color; or 2) is a calque on Occitan *capelan,* both 'cured fish' and 'priest' (cf. *cabilhau);* or 3) is in imitation of *curadillo* 'cured cod', perceived as a diminutive of *cura* 'curate' but in reality drawn from *curar* 'to cure'; or, lastly, 5) derives from Late Latin *abbadagium* 'rents in kind paid to abbeys'. A similar idea underlies Polomé's critical comments (49f.) on the entry for *Kabeljau* in *Etymologisches Wörterbuch der deutschen Sprache.* He proposes a Late Lat. *baccallanus* (as a variant of *baccalarius*) as source, with the fish seen as an abbot or curate on the model of *abadejo* and *curadillo.* The influence of Fr. *chabot/cabot* in the sense of 'big head' is also entertained.

15. Lescarbot, III.367.

16. Egaña Goya, 59.

17. Reproduced in Egaña Goya, 53.

18. *Trésor de la langue française* (1971–94), citing *Glossarium ad scriptores mediae et infimae latinitas*; Charte de Philippe comte de Flandre, Chambre des comptes de Lille, *Cartulaire de Flandre*, I, ch. 325 ds.

19. Early French attestations are *cabellau* 1250 and *cabillau* 1278 (*Trésor de la langue française*), *s.v. cabillaud*. The derivation from Du. *kabeljauw* is in no way supported.

20. See the listing and discussion of ichthyonyms in *FEW*, 5.436f., *s.v. Lucius* 'light', although not all forms may be related to the headword.

21. Kurlansky (35–37) gives a brief summary of popular associations of some of the names for fresh and cured cod. He stresses the sexual connotations of terms such as *morue* 'prostitute' that might lend credence to a derivation of *cod* from Middle English *cod* 'bag, scrotum'. But *morue* makes a late appearance in this sense and *cod* a very early one. While the association of fish with male sexuality is common enough in many languages, the reference here seems to be to dried and cured fish, reflective of the various social and physical conditions attached to female prostitution and not active or hyperactive sexuality.

22. Palsgrave, 206.

23. Eden, III.vi.

24. *Nederlands etymologisch woordenboek, s.v. abberdaan*

25. This term first appears in 1282, *stocfismongere* in 1275–76; *Middle English Dictionary*.

26. Salzman, 261; as concerns the geographical distribution of cod fishing, it is of interest to note that a document recording the 1427 agreement between the Abbot of the Monastery of St Peter, Abbotsbury, Dorset, and the fishermen of Abbotsbury concerning the kinds and numbers of fish to be delivered to the abbot in exchange for customary dues and payments lists twenty-five species of fish, some of them sea fish, but none suggestive of large cod, unless this is the identity of the *mildell* (*milell?*) (Mills).

27. *An Irish-English Dictionary* and *The Illustrated Gaelic-English Dictionary;* Irish has the fish name *codlatan* 'trout' but this is on the root *codl-* and the designation 'sleeper' refers to the trout's still manner and preference to keep among submerged objects in deep pools. English *cod* is unlikely to derive from this root.

28. Another possible explanation is Irish *cud-* 'head'; cf. Fr. *cabot < caput*; see *Dictionary of the Irish Language*.

29. Evidence for what may be judged commercial-scale cod fishing and curing in Orkney in the post-Viking and medieval period is reviewed in Barrett.

30. Ó Baoill, 172f.

Mackerel & great auks

In Geffrei Gaimar's *L'Estoire des Engleis*, a versified chronicle in Anglo-Norman French from about 1140, the historian incorporates the story of Havelock the Dane, perhaps circulating in popular story-telling tradition in support of Danish claims on the kingship of Britain. The story is set well before the Anglo-Saxon invasions of the fifth century but, with the faint concern for anachronism characteristic of medieval literature, we are best advised to view its details as those familiar to the mid-twelfth century and the preceding few generations. Early in the Havelock story, a ship from Denmark is lost at sea. A single family of survivors builds a cabin from the wreckage and sets up on the British shore, first as fishermen, then as salters. Their early diet is described as follows:

> Par un batel bien garesimes,
> Dunt nostre pere alad peschier.
> Peissuns eümes a mangier,
> Turbuz, salmuns e mulüels,
> Graspeis, porpeis e makerels;
> A grant plenté e a fuisun
> Oümes pain e bon peissun.[1]

[We supplied ourselves well by means of a boat in which our father went fishing. We had fish to eat: turbot, salmon and mulwell, grampus, porpoise, and mackerel. In great quantities and abundance we had bread and good fish.]

We may then conclude that even with the modest nautical resources that are represented by a ship's boat salvaged from a storm, inshore fishing on Britain's east coast in the twelfth century brought fishermen into contact with a diverse maritime population of fish, whales, and porpoises. Gaimar's text is the first in a western European vernacular language to mention the mackerel, although his term, *makerel*, bears a striking resemblance to the modern English name.

The etymological situation, however, is a good deal more complex than might appear. Contemporary lexicographical authorities such as *Oxford English Dictionary* and *Trésor de la langue française* are in agreement that English *mackerel* is a loan from Anglo-Norman French – the *makerel* of Gaimar's chronicle, seen above – and that Late Latin *makerellus*, Middle Dutch *makereel*, and Middle Low German *makkerele* are all ultimately derivative of French, while Danish *makrel*, Norwegian *makrell*, Swedish *makrill*, early modern German *makrel*, Russian *makrel'* are probably modeled on one or more of these medieval seaboard terms.[2] Both dictionaries also reject the association of *mackerel* with French *maquereau* in the sense of 'pimp', pointing up that the popular belief in the mackerel's role in promoting mating between male and female herring is a recent invention.[3] For similar chronological reasons, the dictionaries also reject the association with Middle French *macher* (Mod. Fr. *mâcher*) 'crush, bruise' (homonymous with *mâcher* 'chew', although with a different, still unexplained, etymology) on the grounds that the appearance of this word in northern French post-dates Gaimar's use of *makerel*. Thus the spotted or blotched appearance of some species of mackerel cannot convincingly be matched up with words referencing bruising.

Troubling these etymological waters are also various other post-medieval associations with French *maquereau* (in addition to that of 'pimp', above): that gooseberries, because of their clouded, mottled appearance, had an affinity with mackerels, leading to the creation of a culinary dish with these two constituents, and the entry in a sixteenth-century French dictionary that cites *maquereaux* as a descriptive term for the red blotches that appear on the legs of people who sit too close to the fire.[4]

In pursuing a new and more satisfactory etymology for *mackerel*, we may begin by filling out the icthyonymic picture for the remainder of Atlantic and Mediterranean Europe. The Greeks called the fish *skombros* and the Romans *scomber*.[5] In medieval Provence the name was *vairat*, which would seem to reference the variable colors of the fish. In Portuguese we find *cavala*, in Spanish *caballa* (along with *escombro*), reflecting Latin *caballa* 'mare'. This equine reference has been retained in the scientific name *Scomberomorus cavalla* for the king mackerel, which is the largest species. Finally, we should remember the Basque fishing industry operating along the northern coast of Iberia. Here one name for the mackerel was *verdel*, a loan from Latin *veridis* 'green', no doubt with the influence of Spanish *verde*. Again, the coloration of the fish is singled out. Some would distinguish between the *caballa* and *verdel* as two distinct species.[6] And to list a last minority language name, the mackerel is called *brezhell* in Brittany, apparently because of its qualities as a fighter (cf. Breton *brezelin* 'to make war'). Yet none of the above names can be viewed as a plausible source of Norman French *makerel*.

Mackerel are found in all temperate and tropical seas, although only a few species leave the oceanic environment to come close to shore in search of food, as we must imagine the fish caught by Gaimar's fisherman in his small boat. Among these is the Spanish mackerel (*Scomberomorus maculatus*).[7] The mackerel is an oily fish and does not keep well in its fresh state. Some degree of curing would then have been necessary for fish not sold or bartered and consumed on the day they were caught. For this reason, the mackerel did not become an important trade commodity until the late Middle Ages, with improved transportation resources.[8] Fish that were traded occasionally went by the name of the community that brought them ashore and cured them, since the climactic conditions of curing, combinations of salting and drying, etc. would have been factors determining the properties of the end product. One example is *haberdine* for salt cod, thought to be based on Labourd, the name of a district in the Basque country, of which Bayonne is the capital.[9]

Since the Spanish mackerel is known to have frequented inshore waters, I now explore two possible derivations of *mackerel* from the Basque language, although records for the period under consideration are of the slimmest. Noting that the mackerel was on occasion named for its color, e.g. *verdel*, another Basque word for green, *musker*, could have generated a trade name, although we should have to account for the loss of -*s*-. More plausible, I judge, is the etymology that can be constructed on the clue give by the modern scientific name for the Spanish mackerel, *Scomberomorus maculatus*, the second element of which refers to the spotted appearance of the fish (cf. Fr. *maquereaux* as 'blotches'). In Latin *macula* meant 'spot',[10] *maculare* 'to make spotted', *maculosus, maculatus* 'full of spots, spotted, speckled'. Modern Basque has a word *makel* which seems an early loan from Latin. It means, variously, 'crippled, disfigured, weakened', that is, marked in significant, often negative fashion. A variant form, with slightly different extended meanings although still centered on deformation, is *maker*.[11] In loans from Latin, Basque often changed intervocalic -*l*- to -*r*-, so that Latin *maculatus* or *maculosus* could have yielded both *maker* and *makel*.[12] Of these two, the latter is still found in Basque as a noun, a synonym for *verdel*, the more common name for the mackerel.

It is then proposed Norman French *makerel* is an extended form of medieval Basque *maker as a name for the mackerel, exhibiting the same suffixation as found in *pickerel*, a word first attested in documents from the year 1200.[13] One objection that must be raised to this proposed etymology is that the oily mackerel did not travel well, and may have been exported from the Basque country in only modest amounts in the twelfth century. If *makerel* did reach Normandy in the fashion proposed here, was it as a name for the fresh or for the cured fish? As with the several European names for the cod, more evidence and more analysis is required before a fully satisfactory explanation can be established. But unlike the anecdotal association of the pandering mackerel with the herring or the explanation of the name by references to its 'bruised' appearance, the derivation here advanced is founded squarely on an appreciation of the spotted appearance of the Spanish mackerel and is drawn from one of the pre-eminent fishing and whaling communities of the early Middle Ages.[14]

******

The interplay of languages along the European Atlantic seaboard that we have observed in the case of *mackerel*, an interplay facilitated by the very mobility of ships and the fundamentals of commerce, will assist in our orientation toward another North Atlantic etymological puzzle, the origins and original referent of the word *penguin*. Like *mackerel*, this will be seen to be an international word, with largely the same phonological contours in several languages, an apparently simple situation that both multiplies and complicates the search for the geographical, cultural, and linguistic matrix where it was coined.

Although our first attestation does not come from medieval England and a mixed Norman French–Old English linguistic environment, the search will started from the unusually generous etymological note accompanying the *OED* entry for *penguin*.[15] The entry provides a great deal of, ultimately, unresolved pieces of information but, complemented with some practical geographical information and awareness of late-medieval navigational practices, will yield a satisfactory solution.

The 'penguin word' is first found in English in Francis Fletcher's log of Sir Francis Drake's *Golden Hind* from 1577, but it is already being seen as an international term: '… Infinite were the Numbers of the foule, wch the Welsh men name Pengwin. & Maglanus [Magellan] tearmed them Geese'.[16] As early, then, as the late sixteenth century, it was believed that *penguin* originated in a Welsh term for a species of North Atlantic fowl. The birds in question have convincingly been identified with the great auk (*Alca impennis*), a large, flightless, black and white bird, prized for its fat, which was rendered as a valuable oil.[17] This led early lexicographers to deconstruct the word as derived from Welsh *penn* 'head' + *gwynn* 'white', a derivation that still enjoys considerable currency. Two decades after Fletcher, the term appears in an account of Dutch exploration in the southern hemisphere, albeit in the form *fenguin*.[18] This work was translated into French the same year, and the equivalent form is *pinguyn*.[19] In this instance a term first used of northern fowl is being applied to comparable flightless, black and white birds met in southern seas, those today called *penguins* in English.

The great auk, along with gannets, murres and razorbills, was found in enormous numbers on a rocky islet off the north-eastern coast of Newfoundland now known as Funk Island, purportedly because of the offensive odor of nitrate and sulphate from the vast amounts of guano and fresh bird droppings found at the roosting and nesting sites there.[20] This resulted in the island early being called Penguin Island, *L'Île aux pingouins*. Yet almost a century earlier, Renaissance cartography knew of this 'Bird Island' independently of any reference to a specific species. It is identified in maps by the Portuguese cartographer Pedro Reinel as *Y Dos Saues* (1504) and his countryman Lopo Homen as *Ylhas das aves* (1519).[21]

Two observations may now be made of this popular knowledge. Welsh seafarers are not specifically known to have been active in North American waters at this early period, although this is a conclusion drawn from our very scant documentary evidence, and fishing boats from Wales cannot be categorically excluded from the British fleets that left Bristol, the port of departure for John Cabot's voyage of 1497. Second, the great auk does not have a white head, although there are prominent white spots in front of its eyes. An excerpt from another contemporary account will assist in our reorientation to these early references to both penguins and insular nesting sites. In the travel accounts published in 1589 by Richard Hakluyt we read: 'They came to part of the West Indies [here North America, not the Caribbean islands] about Cape Breton, shaping their course thence Northeastwards, until they came to the Island of Penguin, which is very full of rockes and stones, whereon they went and found it full of great foules white and gray, as big as geese.'[22] As this reference to Cape Breton, the eastern tip of what is now known as Cape Breton Island, reminds us, Breton fishermen were among the first to exploit the waters off Newfoundland and in the St Lawrence estuary, a claim shared with the Portuguese, Basques, and Normans. *Penn gwynn*, above identified as Welsh, would also have been an acceptable phrase in Breton, and here we should recall that Welsh and Breton *penn* meant 'headland' as well as 'head'.

Returning to Funk Island, we see it located at a point on the

Newfoundland coast where it may have been a significant landmark, near the northeastern tip of the greater island, where ships wishing to sail westward along the north coast would be preparing to alter their course. Funk Island is less than a square kilometer in area and rises only fourteen meters from the sea. The northeastern portion of the island is without vegetation and is composed of feldspathic granite (cf. 'full of rockes and stones', above). Centuries of bird droppings have left this exposed pale-colored rock coated white. Our two notions come together in a propagandistic passage from 1584 advancing the notion that Welsh explorers under Prince Madoc were the first reach North America:

> But the Iland of Corroeso, the cape of Bryton, the riuer of Gwyndor, and the white rocks of Pengwyn, which all be Brytish or Welsh words, doo manifestlie shew that it was that countrie which Madoc and his people inhabited.[23]

It is then proposed that *penn gwynn*, whether Welsh or Breton, originally referred to the 'white headland' of Funk Island. Late medieval sailors, with only limited navigational aids, preferred to sail 'on a latitude' and shoot the sun daily as a means to stay on course. Norse sailing from Trondheim to Iceland and, on the Greenland trade route, from Bergen to Cap Farvel (Nunap Isua) at the southern tip of Greenland, and thence to the settlements on the western coast, are well-known instances of the practice.[24] It is then perhaps no coincidence that Brest, the main Breton port, lies just slightly more than one degree of latitude south of Funk Island, while Bristol is located just slightly farther to the north.

Both navigational and provisioning needs brought ships near Funk Island. We can easily imagine interaction, not least linguistic, among the numerous ships' crews from the fact that in the year 1578 alone 350 Spanish and French vessels and fifty English were fishing in these waters. As the passage along the Newfoundland coast became more familiar, the referent of *penn gwynn* in the several languages of North Atlantic seafarers with at best a nodding acquaintance with Breton or Welsh became the island's principal resource – birds – displacing the identification of a topographical feature.[25] In fact, the reference to the 'Island of Birds', first found on the Portuguese charts, predates other written testimony by seven decades. *Penn gwynn* was applied specifically to the great auk that was so characteristic of this landmark and was, indeed, its principal resource, because the easily caught birds were so rich in fat, as well as providing flesh, feathers, and eggs.[26] Just as one understanding of *penn* came to replace another ('head' for 'headland'), so the 'white' of *gwynn* was accepted in popular language as only an approximate descriptor of the coloring of the great auk, not white-headed but with two white spots.

By the time of our earliest vernacular records, first inshore then deep-sea fishing were becoming large-scale, quasi-industrial commercial enterprises, with investors and owners quite distinct in many cases from masters and crews, and from subsequent on-shore processing and marketing procedures – a far cry from Gaimar's subsistence fisherman on the North Sea coast of Britain. Both individual and national competition was taken to the far corners of the globe as new, rich, seemingly inexhaustible, fishing and whaling grounds were discovered. The vocabularies of technology and trade were expanded and exported with these new developments, as was the lexis of the natural world.

The fish name *mackerel* cannot be pinned down with certainty, at least not in geographical terms, although an origin in the concept of 'maculated' seems likely. The tie between fish name and fish species has proved durable. *Penguin*, on the other hand, is seen to have a specific geographical origin, but here the referent is replaced – headland and landmark giving way the island's chief resource, the great auk, colonies of which were also met at other sites. With the extinction of the great auk, the use of *penguin* in English came to be restricted to comparable birds of the southern hemisphere, the third stage, if we will, in the evolving signification of *penn gwynn*. A case can be made for both words originating among lesser known languages of Europe, Basque, and Welsh or Breton. Both went on to become international words, recorded in many languages of the Atlantic seaboard but in the process losing their etymological moorings.

NOTES

1. Geoffroi Gaimar, *L'Estoire des Engleis*, vv. 440–46. This article first appeared as '*Mackerel* and *penguin*: International Words of the North Atlantic', *NOWELE* 56–57 (2009), 41–52, and is reprinted with the permission of the editor.

2. *Oxford English Dictionary*, *s.v. mackerel; Trésor de la langue française, s.v. maquereau*.

3. As late as 1959, *Französisches etymologisches Wörterbuch* still derived French *maquereau* from Middle Low Dutch *makelâre* 'go-between, broker'; *FEW, Germanische Elemente*, Vol. 16, 502–05.

4. On the association with Med. Fr. *macher* 'to bruise' and the putative connection with gooseberries, see Guiraud.

5. No sure etymology has been established; *Griechisches etymologisches Wörterbuch, s.v.* σκόμβρος.

6. See http://es.wikipedia.org/wiki/Caballa.

7. See the brief characterization of inshore fishing for mackerel in the Middle Ages in Brian K. Roberts.

8. Richard C. Hoffmann, pers. comm.

9. In the non-French development of the term, *l-* was perceived as the definite article: *l'abourdin > abourdin > haberdine*. Note, too, the Dutch form *abberdaan*. Fuller discussion in Sayers (2002).

10. Latin *macula* developed in early French as *maille* 'spot, stain; mesh (of a net)', and was then reintroduced as *macule*, a learned loan, in the early fourteenth century; *FEW*, VI.I.12, *s.v. macula*.

11. *Diccionario Vasco-Castellano*, II.1370, *s.v.v. makel, maker*.

12. *A Grammar of Basque*, 2.1.8.2, 'Main changes in old borrowings from Latin and early Romance', 63–65. Such rhotacism is not a feature of Gallo-Romance, where the phenomenon affects mostly *s/z*.

13. *OED, s.v. pickerel*; the word is first found as part of personal names, e.g., *Willelmus Pikerel*.

14. B. K. Roberts, 86–87. English has numerous phrases with mackerel, e.g., *mackerel breeze*, a wind that was thought to bring the fish nearer the surface, but true figurative uses also appear quite early, e.g., *mackerel sky* (1667). Such conditions did not necessarily mean good fishing, and it is the dappled appearance of the cirrocumulus or high altocumulus clouds that is referenced.

15. *OED, s.v. penguin*.

16. Cited from 'Francis Fletcher's Notes' in *The World Encompassed*, 128. Several editors of John Skelton's satirical poem 'Speke Parrot', with its avian allusions, have explained the world 'pendugum' as 'penguin', which, if true, which make this, in the 1520s, the earliest attestation in English. Considine convincingly shows that the term must mean something like 'old gossip'. Could *pendulum* 'wagging tongue' be envisaged?

17. In northern Europe, before the Age of Exploration, the great auk was known by names derived from Old Norse *geirfugl*: Faroese *gorfuglur*, Sw. *garfogel*, Da. *geirfugl*, Eng. *garefowl*. Loans into other languages influenced by Norse yielded Gaelic *gearbhul* and Norman French *gorfou*; *OED, s.v. gare-fowl*. The dictionary

states that the meaning of the first part of the compound is uncertain. ON *geir* 'spear (point)' might be entertained, with reference to the bird's beak, the shape of which is not, however, specific to this species. ON *geir* 'gore, triangular strip' is another possibility. The image, if such it is, was also used in ON *geirfálki*, whence Eng. *gerfalcon*. The term *auk* is first attested in English during the same era here under consideration (1580). It is likely a northernism, with cognates in Sw. *alka*, Da. *alke*, deriving from ON *álka*.

18. Lodewijcksz, *D'eerste boeck, Historie van Indiën*, 410. *OED* promotes the idea that Dutch *fenguin* was borrowed from English.

19. *Premier Livre De l'Histoire De La Navigation Avx Indes Orientales*, 1609.

20. 'Funk Island', in *Encyclopedia of Newfoundland and Labrador*, II.435–39.

21. Reinel's nautical chart of the Atlantic, reproduced in *Portugaliae Monumenta Cartographica*, Vol. 1, Plate 8; Homen's map of western Europe with a portion of the North American coast, *ibid.*, Plate 24.

22. 'The voyage of master Hore and diuers other Gentlemen', in *The principall nauigations, voiages and discoueries*, III.518.

23. *The historie of Cambria, now called Wales*, 229.

24. Marcus.

25. The focus on birds led to further etymological speculation, as when *penguin* was associated with Latin *pinguis* 'fat', e.g. in *Nederlands etymologisch woordenboek*, 522.

26. By the mid-nineteenth century, the great auk had been hunted to extinction.

Spatchcock & salmagundi

The descriptor *spatchcocked* is recently returned to us by novelist Giles Foden who, in *Turbulence* (2010), has his half-Irish narrator/protagonist make a comparison with memories from his childhood in East Africa's Nyasaland. The narrator writes from the vantage point of 1980, the events he describes were in January 1944, more exactly during the run-up to D-Day. Inhaling an office's smell of beeswax polish, he recalls 'Our dog Vickers sliding across the floor on spatchcocked legs'.[1] Context might aid us to interpret the unaccustomed word as 'splayed', the Rhodesian Ridgeback's right and left pairs of legs split along the axis of its spine.

The *OED* defines *spatchcock* as 'a fowl split open and grilled after being killed, plucked, and dressed in a summary fashion'.[2] The derived verb, *to spatchcock*, then meant 'to cook as, or in the manner of, a spatchcock', while figurative uses entered the world of letters: 'to insert, interpolate, or sandwich (a phrase, sentence, etc.); to add to, or modify, by interpolation'. The dictionary states that the word was 'originally in Irish use, later chiefly Anglo-Indian'. As for etymology, the *OED* accepts the explanation of a predecessor, Francis Grose's *A Classical Dictionary of the Vulgar Tongue* from the late eighteenth century: '*Spatch cock*, abbreviation of a dispatch cock, an Irish dish upon any sudden occasion. It is a hen just killed from the roost, or yard, and immediately skinned, split, and broiled'.[3] The *Oxford Dictionary of English Etymology*, however, calls this poppycock, points to the comparable use of *spitchcock* in cooking eels cut in pieces, and states that the origin is then 'unknown'.[4]

In 2009 the origin of *spatchcock* was the object of a casual review at the website *Languagehat*, where recent use in popular and technical food writing is given.[5] Attention there is called to James Joyce's use of the term in *Ulysses*. The reference is worth pursuing. The word occurs in the course of the discussion of Shakespeare in the National Library in *Scylla and Charybdis*. Stephen Daedalus asks: 'Why is the underplot of *King Lear* in which Edmund figures lifted out of Sidney's *Arcadia* and spatchcocked on to a Celtic legend older than history?'[6] The legend in question is that of the Irish sea god Mannanán mac Lyr.

The *OED*'s claim for original currency of *spatchcock* in Ireland, the source of a number of its citations, this reference in Joyce, and, on a symbolic level, librarian Lyster's concern in *Ulysses* (just a few lines earlier) for the needs of Irish lexicographer Patrick S. Dinneen ('O, Father Dineen! Directly.') prompt an investigation into the possible origins of *spatchcock* in the Gaelic of Ireland, whence a loan or loan translation into English. Father Dinneen's *Foclóir Gaedhilge agus Béarla – An Irish-English Dictionary* (Joyce had a copy in his personal library) offers a number of interesting leads: 1) *speac* 'bar, spike', 2) *spéice* 'sharpened pole, stake', 3) *spíce* 'spike', all of which might qualify as a spit, as well as *spot* 'eunuch', which is also glossed with the intriguing Hiberno-English term *spate*.[7] *Spot* is the past participle of the verb *spothaim* 'I split, cut', which had a variant or synonymous form *spochaim*, with past participle *spoctha*. *Coc* is a common Irish word for 'cock, a tuft, a cock's comb'.[8] Although Dinneen's dictionary offers no example of the likely antecedent of *spatchcock*, a combination of *spocht-* or *spot* and *coc* in the sense of 'fresh young (or small) bird split for broiling' can be entertained without too much forcing of the available evidence. The second element of the compound would have a lenited initial consonant, so that something like **spocht-choc* or **spot-choc* may be imagined, with folk etymology reshaping this second element as *cock* in the English of Ireland. While the original meaning would seem to have referred to splitting the bird, its subsequent handling has come to predominate, the bird either spitted over the fire, held in place by crossed skewers, or placed on a gridiron, with the split carcass splayed out or in two separate parts.

This solves the problem of the origin of *spatchcock* in economical fashion but does not explain the term or form *spitchcock* as used in preparing eels. Recipes such as that in Nathan Bailey's *Dictionarium domesticum* (1736) give no indication of skewering the pieces of eel, so that the notion of a *spit* can be ruled out in explaining the form, which might otherwise be judged an eel-specific variant of *spatchcock*.[9] The most likely explanation is that the pieces of eels were split before grilling. A continuing difficulty is the dating. *Spechcock* is attested from 1597, *spitchcoke* from 1601, *spatchcock* from no earlier than 1785.

******

The *Oxford English Dictionary* defines *salmagundi* as 'a dish composed of chopped meat, anchovies, eggs, onions with oil and condiments'.[10] First attestations date from the latter part of the seventeenth century and variant spellings such as *salmagondi, salamongundy, sallad-*

magundy, Solomon Gundy, salmogundy, salmagunda, salmagundy suggest a perception of foreign origins for the dish and name. The culinary term is traced by the *OED* to 'French *salmigondis* (in the 16th cent. *salmiguondin, salmingondin)*', this, in turn, called 'of obscure origin'. The dictionary gives no cross-references to other entries, of which more below.

The earliest reference to a comparable term in French dates to 1627 in which *salmigondis* is given as the name of a stew of beef loin: *salmigondis de l'aloyau.*[11] A form with a variant suffix, *salmiguondin,* was earlier used by Rabelais as the name for a stew or *ragout* in one his passages of gastronomical fantasy.[12] The French term is to be recognized as a compound. The first element is found earlier in the treatise of household economy *Le Ménagier de Paris*, in the section on recipes, as *salamine*, a fish dish.[13] *Salaminée* is also found and seems to be a related sauce. The semantic nucleus here is Latin *sal* 'salt' or *salsus* 'salty', the means of preservation of some of the ingredients, e.g., fish, apparently giving its name to the dishes. In classical Latin, *salsamentum* signified 'brine for pickling fish' or fish so preserved. Yet in medieval Latin the term shifts semantics, becoming both more general and more specific, now designating a sauce or condiment.[14] The semantics, like the ingredients of the dishes under consideration, seem continuously astir.

In late medieval French, *salamine* seems to have been abbreviated and complemented with a second element, *-gondin*, plausibly derived from the Old French verb *condir* 'to season' (cf. English *condiment*).[15] The short French forms *salmis* and *salmi* for a dish of game birds do not appear until the eighteenth century. Although *salmagundi* makes a relatively late appearance in English, French *salamine* is represented in Britain much earlier. In a separate entry for *salomene*, the *OED* lists the Middle English forms *salome, salomere*, but by way of definition offers only a recipe from 1430: 'Salomene. Take gode Wyne, an ... pouder, & Brede y-ground, an sugre ...; þan take Trowtys, Rochys, Perchys, oþer Carpys, ... an ... roste hem ...; þan hewe hem in gobettys: ... fry hem in oyle a lytil, þen caste in þe brwet; ... take Maces, Clowes [etc.] ... an cast a-boue, & serue forth'.[16] We are again in the presence of a fish dish Yet here too, etymology is not pursued much past the Channel: 'Of obscure origin: compare Italian *salame* (see *salami* n.); also French *salmis* (see *salmi* n.), which agrees closely in sense' (*OED*).

The *Middle English Dictionary,* under the head word *salomene* (var. *salmene*), has located a considerably earlier instance, from about 1325: 'Bruet salmene: Vinegre, galyngal, kanel, poudre of clouwes & poudre of gilofre, muche plente of ayren monie, & sucre gret plente vorte abaten þe streynþe of þe spicerie; meddlee wyþ þe speces gyngeree'.[17] The Middle English forms are traceable to Anglo-French culinary texts, where we find, for example, *browet salmené*, a kind of fish broth. The *Anglo-Norman Dictionary*'s entry for *salmené* must be pursued to *bruet*, defined as 'broth, soup, stock, brose', for a more detailed picture to emerge.[18] Here we read: '*bruet salmené*, (culin.) salamine, a spicy sauce', with a quotation from a cookery book: 'Browet salmenee. Vinegre, galyngal, canele, poudre de clous de gylofre, grant plenté; des eofs moltz, e sucre grant plenté pur abatre la force de le especerie; lyé ou les especes de gyngyvre; colour, neyr ou vert' ('*Salmenee* broth: Vinegar, galingale, cinnamon, a goodly amount of ground cloves; many eggs, and a goodly quantity of sugar to reduce the strength of the spices; water of lye or essence of ginger; color: black or green').[19]

The various words here under consideration cover both sauces and individual dishes, with the boundaries not always clear. English *salomene* did not survive the late medieval period. *Salmagundi* enters the language considerably later and is not to be considered a true successor. It is clearly a loan from the continent, and an isolated one; the exact circumstances of the transfer remain obscure. Still, its prior history and lexical affinities are better known than the pertinent *OED* entry would suggest. By the seventeenth century, *salmagundi* designated a dish with a spicy, salty, fish-based sauce, perhaps incoporating meat left from an earlier meal. The apparently indeterminate ingredients (note the occasional replacement of the first lexical element by *sallad* in some instances of the name) quickly led to figurative use as a synonym for a hodge-podge: 'After all this salmagondis of quotation, can you bear another slice of Aristotle?'[20]

NOTES

1. Giles Foden, *Turbulence*, 33. This note was first published in 'Challenges Facing English Etymology in the Twenty-First Century, with Illustrations', *Studia Neophilologica* 84 (2012), 1–25, and is reproduced with the permission of the editor.
2. *OED, s.v. spatchcock*, n.
3. Grose, *A Dictionary of the Vulgar Tongue.*
4. *Oxford Dictionary of English Etymology*, 850, *s.v. spatchcock.*
5. '*Spatchcock*', at *Languagehat*, http://www.languagehat.com/archives/003406.php (posted 14 February 2009); see Davidson, *The Penguin Companion to Food.*
6. James Joyce, *Ulysses,* 9.174, ll. 990–992.
7. *Foclóir Gaedhilge agus Béarla – An Irish-English Dictionary, s. vv.* In *spot > spate* we note the further raising of the high Irish *-o-* to English *-a-*, relevant to the development of *spatchcock*. Although English *spate* 'torrent' is not relevant to present concerns, it should be noted that, while the *OED* calls the usage Scottish and northern, and the origin obscure, the word is found in Scots Gaelic as *speid* and is more marginally represented in Irish as *spid.*
8. The morphology of verb forms in Irish has led to the convention of citing first person singular present tense forms in reference works.
9. Bailey, 'To spitchcock eels', in *Dictionarium domesticum, s.v. Eel.* Is there some echoic effect, the vowel of *eel* replicated in modified form in *spitch-?*
10. *The Oxford English Dictionary, s.v. salmagundi*, n. This note was first published as '*Salmagundi*', *Notes & Queries* 59.3 (2012), 335–37, and is reproduced with the permission of the publisher.
11. *Variétés historiques et littéraires*, 1.363.
12. François Rabelais, *Le Quart Livre*, ed. Marichal, 239. *Salmigondin* also occurs in Rabelais as a proper name; *Pantagruel*, ed. Saulnier, 174. Additional early examples in *Trésor de la langue française, s.v. salmigondis.*
13. *Le Mesnagier de Paris*, 180.
14. *Mediae Latinitatis lexicon minus, s.v. salsamentum.*
15. See *Französisches etymologisches Wörterbuch*, 11, 84b; exemplification from about 1265 in Brunetto Latini, *Le Livre du Trésor*, II, 239.
16. *Two Fifteenth-Century Cookery-Books*, 21.
17. *Curye on Inglysch: English Culinary Manuscripts of the Fourteenth Century*, 47.
18. *Anglo-Norman Dictionary, s.v. bruet.*
19. Quoted from Hieatt and Jones, 'Culinary Collections', (B) 18.
20. Thomas Twining, 18, from 1761. The *OED* has a good etymological note on *hotchpot*, tracing it to Old French and Norman *hochepot*. The dictionary might have stated that French *hocher* (Englished as *hotch*) meant 'to shake, jerk up and down', so that the kinetic image of a jumble dominates the term, rather than any specific ingredients.

Chitterlings & dumplings

Chitterling is defined in the *OED* as 'the smaller intestines of beasts, as of the pig, *esp.* as an article of food prepared by frying or boiling. Sometimes filled with mince-meat or force-meat, as a kind of sausage'.[1] Of interest for the subsequent discussion is what we might call the radiating semantics of the word: part of the body; culinary dish; implied way of preparation. The word is attested from the late thirteenth century, that is, the Middle English period, and the following late medieval spellings have been noted: *cheterling, chytyrlynge, chiterlynge, chyterling*. More recent dialect forms include *chidling, chitling, chitter, chitteril*.[2] The unstable quality of the *-r-* is worth noting. As concerns etymology, the dictionary states that 'the primary form and derivation are doubtful'. German *kutteln* 'chawdrons' and Middle High German *kutel* agree in general sense but can have 'only a remote relation phonetically'.[3] The social company that chitterlings kept in the early seventeenth century is suggested by a line from Dekker and Middleton's *The Honest Whore*: 'How fare I? – as wel as heart can wish, with calues chaldrons and chitterlings'.[4]

The absence of any evidence from Old English, even for the putative root element *chitter-*, suggests a loan or import of some kind. Norman French has no plausible antecedents and such Old Norse diminutives in *-ling* as entered the language of the future Normandy and survived display a reduction of the suffix to *-lin*. This said, *-ling* was still a productive suffix in Middle English and a native English neologism in the late Middle Ages cannot be excluded as a possibility (see further below).[5]

Norse words entered Old English in more direct fashion, however, than via Norman French. It is proposed that *chitterling* represents a diminutive of Old Norse *ketill* 'kettle, pot, cauldron', viz. **ketillingr*, that was introduced in the Danelaw. Attested native compounds on the base word are, however, limited to *ketilhadda* 'kettle-handle', *ketilhrím* 'pot soot', and *ketiltak*, a judicial ordeal in which women were required to take hot stones from a pot of boiling water.[6] Before addressing the semantic development that such a derivation would imply, an anecdote from medieval Icelandic literature will illustrate spontaneous word formation and the trope of metonymy often thereby involved.

Early in *Kormáks saga* the feckless young poet is mocked by a farmhand, now serving as kitchen helper, for hanging around the women's part of the central building in the hope of running into the girl Steingerð.[7] Holding up a length of chitterling or sausage from the cooking pot, Narfi slyly asks in an impromptu couplet how Kormák likes these *ketils … ormar* 'kettle's snakes'. The seemingly innocuous remark is a slur on the poet's masculinity, since boiling sausage is women's work, and further sexual innuendo seems implied in the choice of foodstuff for mention. The elements of the implied compound, 'kettle' and 'snakes', are here separated in the disjointed syntax of skaldic verse and are not explicitly given full linguistic status until Kormák extemporizes a stanza containing the form *ketilormar* 'kettle-snakes' – but not before capping Narfi's couplet with one of his own and giving the insolent cook's-boy a blow on the head with the back of his hand-axe.

The scene is played out in the autumn when the sheep are slaughtered and the meat prepared for the coming winter season. Thus, we may assume relatively large quantities of chitterlings being processed. Just as Narfi gives them a provisional name, kettle snakes, so we might imagine a less poetic *ketillingar* as customary contents of a cauldron. European languages have no lack of culinary terminology metonymically based on where or how the dish is prepared: biscuit, *brochette*, cookie, *fondue*, *frites*, fritter, roast, steak, plus hot-pot, *pot au feu*, *olla podrida*. Naturally, sausages would not be the only food to have been cooked in the Icelandic pot and we can only speculate why such a name as the proposed *ketellingar* might have been reserved for them.

In an adaptation into early Middle English, the two *l* sounds (of the root and suffix) could have been dissimulated in some regions of England, leading to the replacement of one liquid by another, *l* > *r*, as in *cheterling*, or the *ls* resolved as a single sound, as in *chidling, chitling*. Although not causally related, the transfer of the name of the cooking utensil to some typical contents in the North is paralleled in Britain by the transfer of the name of the dish to the part of the animal that supplies a portion of it, the casing – once again the container substituting for the content – as seen in the extended *OED* definition above. The semantic sequence through the two languages would then have been pot to gut, and not the more plausible gut to pot.

Yet is a loan from Norse really necessary or plausible? At a minimum we have the caveat that Old Norse *k-* is regularly preserved in loans into English, e.g., *kid < kið, keel < kjǫlr*. Although the *OED* entry for *chitterling* gives no cross-reference, the dictionary has a separate entry for *chitling*, where we read: 'another form of *chitterling* n.: widely used in English dialects, and in U.S.: cf. also *chidlings* n.'. Also to be noted here is the commonly met African-American form *chitlins*.[8] Most telling, however, is the dictionary's statement that a variant dialect form is *kettlings*. While no proof in itself, this does establish that some speakers of English would have found it plausible that the dish of stuffed intestine or sausage might be named for the manner and place in which it was cooked.[9] Old English *cetel* is preserved in Middle English *chetel* (south) and *cetel* (central and north). Thus, against the intriguing possibility that chitterlings are related to the mutton sausages of the farm at Tungu, we must acknowledge the possibility of a native English formation **chetelling*. On balance, the -*r*- of *chitterling* suggests that a form such as ON *ketillingr* was (also?) in play.

******

With pots on the fire, the dumpling is not so far from chitterling that the history of the term can not be considered and its etymology, to the extent one is recognized, scrutinized. Here again the *OED* is our starting point. The definition seems organized to lend support to the suggested etymology: 'A kind of pudding consisting of a mass of paste or dough, more or less globular in form, either plain and boiled, or enclosing fruit and boiled or baked'; 'Etymology: probably < same source as *dump* adj.'[10] For *dump* as adjective, two meanings are proposed: 1) 'in a "dump", amazed, perplexed'; 2) 'of the consistence of dough or dumpling; without elasticity or spring'. In the first case, one wonders, with the dictionary, whether this is not a variation on *dumb*; in the second, the late first attestation (1852) prompts the thought that this may be a back formation from *dumpling* itself, rather than its source. The *OED* also notes that Norfolk is popularly seen as the home of the British dumpling.

The dumpling is widely represented in European cuisine. To look only to German cooking, we find the base terms *Kloss*, *Knödel*, and *Nudel* in numerous compounds. Of these, *Dampfnudel* as 'yeast dumpling' (usually sweet but, in some regions, salty) commands attention. Without proposing any too close equivalence between Norfolk and Tirolean dumplings, *dampf-* is here to be recognized as 'steam'. In late Middle English (1480), *damp*, as noun, had the negative connotation that was subsequently associated with the air of underground workings, i.e., mine damp, and meant 'an exhalation, a vapour or gas, of a noxious kind'. No corresponding Old English noun is recorded.[11] A primary meaning of *damp* as a verb is 'to affect with "damp", to stifle, choke, extinguish; to dull, deaden (fire, sound, etc.)' (from 1504); a narrower application is 'to cover or fill it with small coal, ashes, or coke, so as to check combustion and prevent its going out, when not required for some time'. The verb *dampen*, seen as a derivative, is found from 1630 onwards.

To turn now to the practical considerations of making dumplings, traditional Norfolk recipes call for the small quantities of dough, the future dumplings, to be steamed in a greased steamer. Other recipes call for the dough to be placed on top of a vegetable and/or meat stew. In any case, the dumplings will rise to the surface. The information, however, does not authorize us to posit a lost and positive history for *damp* in English and recognize dumplings as 'steamies'. One could consider the boiling pot, with the lid firmly on to retain steam, as 'damped' but the term more properly refers to fires. Norfolk's location on the coast would make it a plausible entry point for a lexical loan from the Netherlands or Germany (*dampling, *dampfling) but one wonders whether such a simple dish, flour and water, was not a feature of English cooking before 1600 and such enhancements as given by the cooks of Norfolk.

It then seems probable that *dumpling* is to be traced to the late attested *dump* and *dumpy* (used of globular metal coins and counters, nail, sweets and even short, stout persons) and not to **damp* 'steam' or *to damp*, shape trumping process.[12] German *dumpf* 'airless, close, dull, hollow, muffled' corresponds so well with the affect of English *dump* that a common Germanic source seems likely, although this must be weighed against the likelihood of a lengthy underground existence for the latter. Another early name for the dumpling was *pot-ball* (cf. German *Kloss*).[13] *Dumpling* is best seen as a late and possibly local neologism that caught on, perhaps aided by a refined cooking process like that attributed to the county of Norfolk.

NOTES

1. *Oxford English Dictionary, s.v. chitterling.*.
2. *Middle English Dictionary* backdates the *OED*'s earliest reference from *ca.* 1400 to about 1280. The text in Latin describes women washing *cheterlingis* (a Middle English form inserted in the Latin) in a stream, quarreling all the while; *Inventories and Account Rolls ... Jarrow*, 57. The *MED* also calls attention to Old English *cīete, cŷte* 'hut', of which *chitterling* might be considered a derivative.
3. The *OED* suggests the possible influence of *chaldron* on the development of both the form and meaning of *chawdron*, a sauce or dish of chopped entrails and spices, etc. See below for another example of the name for a utensil being transferred to the dish and its constituents.
4. Dekker and Middleton, III.i.16.
5. *MED, s.v. -ling* (suf.).
6. *Concise Dictionary of Old Icelandic, s.v. ketill.*
7. *Kormáks saga*, Ch. 4.
8. *American Heritage Dictionary, s.v. chitlins.* In Scots, *chitterlin'* may refer to a morsel of any food; *Dictionary of the Scots Language.*
9. *Kettling* is first recorded from 1869: 'Then there are the delusive "kettlings", among the "low-down" people. ... I will simply say that it is fried sausages, minus all the unhealthy and absurd meat which most people insist on stuffing into the intestinal integuments'; *Overland Monthly* (August, 1869), 130/1.
10. *OED, s.v. dumpling.*
11. *OED*: 'Corresponds with Middle Low German and modern Dutch and Danish *damp* vapour, steam, smoke, modern Icelandic *dampr* steam, Middle High German *dampf, tampf*, modern German *dampf* vapour, steam; compare also Swedish *damb* dust. The word is not known in the earlier stages of the languages, and its history in English before its appearance in 1480 is unknown; it is difficult to conceive of its having come down from Old English times without appearing in writing'.
12. See *Indogermanisches etymologisches Wörterbuch*, II. 1080, *s.v. tumo* 'thick' While a definitive etymological statement on *dump* is still outstanding, it continues in a phono-semantic cluster of words with different origins and histories but all affectively washed with the same lightly negative coloring, expressive of clumsiness, squat, globular shape, and the like: *bump, clump, frump, grump, lump, mumps, plump, rump, slump, sump, stump, thump, tump.*
13. 'A Dumpling, or Pot-Ball is made either long or round, as the maker pleaseth'; Holme (1688), iii. 293/2.

Haggis & tripe

Our standard lexicographical reference works have firm views about *haggis*. *Oxford English Dictionary* states categorically 'derivation unknown'. *Middle English Dictionary*: 'Prob. from *haggen* … AF [Anglo-French] *hagiz* is no doubt from ME [Middle English]'. *Dictionary of the Scots Language*: 'Orig. uncertain but prob. a deriv. of *HAG*, v[1], n[1], to chop'.[1] *OED* continues:

> The analogy of most terms of cookery suggests a French source; but no corresp. F. word or form has been found. The conjecture that it represents F. *hachis* 'hash', with assimilation to *hag, hack*, to chop, has app. no basis of fact; F. *hachis* is not known so early, and the earliest forms of the Eng. word are more remote from it. Whether the word is connected with *hag*, vb., evidence does not show.

Would *OED* chief-editor Murray, a Scot, have been defending the ancestry of the haggis, deferring to Burns rather than philological evidence?

The first attestation of a haggis word noted by *OED* is from 1420. This is in *Liber Cure Cocorum* and the passage is worth quoting in full:

> *For hagese*
> Þe hert of schepe, þe nere þou take,
> Þo bowel nogt þou shalle forsake,
> On þe turbilen made, and boyled wele,
> Hacke alle togeder with gode persole,
> Isop, saveray, þou schalle take þen,

And suet of schepe take in, I ken,
With powder of peper and egges gode wonne,
And sethe hit wele and serve hit þenne,
Loke hit be saltyd for gode menne.
In wyntur tyme when erbs ben gode,
Take powder of hom I wot in dede,
As saveray, mynt and tyme, fulle gode,
Isop and sauge I wot by þe rode.[2]

Nere are kidneys and the *turbilen* is likely *court bouillon*. Unlike stock or broth, which might be used in an accompanying sauce, *court bouillon* was often discarded, and might have a higher salt or acid content. It was traditionally used in cooking offal, in particular organ meat.[3] The insistence on seasoning – pepper plus fresh herbs in summer, dried and ground herbs in winter, no fewer than six of which are named – underlines the bland (or lightly unpalatable) nature of much organ meat and the practical, economical basis of this and comparable recipes. We note that there is no mention of the addition of grain or pulse, which would have served a similar practical purpose, to eke out the meat.

This text then establishes the status of the dish at the court of Henry VI. And we cannot fail to note, whether intentional or unconscious, the juxtaposition of *hagese* and *hacke*. *MED* has a somewhat earlier instance: 'Draweþ out þe hagys of þe posnet'. This is from *Femina*, a hybrid Anglo-Norman or Anglo-French text in several senses, that offers English verse paraphrases of didactic material from various French sources. It is dated to about 1400. The matching French verse is 'estreiez le hagyz du posnet'.[4] The tract's *posnet* is not a native English term and is rather a loan from Norman *possonet* 'cooking pot'. There may be good reason to claim that *hagyz* is a similar loan. Before looking to *Femina*'s source in this regard, we may note that the first attestation of *haggis* in Scots is from 1699 and can then not help with etymology or early history.[5]

Femina draws on the *Tretiz* of Walter of Bibbesworth, who in about 1275 sought to provide a working vocabulary in French for the English-speaking mistresses of rural estates, or so the authorial conceit would have it.[6] Walter provides invaluable insight into the late thirteenth-century vocabulary in French and English (here in the form of interlinear glosses, not full paraphrases) for such household operations as baking, dressing flax, spinning, and brewing but is more laconic as concerns actual processes. In a section entitled 'Ore pur attirer bel la mesoun' ('Now [the French] for decorating the house [for a feast]'), Walter has a great deal to say about spreading layers of tablecloths – the cleanest on top – washing out drinking cups and bowls,[7] and cutting fingernails with scissors, perhaps those of the servants! He enlivens the imagined scene with an apostrophe to the scullion: 'Va t'en, quistroun, ou toun havez Estrere le hagis del postnez' (vv 1035–36). *Havez*, elsewhere found as *havet*, means 'meat-hook' and the English gloss is appropriately *fleyschhock*. *Estrere* is readily seen as allied to *extract*, and *postnez* we have already identified as a cooking pot. The verse then translates as 'Off you go, cook's boy, and bring the haggis out out the cooking pot with your meat hook.' A meat hook could be used for many kitchen tasks but here its immediate signification for haggis studies is that the object to be recovered is too large or heavy to be managed with a ladle, spoon, or tongs. We might imagine the scullion hooking the fork into a loop of the cord with which the casing was trussed up. Walter then goes on to exhort the kitchen boy to put an old bee-hive (Anglo-Norman *rouche*, Middle English *hivve*) under his pots and not a *ladle* (AN *louche*, ME *ladil*). Perhaps old coiled-straw bee-hives are being used to keep the fire going and the lad is being warned not to let the ladle slip into the fire. Whatever is meant here exactly – and it may just be the French word *rouche* being played off against *louche* – it seems unrelated to the retrieval of the haggis.[8]

Skeat proposed that *haggis* was derived from Old Norse *höggva* 'to hew, strike',[9] but even when found in a non-martial context, e.g. with reference to felling trees, its medieval use is not attested for cutting and mincing activity on the scale and in the domestic environment here envisaged.[10] Nor has the verb generated a name for any of the modern Scandinavian equivalents of the haggis: Icelandic *slátur*,

Faroese *gartálg*, Norwegian *lungemos*, Swedish *pölsa*. Walter's modern editor, William Rothwell thinks the word a loan from English.[11]

In medieval continental French, the verb *hacher* (var. *hagier*) is attested from about 1225 in the sense of cutting into pieces.[12] It is traced to a Frankish noun *hâppia*, a curved kitchen knife.[13] Aside from Walter of Bibbesworth, the first example of its use in a culinary context is from the fourteenth-century household manual, *Le Mesnagier de Paris*.[14] In the section on preparing the house for a celebration, Walter or a later scribe averages about one English gloss every two verses. While meathooks, ladles, and hives are all the object of such glossing, the French term *hagis* is not, suggesting that the word was well known to both speech communities, and even this is perhaps too categorical a phrasing for a landed aristocracy whose members might simply occupy differing positions on a scale of French-language competency. Walter's French and its 'absent' English gloss remain our earliest example of a reference to haggis. First attestations have little evidentiary value and in reality only establish *termini post quem*. We are not authorized to claim Walter's *Tretiz* as the context for a first instance of *hagis* 125 years before the English verse of *Femina*, as noted in *MED*, but the lack of a gloss does point to the word having been in common currency.

As *OED* concedes, most culinary terminology and attendant cooking processes and products crossed the Channel in only one direction, from France to England. Given long-standing attitudes toward perfidious Albion, it is difficult to imagine the haggis, as minced organ meat mixed with grain and herbs and cooked in a sheep's stomach, being adopted from British to French dining halls. To look in the other direction, there is no need to assume a taste for haggis moving from northern England into Scotland, as ties between Scotland and France in these centuries were sufficiently close for such a dish to have been taken up directly from France. Innovative uses of the less-prized cuts of meat – the heart, lungs, liver, intestines, brains, testicles – are a feature of most food cultures. In Iberia, for example, we find *camaïot* in the Balearic Islands, *chireta* in Aragon, *girella* in Catalonia, *buchos* in Portugal and Galicia, and doubtless many more.

In medieval French and English haggis we may have something in the nature of a specific recipe – the kinds of meat chopped up, the choice of grains or vegetables incorporated, the nature of the seasoning, use of the stomach as casing – rather than a distinct dish.

To conclude, with reference to the historical dictionaries first cited, *haggis* is shown to have been a well-understood term in a late thirteenth-century social context in which both Anglo-Norman French and English were used. The variety of early spellings, *hagis, hagiz, hagyz*; *hagays*; *agys*; plural *hegges, hacys*,[15] suggests an origin in the French verb *hacher, hager* (derived from a Frankish verb meaning 'to hack') plus the suffix *-ëis*, yielding **hagëis* 'chopped, minced matter'.[16] The term for the processing of the chief ingredient was then extended to the dish itself. English *pasty* offers a comparable development. This term for a seasoned meat pie (often of venison) is derived from Anglo-Norman *paste* 'dough', i.e., the pastry crust enclosing the pie. Just as the container of the pasty – the crust – gave a name to the dish as a whole, the status of the contents – minced – determined the name of the haggis.

******

Close to *haggis*, in terms of food register and anatomy, is *tripe*. Of *tripe* as '[t]he first or second stomach of a ruminant, esp. of the ox, prepared as food; formerly including also the entrails of swine and fish', the *Oxford English Dictionary* states that, while the immediate antecedent of the English term is Old French *tripe, trippe* 'entrails of an animal', the ulterior source is 'uncertain'.[17] Our earliest Middle English attestation is actually from the English settlements in early fourteenth-century Ireland in the poem called 'Satire on the People of Kildare': 'Hail be ȝe hokesters dun bi þe lake, Wiþ candles and golokes and þe pottes blak, Tripis and kine fete and schepen heuedes.'[18] From a later century, a cautionary note: 'Bryng vs in no mutton, for that is often lene, Nor bryng vs in no trypys, for thei be syldom clene'.[19]

As well as in glossary entries, *tripe, trippe* is found in one manuscript of Walter of Bibbesworth's late thirteenth-century work on the French vocabulary of estate management, in a cameo scene devoted to the preparations for a feast: 'Le quistroun ov soun havet Trait la tripe del poconet' ('The cook's boy with his meat-hook pulls the tripe from the cooking pot').[20] Authoritative French lexicographical works note *tripe* in texts from the latter half of the thirteenth century but also call the origin 'obscure'.[21] Sources in Arabic *therb* 'suet' (or 'fold of cloth') or Latin *exstirpare* are rejected, and a possible Vulgar Latin **trippa*, 'd'origine expressive', is tentatively proposed, in view of parallels in Italian *trippa*, Spanish, Catalan, and Portuguese *tripa*. An early French attestation is in the anonymous *fit* called *La Bataille de Caresme et de Charnage* (The Fight Between Lenten-time and Flesh-time), in which 'tripes de porc et de mouton' are enlisted among the troops of Lord Carnivore, as we might call *Baron Charnage*.[22]

In light of the well-known Norman culinary dish *tripes à la mode de Caen*,[23] one might speculate that the origins of the term lay in Old Norse and in the culture of early medieval Scandinavia. But there is no plausible correspondence with Norman *tripe*, *þarmr* being the usual word for 'entrails' (cf. Old English *þearmas*). Still, the notion of a Germanic connection need not be rejected. If we turn from cuisine to anatomy, we may adduce the functions of the intestine in the alimentary canal system, among which is the propulsion of digested matter through the system by means of peristalsis, the contraction of the smooth muscles of the gut. The idea of propulsion is expressed in Old High German by the verb *trîban*, cognate with English *drive*, modern German *Trieb*, *treiben*.[24] The elements *trib-*, *trîb-* are also found in OHG compounds such as *ûztrîban* 'to expel'. An Old Frankish form that might be figured as **tribba* (perhaps an abbreviation; cf. OHG *trîbari* 'driver'), although unattested in our source materials, may be entertained as a source for Gallo-Romance *trippe* and further Romance forms.[25] This would entail a multi-faceted semantic development. Initially a term for a part of the body based on function and process ('pusher'), *trippe* would have had to become attached to a culinary dish incorporating such offal and, one would think, have lost much of its original signifying and affective value. It is hard to imagine a dish simply called 'guts'. The later shift in designation in English is from intestines to stomach parts and from a range of animals to bovines. The North American term *chitterlings* for sausages in natural, intestine casings is more of a conventional euphemism, apparently having originated as 'kettle-boiled (sausages)'. *Force-meat*, 'meat chopped fine, spiced, and highly seasoned, chiefly used for stuffing or as a garnish' (*OED*), reverses the imagery of a Germanic **tribba* and its original notion of expulsion.

The tripe and onions extolled by Samuel Butler (*The Way of All Flesh*) and Charles Dickens (*Barnaby Rudge*) is now a rarely met dish, at least in Britain.[26] *Tripe*, once used contemptuously of a person, began to be applied in a figurative sense to 'worthless stuff, rubbish, especially artistic work, opinions, conversation' (*OED*) in the late seventeenth century. Today, dish, name, and metaphor are all marginalized.

NOTES

1. *Oxford English Dictionary, s.v. haggis*; *Middle English Dictionary, s.v. hagis*; *Dictionary of the Scots Language, s.v. haggis*. Other English etymological dictionaries range from no entry at all (*The Barnhard Concise Dictionary of Etymology*) to stating that the origin is unknown (Klein) and on to a far-fetched and unsupported origin in Old French *agace* 'magpie' (*The Oxford Dictionary of English Etymology*). See further below. This article was first published as 'The Genealogy of the Haggis', *Miscelánea* 39 (2009), 103–10, and is reproduced with the permission of the editors.
2. *Liber Cure Cocorum*, 52–53.
3. *Middle English Dictionary* speculates that the term *turbilen* is probably drawn from Old French *torbillon* 'whirlwind', in the sense of a seething pot of liquid, but it is much more likely a distortion of *court bouillon*, literally 'short boil(ed)'. If this were true, it would be the earliest attestation of the phrase, albeit in garbled form, in either French or English. My thanks to Jennifer Sayers for differentiating for me among *court bouillon*, stock, and broth. See further *Larousse Gastronomique*, 352.
4. *Femina* (2005), 74.
5. 'He saw Carnegie himself have in his hand a hot sheep's haggis'; *The Black Book of Kincardineshire*, 94.
6. Walter of Bibbesworth (1990), 1.
7. Walter's term for bowl is *queles* (v. 1033). *Anglo-Norman Dictionary* has an entry under the head-word *escuele* but seems not to have noticed this variant form.
8. On the kitchen as a frequent site for medieval humor, see Gordon. At the end of the haggis episode, Walter returns to the vocabulary of bee-keeping; see 'Beehives & honey' in this volume.

9. *A Concise Etymological Dictionary of the English Language.*
10. *An Icelandic English Dictionary, s.v. höggva.*
11. Rothwell (1984), 174.
12. *Altfranzösisches Wörterbuch, s.v. hacher.*
13. *Französisches etymologisches Wörterbuch*, Vol. 16, 144–48, *s.v. hâppia*, at 146b. See further *Indogermanisches etymologisches Wörterbuch*, II.932, *s.v. (s)skep, (s)kop* 'to cut, split with a sharp instrument'. The *FEW* evolution – from a nominal formation, through a verbal form, to finally designate the end product of the verbal action – is rather roundabout. A more direct derivation would be from a Frankish verb cognate with Middle High German *hacken* 'to hack into pieces'; *IEW*, II. 537, *s.v. keg-/kek-, keng-/kenk-*. *Dictionnaire étymologique de l'ancien français*, the most recent reference work to address the word *haggis*, has a disappointing entry *s.v. haguier*, which it would derive, with no justification offered, from a Middle Dutch *hacken* 'to chop'. Its discussion of *haggis* reviews some earlier secondary literature but makes no effort to place the dish in a bilingual cultural environment.
14. *Mesnagier de Paris*, 684, l. 1619.
15. *Anglo-Norman Dictionary, s.v. hagis.*
16. See Lodge, who recognizes the worth of Walter of Bibbesworth's early testimony and speculates on possible medieval pronunciations of the haggis word in France and England, i.e., whether the intervocalic consonant(s) was pronounced -*g*-, -*dz*- or -*ch*-. But here too a discussion of the wider cultural context is lacking.
17. *OED, s.v. tripe*, n.i.
18. *The Satire on the People of Kildare*, 155.
19. 'Bring us', in *The Early English Carols*, 286.
20. This variant reading of a line that is devoted to the haggis in most manuscripts of Walter's treatise is found in MS (B), Cambridge Trinity Coll. B.14.40.
21. *Trésor de la langue française, s.v. tripe*, citing *Französisches etymologisches Wörterbuch*, vol. 13, 2, p. 300b.
22. *La Bataille de Caresme et de Charnage*, v. 247.
23. The traditional French dish consists of tripe cooked with carrots, onions, and cow heels in cider or white wine.
24. *Althochdeutsches Wörterbuch, s.v. triban.*
25. *FEW, Germanische Elemente*, Vol. 17, S–Z, lists no Gallo-Romance derivatives of Germanic *triban*.
26. For the dish's continued popularity in other parts of the world, see http://en.wikipedia.org/wiki/Tripe.

Pork

This note is devoted to the English terminology of a few basic products of the pig. It does not include the names of butcher's cuts or of the multitude of dishes based on or incorporating pork, all of which have followed their own dynamic, with French cuisine and its vocabulary playing a substantial role in their historical development. This briefer academic menu includes *ham, gammon, sausage, bacon* (with its *flitches, rashers,* and *collops*), *lard* and *lardons*. But, first, we do well to consider the name of the animal itself, *pig*.

Pig, as a designation of *Sus domestica*, is the object of a recently updated entry in the New Edition of the *Oxford English Dictionary* being published online.[1] The etymological note is ample but inconclusive and the dictionary's summary conclusion is 'origin uncertain'. Nonetheless, there is a quite full range of Germanic, especially Dutch, cognates of *pig*, although they exhibit considerable variety. Reflexes include Middle Dutch dialect forms *bagge, pogge, pegsken, puggen, vigghe*, early modern regional Dutch *bigge, pigge, pogge*, modern Dutch *big, biggele, biggeken, biggetje* – all in the sense 'young pig'. To this evidence may be added Middle Low German *bachelken, baggelken*, Low German *Pogge, Bigg*. The tacit conclusion from the *OED* entry for *pig* is that the word is without cognates beyond the sphere of western European Germanic languages. This may not be unconditionally the case.

The following discussion of English *pig* is guided by three considerations: 1) evidence that *pig* and related words were first used of young animals; 2) the *OED*'s suggestion of 'borrowing from a common (perhaps substratal) source'; and 3) the Dictionary's sense of the word possibly having 'a very familiar, affective character spread from one locality to another'.

Early continental Celtic, in the form of Gaulish, has a number of terms for swine: *banuos* 'young pig', *moccos* 'pig, wild boar', *orco-* 'young pig', *succos* 'pig', *turcos* 'boar, wild boar'.[2] Of these, the *orco-* forms are cognate with Latin *porcus* and Old English *fearh*, whence *farrow*. The notion of a loan from Gaulish to Germanic, 'adstratal' rather than substratal, should not be dismissed out of hand. We need think only of such Gaulish loans into German as *Amt* 'office, function' and *Reich* 'kingdom' on the one hand, *Eisen* 'iron', *Karre* 'cart', and *Pferd* 'horse' on the other to recognize the possible range of cultural exports. *Moccos* 'pig, wild boar' is found as a theonym in Gaulish inscriptions and as an element of personal names, e.g., *Cato-mocus* 'Battle-Boar'.[3] English *pig* is not so distant from *moccos,* when we consider the points of articulation and nasal, voiced or unvoiced quality of the sounds *m-* and *p-*, *-kk-* and *-g*. A Gaulish diminutive form designating young swine, e.g., *moccillos*, could also well carry some of the affect that the *OED* suggests for *pig* and its cognates. We need only think of *piggy, piglet,* and, on a larger scale, *porker* in current English. Trade in livestock across the lower Rhine between Celts and Germans can be imagined, although we have little in the way of evidence for such intercultural interaction. The subsequent spread of a *pig* word through numerous Germanic dialects in a variety of forms, ultimately via the Angles and Saxons to Britain, and its emergence as the generic word for swine in English reflect a dynamic that is neither fully documented nor fully understood. An ultimate Gaulish origin for the English name of *Sus domestica* must then remain speculative.

In a fuller study, other pig words might well be examined. e.g., *sow, boar, farrow*. Etymologies are relatively transparent for most of these but this is not the case for *hog*. The *OED* states that the origin is unknown and offers this etymological note:

> The suggestion that Old English *hogg* was borrowed < Old Welsh *huch* pig, swine (Welsh *hwch*, now only in sense 'sow') or its cognate Old Cornish *hoch* (Middle Cornish *hoch* ; < the same Indo-European base as *sow* ...) is unlikely on phonological grounds, unless the word

showed alteration in form as a result of association with the group
of animal names in *-cga, -gga* listed at *dog* ...[4]

Yet, if we imagine that the word was adopted in the fifth or sixth
centuries by the invading Angles and Saxons from the native British
who spoke Brittonic or Old British, a Celtic language close to Gaulish,
a term akin to Gaulish *succos* 'pig' could have been adopted at a much
earlier date than the subsequent emergence of the Cornish and Welsh
forms.[5]

In comparison with *pig* and *hog*, *pork* has a more readily identified
origin. The set *cow/ beef, calf/ veal, sheep/ mutton*, and *pig/ pork* is well
known: native English terms for the animals, Anglo-Norman French
for their meat (reflecting, we might imagine, social and dietary differences between early producers and consumers). English *pork* is then
to be traced to the Norman Conquest and Anglo-Norman French
porc, where it designated both the animal and its flesh. French *porc*,
in turn, derives from Latin *porcus*, which was initially the term for
the domesticated animal, while *sus* served as a generic term for both
domesticated and wild pigs.

In Old English, *ham* designated the back of the human knee and the
hock of quadrupeds.[6] In the Middle English period, *hamme, homme,
hambe* continued with this meaning, with no extension to foodstuffs.
It is only in the mid-seventeenth century that a more specialized use
appears in print: 'the thigh of a slaughtered animal, used for food;
spec. that of a hog salted and dried in smoke or otherwise' (*OED*).
For example: 'Mr. Henrie Blyth had such antipathie aganis an ham,
that no sooner did he heare a ham spoken of but he swarfed'.[7] Yet, in
the Anglo-French that was spoken in Britain for centuries, *jambon*
(variant spellings *jambeun, gambon, gambone, gamboun, chamben*) was
being used both of the hock and of the ham or thigh of wild boars.
As the celebrated early fourteenth-century master of game William
Twiti states, the best parts of the boar include 'le qoer e le pomoun
e lez pestles e la eschine ... e les gambouns' (the heart and the lungs
and the foreleg and the spine ... and the hams).[8] Old French *jambon*
is derived from *jambe* 'leg', with the addition of an aggrandizing suffix

-on, here in reference to the fullest part of the leg.[9] It designated a preserved (e.g., smoked, salted) thigh or shoulder of pork. As the antecedent of modern English *gammon* it appears in Middle and Renaissance English, as *gambon(e)*, *gammound*, *gamond*.

It is also possible that the semantics of Anglo-French *jambon* influenced Middle English *hamme* so that in the early modern period *ham* came to be used of the salted and dried thigh of the hog, thus extending the original semantics of Old English *ham* 'back of knee' to include the flesh of the upper thigh. Here it may be proposed that *jambon* could have suggested, to an English ear, *ham-bone* (folk etymology), in which a simplex *ham* could be recognized.

Sausage might well be included with *ham* among the names for basic pork products but the explanation of the name is straightforward and this note will not pause long over it: Middle English *sausige* represents the loan of Old Northern French *saussiche* (Central Old French, modern French *saucisse*) and has cognates in Spanish *salchicha*, Portuguese *salchicha*, Italian *salsiccia*. All derive from < Late Latin *salsīcia* 'prepared by salting', < *salsus* 'salted'.

From *ham* via *sausage* to their social inferior *bacon*. Also cured with salt, bacon comes in two main sorts, streaky from the side and belly, and round from the loin. As a lexical item, *bacon* is also a French import. In medieval Anglo-French it could refer to a leg or flitch of pork, even salt pork generally.[10] The qualities of Irish bacon were recognized as early as the second half of the twelfth century, as noted in the chronicle devoted to the twelfth-century Cambrio-Norman invasion of Ireland: 'Tant troverent ... Blé, ferin e bacun' (They found great quantities of wheat, flour, and salt pork).[11] In modern French, *bacon* has been supplanted by *porc salé* or *lard* (on the latter, see further below). Authoritative French lexicographical works trace *bacon* to an Old Frankish lexical import, *bakko*, cognate with Old High German *bahho*, Middle High German *backe*, *bache*, Middle Dutch *bake(n)* 'ham, flitch of bacon'.[12] This was also adopted into medieval Latin as *baco*, *bacho*. These are, in turn, claimed as figurative extensions of Germanic words for 'back', the ultimate origin of which is a hypothetical Germanic **bako-z*. A fatty bacon, called *bardière* in

French, can, indeed, be taken from the back of the hog but is judged inferior to the leaner bacon taken from the belly. *Bakko* would seem to have meant 'rump' in this application, a semantic narrowing that increased with its application to the cured leg of the pig.

Here, one may parenthetically raise the question that must underlie all speculation on early diet: just how common was it to eat fresh meat? Answers will surely differ according to time, region, and social class. One can well imagine British yeomen having some fresh meat at slaughtering time in the fall but appreciable quantities must have been pickled or smoked for the lean winter months. Small game was doubtless eaten at once. And venison, if one had the right to hunt the deer? As concerns linguistic transfers and the names of animals in particular, it seems likely that some techniques of animal husbandry, and food preservation and preparation accompanied the new names of animals likely already represented in communities of the receiving language.

A side or slab of bacon is traditionally called a flitch in many parts of the English-speaking world. The term would seem to derive in a straight line of descent from Old English *flicce* 'fresh or cured side of an animal', most often the pig.[13] But in Old French, *flec* and *fliche, flique* were used of a side of bacon.[14] These words, too, along with the antecedent of bacon, would appear to have been imports from Frankish and thus cognate with the Old English term. The situation in the modern English and French languages is made more complicated by the fact that *flec, fliche* did not survive into modern French, where *flèche* 'arrow' is instead used in the expression *flèche de lard* for a side of bacon, one of several figurative extensions of *flèche* to oblong objects ending in a tapered point. Assuming that *fliche* was also represented in Anglo-French (although it is not preserved in the written record, where *bacon* is used), it will have reinforced native English *flicce* in this application, as Old Norse *flikki* will earlier also have done in the Danelaw. The possibly hybrid forms *flicche, flik, flikke, flucche* emerge in Middle English.[15] Here we find this grim image of a fallen knight: 'On eyther syde his hors he lyes, As it hadde ben two clouen stikkes, Or of a swyn to clouen flikkes'.[16]

From the flitch may be taken individual slices or strips, or, as they are often called in Britain, Ireland, Australia, and New Zealand, *rashers*. The *OED* claims that the etymology is uncertain. *Rasher* is first attested in the last quarter of the sixteenth century. A ready explanation is, however, found in Anglo-French. The Old French verb *racer, racher* 'to tear' (< Latin *radicare*) appears in the French of Britain but more commonly in an expanded version, *arracher* 'to tear out or off' (< Latin *eradicare*). The various forms of the latter attest to the instability of the first prefixal element: *aracer, arascher, arasser, arassher, aracher, enracher, enraser, esracher, esracier, esrachier,* and the like.[17] Under these circumstances, Anglo-French often drops such initial elements. These verbs are represented in Middle English by *arācen, arracen, arasen, arachen.*[18] The English verb *to rash* 'to cut, slash', from a French simplex, *racher,* or an abbreviated version of *aracher,* is attested from the mid-sixteenth century. It is proposed that English *rasher* represents accommodation in English of a French participial form **raché* 'something ripped or sliced off', completed by the typical English agent ending *-r*. As Dryden writes in the Prologue to *All for Love*: 'Drink hearty Draughts of Ale … And snatch the homely Rasher from the Coals.'[19]

Collop is an English term found as early as Langland's *Piers Plowman* (1360s) and designated bacon and eggs, or, originally, an egg cooked on a slice of bacon and in its melted fat.[20] The *OED* calls its derivation 'obscure'. The explanation may lie in a compound or hybrid form, along the line of *dollop*. The Anglo-French verb whose modern French equivalent is *couper* 'to cut' was variously spelled *colper, couper, coeper, colper, coper, copper, cosper, cuper, cupper,* and some of these spellings may reflect subtle differences of pronunciation – or none at all.[21] English *coppice,* earlier *coupis/coupiz,* as a term of sylvan husbandry, derives from this source. Let us posit a first element **colp-* with the meaning 'cut' or, more precisely, 'slice'. The Germanic languages have a range of terms on the model of *lob* that reference something bulky, amorphous, globulous or pendant; an Old English cognate may be fairly safely assumed. In early modern English *lob* designated a lump, clump, large piece, or viscous liquid; we even have lob-grass, a hooded grass species, *Bromus mollis*. *Dollop* can also be associated with this lexical element.[22] Let us then accept *lob* with de-aspirated -*b*, i.e., *lop*, as a plausible antecedent for a reconstructed compound that may be figured as **colp-lop*, later *collop*, with the basic meaning 'piece of indeterminate shape cut off a larger body' and more specifically a slice from a flitch of bacon.

With English *lard* we are still among the complex currents of lexical interplay between French and English, and also the shifts of meaning, status, relative frequency, and distribution over time, space, and dialect within each of these languages. In Old French and Anglo-French, *lard* meant salt pork from a variety of cuts. It is tempting to think that with time, the French distinguished between the fleshier *bacon* of the side and belly, and the fatter bacon of the back, *la bardière* (cf. the English culinary term, *to bard*). *Lard* (< Latin *lardum, laridum)* was retained in French for salt pork generally, including streaked bacon, while a new term, *saindoux*, was coined some time before the thirteenth century for the rendered product that could be taken from the back and elsewhere. It consists of *sain* (< late Latin *sagimen* < classical Latin *sagima*), 'the grease of wild boars, foxes, and wolves', plus *doux* 'mild, sweet', as an attenuating, domesticating qualifier.[23] In English, while we have a neat match between *porc salé* and salt pork, bacon came to refer to streaky bacon and even better cuts such as Canadian or back bacon, while *lard*, the old term for salt pork generally, took the narrower meaning of the fat or grease recovered from a pig carcass. The term is attested from about 1440 ('Take þo ox tonge ... Sethe hit, broche hit in larde yche dele').[24] It should also be recalled that the medieval Latin spoken and written in Britain would often have added its weight to Anglo-French in the case of Latin-derived words, promoting their adoption in the English vernacular.[25] *Lardons*, pieces of bacon or pork inserted in meat, are also noted in writing from the mid-fifteenth century, and the term is originally a French formation.

As this cursory examination illustrates, many English words are still judged without full and satisfactory historical explanation and, ironically, this is the case for numerous everyday terms: *dog, frog, girl, colt, pig, hog.*[26] The pig- and pork-related words discussed here, while associated in our mental vocabularies, have individual histories, although it is striking how many words in this set are the result of borrowings between cultures in contact—from Celtic (Gaulish, British) to western Germanic, from Frankish to Gallo-Romance, from Norman French to English. In some cases, the newly introduced words may have had a distinct affective value (as does baby talk), have been loans from a subaltern population or, alternately, from a culture perceived as superior in some respect (e.g., French vs British cuisine). In some cases the introduction of new vocabulary may have been accompanied by changes in animal husbandry and curing techniques. Adding to the dynamic, words may undergo semantic shifts, moving to designate a different part of a carcass. Nonetheless, the relative value attached to the various pork products seems about the same, to the degree such assessments are possible. The various curing techniques, these too the object of intercultural transfer, also made it possible for agrarian tenant farmers to pay rent with hams, bacon, etc., setting the stage for later commercialization and medium- and long-distance trade – hams from Parma, Bayonne, Guijuelo, and so on.

The set of English words reviewed here also represents the survivors in the Darwinian lexical world – much vocabulary must have been lost over time and across space, as browsing Joseph Wright's *English Dialect Dictionary*, looking for pigs in out-of-the way pokes, quickly illustrates.[27]

NOTES

1. *The Oxford English Dictionary*, New Edition (Oxford: Oxford University Press, 2012), *OED Online, s.v. pig*, <http://www.oed.com/view/Entry/143654, accessed 24 February, 2013. This article first appeared as 'The Early History of Some Traditional Names for Pork Products', in *Petits Propos Culinaires* 98 (2013), pp. 78–88.

2. Xavier Delamarre, *Dictionnaire de la langue gauloise*, 2ⁿᵈ ed. (Paris: Errance, 2003), *s.vv.*; see also Karl-Horst Schmidt, 'Zum "Schwein" im Keltischen', *Man and the Animal World: Studies in Archaeozoology, Archaeology, Anthropology and Palaeolinguistics in Memoriam Sándor Bökönyi*, edited by Peter Anreiter (Budapest: Archaeolingua Alapítvány, 1998), pp. 713–16.

3. Delamarre, *Dictionnaire de la langue gauloise*, 228, *s.v. moccos*. Some have seen a porcine deity, *Baco*, behind the reference to 'deo Baconis' in an inscription from Châlon. But this is more surely a reference to the beech, *bagos* in Gaulish, and as a cult tree often found in place-names (Delamarre, 64). Among neo-Celtic enthusiasts, such fragmentary evidence is soon hoisted into the pantheon; see, e.g., http://en.wikipedia.org/wiki/Baco_%28god%29.

4. *OED Online* (December 2012), *s.v. hog*, http://www.oed.com/view/Entry/87576, accessed February 24, 2013.

5. While phonological mutation in Gaulish is a bit too complicated to detail here, its contribution to the assumed passage of *s-* to *h-* is not problematic; see Peter Schrijver, *Studies in British Celtic Historical Phonology* (Amsterdam; Atlanta, GA: Rodopi, 1995).

6. *Dictionary of Old English*, edited by Antonette diPaolo-Healey et al. (Toronto: University of Toronto Press, 2007–), *s.v. ham*.

7. John Row, *The historie of the Kirk of Scotland, M.D.LVIII.-M.DC.XXXVII* (Edinburgh: Maitland Club, 1842), 324.

8. William Twiti, *The Middle English Text of 'The Art of Hunting' by William Twiti, with a Parallel Text of the Anglo-Norman 'L'art de venerie' by William Twiti*, edited by D. Scott-Macnab, Middle English Texts 40 (Heidelberg: Winter, 2009), 182.

9. *Trésor de la langue française*, edited by Paul Imbs (Paris: Centre national de la recherche scientifique, 1971–94), *s.v. jambon*. See, now, *Dictionnaire étymologique de l'ancien français*, edited by Kurt Baldinger e. al. (Québec: Presses de l'Université Laval; Tübingen: Niemeyer; Paris: Klincksieck, 1974–), *s.v. jambon*. This work is thus far limited to the range G to K and of little direct help to other words here under review.

10. *Anglo-Norman Dictionary*, 2ⁿᵈ ed., edited by William Rothwell et al. (Aberystwyth: Modern Humanities Research Association 2005), *s.v. bacon*.

11. *The Deeds of the Normans in Ireland: La Geste des Engleis en Yrlande*, ed. E. Mullaly (Dublin: Four Courts, 2002), v. 1960.

12. *Französisches etymologisches Wörterbuch*, edited by Walther von Wartburg et al. (Bonn: F. Klopp [several subsequent places of publication and publishers], 1928–2000), *Germanische Elemente*, vol.15, pt. 1, 29b, *s.v. bakko*.

13. *Dictionary of Old English, s.v. flicce*.

14. Frédéric Godefroy, *Dictionnaire de l'ancienne langue française* (Paris: F. Vierweg, 1881–1902), *s.vv. flec, fliche.*

15 'Tak þe fatt bakon of an alde swyn flyk & melte it', *The Liber de Diversis Medicinis in the Thornton Manuscript,* edited by M. S. Ogden, EETS 207 (London: Oxford University Press, 1938; rev. reprint 1969), 55/1, cited from *Middle English Dictionary,* edited by Hans Kunrath et al. (Ann Arbor, Michigan: University of Michigan Press, 1952–2001), *s.v. flicche.*

16. *The Laud Troy Book,* edited by J. E. Wülfing, EETS 121, 122 (London: K. Paul, Trench, Trübner & co., 1902, 1903; reprint as one vol. 1988), v. 6284.

17. *Anglo-Norman Dictionary, s.v. aracer.*

18. *Middle English Dictionary, s.v. arācen.*

19. John Dryden, *All for love; or, The world well lost* (London: T. Warren, 1696).

20. *OED Online* (December 2012), *s.v. collop,* <http://www.oed.com/view/Entry/36423, accessed 25 February 2013. 'I haue no salt Bacon, Ne no Cokeneyes, bi Crist Colopus to maken'; William Langland, *The Vision of William Concerning Piers Plowman,* edited by William Skeat (London: N. Trübner, 1867–85, 1886), A.VII.272.

21. *Anglo-Norman Dictionary, s.v. couper.*

22. See *dollop* in William Sayers, 'Challenges Facing English Etymology in the Twenty-First Century, with Illustrations,' *Studia Neophilologica* 84 (2012), 1–25.

23. *Französisches etymologisches Wörterbuch, s.v. sagima.*

24. *Liber cure cocorum, Copied and edited from the Sloane MS. 1986,* edited by Richard Morris (Berlin: Asher, 1862),26, from about 1475; *OED,* OED Online. December 2012, *s.v. lard,* <http://www.oed.com/view/Entry/105810, accessed 24 February 2013.

25. The medieval Latin of such utilitarian British documents as inventories and invoices contains many vernacular words given a light Latin wash, as well as the classical and medieval Latin equivalents of the vocabulary dicussed here; see *Dictionary of Medieval Latin from British Sources,* edited by R.E. Latham (London: Oxford University Press, 1975–2013).

26. To further illustrate the difficulties of research on such lexical 'isolates', see William Sayers, 'The Etymologies of *dog* and *cur*', *The Journal of Indo-European Studies.* 36 (2008), 401–10, and 'Challenges Facing English Etymology in the Twenty-First Century, with Illustrations,' *Studia Neophilologica* 84 (2012), 1–25.

27. Joseph Wright, *The English Dialect Dictionary, being the complete vocabulary of all dialect words still in use, or known to have been in use during the last two hundred years,* 6 vols (London: H. Frowde; New York, G. P. Putnam's Sons, 1898–1905).

Steak & grill

The familiar words *steak* and *grill* are so closely associated that one might be tempted to think that they had evolved in tandem. A closer look at their presumed origins and early histories will, however, illustrate that such pairings are usually the outcome of quite disparate evolutionary paths and that neat parallelism is rarely the case in the dynamic, often apparently chaotic, mix and flux of linguistic, including lexical, development.

Grill is the better documented of the two words and has an ultimate source in the *craticulum* (variant *craticula*) of classical Latin, this derived from Latin *cratis* 'hurdle, lattice', the same word that is at the source of English *grate* in a sense comparable to *grill* as a 'cooking utensil formed of parallel bars of iron or other metal in a frame, usually supported on short legs'.[1] With the loss of intervocalic consonants that is typical of the evolving sound system of Gallo-Romance or early French, *craticulum/a* developed in French into what seem two distinct forms, although they might also represent an earlier and a later stage or regional variants, even terms in differing registers. A longer form, retaining more of the phonic matter of the 'original', is *gradil*. It is found in the Old French glosses of Rashi (Rabbi Shlomo Itzhaki) from the eleventh century on difficult words in the Hebrew *Talmud*, proof that French was the likely vernacular in Jewish homes in early medieval France.[2] But in other medieval glossarial lists, where French equivalents of Latin are given, *cratis* and *craticula* are equated with *grëil*.[3] It is evident from somewhat later texts such as the treatise on household economy, *Le Mesnagier de Paris* (1393), that *gril* refers to a kitchen utensil that permitted food to be roasted by direct exposure to fire.[4] But, on a larger scale and in a grimmer context, *grëil* and *graïl* were also used of the iron frames on which martyrs were believed to have been tortured and killed for their Christian faith.[5]

In the period after the Norman conquest French became acclimatized in Britain. In this Anglo-French, both a spoken and written medium, *grill* appears in a wide variety of orthographies and probably a somewhat more limited range of pronunciations: *greil, greile, greille, grail, graille, graylle, gril, gredil, gredile, grideil, gridel, gridil, gridile, gerdil, gerdile.* In the Middle English that evolved in parallel to Anglo-French and then supplanted it in most spheres of British life except law, the phonological slot for a 'grill word' was occupied by two potential homonyms and thus rivals: 1) *grille* with the meanings 'annoyance, anger; ill feeling; suffering, misfortune; harm' and possibly 'violence', and 2) *grille* (variant *grulle*) 'cricket', also, a venomous insect resembling a cricket.[6] This may account for the above-noted 'longer' French form appearing first in Middle English, as *gridel, gridelle, griddil, gridilie, gredel(le), gredle, girdul, gurdel.* Griddle is the readily identified descendant of this word cluster.[7] ME *gridel* and congeners were used of a grating or lattice; of a grill for roasting or broiling, of an iron plate on which bread was baked; and for the gridiron used as an instrument of torture. *Gridel* was also used of a grid or draw-plate employed in making wire.

Yet, in addition to *gridel*, a superficially transparent Middle English term also appeared, one whose nonetheless eventful development culminated in the form *gridiron*, which was not always the simple compound it appears. The variety of ME forms include *gridēre, greder, gridir(e), gredire, gridirne, gridern(e), girdirin, girderen, gredirn(e),* with additional variants for the second half of the word: *-iron, -ern, -eroun, -eirne, -eiren, -ren, -rin.* The *OED* calls *gridiron* 'of obscure formation'; the modern form *grid* is considered a back formation from *gridiron*, that is, knowledge of the latter led to the assumption that a simpler form (or simplex) must also exist. *Middle English Dictionary*, on the other hand, would derive these forms of *gridiron* from *gridel*, with a substitution of the suffix *-ēre* for *-el* and a subsequent confusion of this suffix with the ME word for 'iron', viz. *īren (īre, īroun, īrne, iren, eire,* etc.).[8] In many European languages, the lateral sounds *r* and *l* are often exchanged for one another, and this kind of slide, conceivably resulting in **gridere* (the asterisk identifies a hypothetical form), may have preceded the identification with a familiar suffix or of a compound with *iron*. The ME collocation is even returned to an Anglo-French context (with some disregard for the idea of iron) in items from a late thirteenth-century inventory: 'Item, I Grediron d'argent, cont' XI peces' ('one silver gridiron made up of 11 pieces').[9]

Gridirons are regularly mentioned in the cookery books of the age: 'Scher yt on schyverys and roste yt on a grydern' ('Cut it into slices and roast it on a gridiron');[10] 'Wan they be ysodyn, nym and rosty hem in a grydere' ('When they are boiled, take and roast them on a gridiron').[11] 'Cutt bred in schyves and toist it upon a gridirne' ('cut bread in slices and toast it on a gridiron').[12] From 1440 we have this inventory of related kitchen utensils: 'Aundrons, spites, rakks, cobbards, trevetts, grederns' ('andirons, spits, racks, spit-holders, trivets, gridirons').[13] The verb *to grill* is not attested before the 1660s and seems modelled on the noun, as was early modern French *griller*.[14] Norman French *grediller* did not survive and Modern French, in its turn, now uses the form *grésiller* but in the sense 'to scorch'.

In summary, English *grill*, despite the phonic reduction, descends in a relatively straight line from Latin *craticulum*, with a *grill/griddle* fork in the medieval period and the recast form *gridiron*. The semantics are equally true to origins, with the form, function, and context (fire) of the utensil largely unchanged, save for size and the possible addition of features such as legs (and the extension to wire-drawing, etc.). The adornment of the grill, the steak, will, lexically, display some of the same consistency but an even more roundabout, multilingual development and adaptation as a culinary term. The thesis to be tested below is that even at an early date *steak* referred to fairly specific cuts of meat and, preferentially but not exclusively, the flesh of specific animals, and to distinct butchering and cooking techniques, perhaps even to a common context where such procedures were practised.

According to the *OED*, *steak* is a loan from Old Norse and would have been introduced to Britain in the course of the Scandinavian invasions of the ninth century, which resulted in the establishment of the Danelaw or Danish-ruled territories in central and eastern England. *Steak* does not, however, appear in written English until the early 1400s, many centuries later. These early attestations will serve to establish some important distinctions. An early cookbook calls for steaks from beef or venison, while a later text includes mutton.[15] In John Lydgate's 1426 translation of Guillaume de Guileville's *Le pèlerinage de vie humaine* under the title *The Pilgrimage of the life of man*, he writes, 'Now to ffrye, now steykës make, And many other soteltes', thus distinguishing frying from the preparation of steak.[16] The verb *roast* is also associated with steaks.[17] John Palsgrave's dictionary from 1530 clearly establishes that steaks were prepared by direct exposure to fire since 'steke of flesshe' is glossed with French *charbonnee* 'scorched, marked by carbon'.[18]

How does this match up with usage in northern Europe where Norse (doubtless with Danish, Norwegian and Swedish dialectal features) was spoken? Our written early medieval evidence is limited to texts composed largely in Iceland although some have a Norwegian provenance. The Norse verb *steikja* 'to roast' is cognate with English *to stoke*, although the latter now applies to tending to a fire (cf. *stoker*) rather than to what is cooked over it. *Steik* in such Norse compounds as *lambasteik* and *kálfasteik*, transparently lamb and veal steaks, is frequently met in the earliest Norwegian law tracts.[19] Another compound *steikiteinn* (cf. Eng. *tine*) designates a spit for roasting steaks. A telling image is met in the poem from the *Edda*, *Fáfnismál* (*The Lay of Fáfnir*), on the encounter between the hero Sigurd and the dragon Fafnir. The dragon is wounded and, after much discussion, killed and its heart cut out. 'Sigurd took Fafnir's heart and roasted (*steicþi*) it on a spit (*á teini*). And when he thought it was done (*fullsteict*), and the juice was dripping out of the heart, he prodded it with his finger to see if it was done.'[20] Licking his hot finger, Sigurd can now understand the speech of the birds. Other examples of the verb *steikja* support this impression of an impromptu meal in the open, far from kitchen amenities, the kind of meal that travellers, shepherds, hunters, and the like may have cooked. Yet this distinction is only an impression, since sources are so scant. It must be borne in mind that such roasting would have entailed the loss of melted fat and then had some slight nutritional and economic consequences. As well, only the tenderest or well-hung cuts – and not hearts – would lend themselves to such direct exposure to the flames. And it should be recalled that only relatively thin cuts of meat would lend themselves to this fairly rapid means of cooking.

Since the Northmen settled Neustria on the European continent, the future Normandy, one might have looked for Old Norse *steik* to have been adopted there, always assuming a need for both the cooking procedure and the descriptive term. A hypothetical development, in line with other adaptations in Gallo-Romance, would yield forms such as **esteic, estei* but no such words are found in Norman French and thus none was carried to Britain and Anglo-French. A purely linguistic explanation for this lack may have been the threat to clarity posed by the presence in Norman French of many near-homonyms of a theoretical *estei*, e.g., *esté, estei, estei* 'summer'. Yet other factors must surely also have been at work in early Normandy, one of which may have been more restricted access to game that could be cooked and eaten in the field.

The Norse language was also carried to the Faroes, Shetland, Orkney, Sutherland, the Hebrides, and Ireland. Of these, only the last-named provides written evidence of cross-cultural contacts between the invaders/traders and natives. In one of the tales of Finn mac Cumhail, preserved from the twelfth century, Finn is invited by Molling the Swift to an impromptu feast assembled magically from all over Ireland. As for the promised menu:

Thou shalt have in Brocc-ross, O Find of the battle!
The berries of the bog, the bacon of Slanga's swine.
Acorns from the wilderness, a steak of the boar of the wave,
Birds of Airer Lemna, salmon on Barrow's bosom ...[21]

Behind the translator's 'steak of the boar of the waves' is Irish 'stáec thuirc na tuinne', which Whitley Stokes, the nineteenth-century editor of the tale, speculates was from a porpoise. Other delicacies includes fish, venison, smoked badger, bacon, nuts, blackberries, apples, sloes, and strawberries. Finn and his men live largely in the wilderness and the proposed banquet draws mainly from non-cultivated or non-domesticated sources of food, evidence for the earlier speculation that steaks were associated with camp fires and the like. In the Irish *dindsenchas*, narrative accounts of the origin of toponyms or place names, *stáic* is again found in apparently fully integrated fashion, that is, there is no sense of the use of a loan word with overtones of foreign cooking practices. In the verse account of the origin of the name of *Duma Selga*, conceivably as early as from the twelfth century, the warrior Fland and his male and female companions are magically transformed into wild swine. His new porcine name is Brogarbán. The swine, who retain the ability to speak, are protected by a chieftain, Buichet, but his wife 'was seized with longing for a steak off Brogarbán's belly' ('im stáic do broinn Brogarbáin'). Fland/Brogarbán is prepared to grant her wish 'for a steak from his tender flesh' ('lé stáic dom fheóil máith'), but succeeds in surviving the woman's overtly sexual appetite to root and fight another day.[22]

Yet it is in the satirical account of the impoverished student Mac Conglinne that steaks assume pride of place. The itinerant scholar has undertaken to lure a demon of gluttony from the innards of his host King Cathal mac Finguine. Just beyond the mouth of the human host of the demon, he grills mutton steaks (*staci*), rubbed with honey and salt, on white hazel spits over an ash-wood fire. 'And as huge as the pieces on the fire were, not one of the four steaks dripped enough to quench the spark of a candle, but they absorbed their own juices into their very core'.[23] He then tempts the attentive demon with an account of a dream vision of a Land of Cockaigne, where a welcoming castle is made of foodstuffs. The demon is eventually lured out of Cathal's mouth by the tantalizing smells and graphic account and, its claws fast in a steak, is thrown into the fire. An inverted cooking pot is secured over the demon, a neat inversion of the Celtic cauldrons of plenty and rebirth.

We then have the puzzling situation of steak being well attested

in the precocious vernacular literature of one region where the
Norse settled (Ireland) but not in another (Normandy), and the
term apparently surfacing in yet a third colony (central and eastern
England) centuries after the fact of invasion. Shane McLeod has
recently advanced the provocative thesis that the apparently smooth
cultural acclimatization of the Danes in England was the result of
many settler families having had prior colonial experience elsewhere
in the North Sea zone, in particular in Ireland and northern Francia
(Normandy).[24] It cannot be ruled out, then, that the grilled cuts of
loin and rump enjoyed in England may owe something to tastes, and
culinary and lexical practices brought to, and further developed in,
Ireland.

While the following passage offers no evidence for the culinary
term *steak* or an exact French equivalent, an account in Chrétien de
Troyes' verse romance, *Yvain*, of an impromptu meal in the wilds
is suggestive of the context in which *steak* could have developed in
neighbouring cultures. During a period of mental aberration the
knight Yvain lives in the wilderness, where he saves a lion from
a serpent (dragon?) and is later helped by the lion. One evening
his new companion brings a freshly killed roe-deer back to Yvain's
encampment.

> Since it was now near nightfall, Yvain chose to spend the night there,
> where he could skin as much of the deer as he wished to eat. Then
> he began to skin it: he split the hide above the ribs and stripped a
> roast (*lardé*) from the loin (*longe*). He struck a spark from a piece of
> flint and with it got some dry sticks to catch fire; then straight away
> he put his roast on a spit (*broche*) over the fire to cook. He roasted
> (*rostit*) it until it was done, but there was no pleasure in eating it,
> for he had neither bread nor wine nor salt, nor table-cloth nor knife
> nor anything else.[25]

The steak removed (before the effects of the adrenaline and lactic
acid build-up, one hopes), roasted and consumed, the lion eats up the
rest of the carcass. Since *lard* was used in Old French of bacon and

salt pork, strips of which were often 'larded' into, or laced around, other cuts of meat, *lardé* would here seem to refer as much to the butchering technique (stripping out) as to the cut or body part.[26]

Recovering a 'rationale' for the introduction of loan words from one language to another is always a bit of a puzzle. Fashion and taste often seem to play a large role. A new mode, new technology, new practice, new object bring new terminology in their wake. But cuts from the loin of beef, pork, and venison were surely eaten before the incursions of the Scandinavians in southern Europe. And the impromptu meals of hunters, travellers, and soldiers around camp-fires can hardly have been an innovation. A number of factors are doubtless at work and it is not entirely certain just what kind of niche Old Norse *steik* first occupied in Irish and English. It is possible that the introduction of *steik* also represents a change in butchering techniques, a new cut in other words. Perhaps it is best to reverse the perspective and speak of Hiberno-Norse and Anglo-Norse lexical and culinary conservatism, the word for steaks and chops and the manner of their cooking being retained among Scandinavian settlers and their descendants in Ireland and the Danelaw after other vocabulary had been surrendered in favour of English. Thereafter, a gradual spread to mainstream Irish and English, just as *grill* was taken up from Anglo-French into Middle English.

Grill and *steak* seem a fixed collocation in English but language is a dynamic presence on stage, with lexical newcomers always in the wings. For example, *barbecue* is attested in English in the late seventeenth century for a wooden frame for smoking meat and fish over a fire (originating in Spanish *barbacoa* and thought to have been borrowed from a indigenous language of the Caribbean) but by 1736 is being used of 'an iron frame for broiling very large joints' (and a carcass thus roasted; *OED*) and has now been further reduced to more modest backyard structures and apparatus for cooking food over an open fire.

NOTES

1. The definition is taken from the *OED* entry for *gridiron*, on which see further below. *Oxford English Dictionary*, 2nd ed. (Oxford: Oxford University Press, 1989), Online edition (2013), *s.v.* grill *n.³*. The *OED* is content to trace *grill* to Old French and no further. *Grate* and *grating* apparently derive from medieval Latin *grata,* from classical Latin *crātis* 'hurdle'.

2. *Les gloses françaises dans les commentaires talmudiques de Raschi*, edited by Arsène Darmsteter and D.S. Blondheim (Paris: l'Ecole des hautes études, 1929), gl. 557.

3. *Trésor de la langue française*, edited by Paul Imbs (Paris: Centre national de la recherche scientifique, 1971–94), citing *Ms. Bibl. Nat. lat.* 8246, 16, in *Anciennes gloses français*, edited by Paul Meyer (Paris: [s.n.], 1895).

4. *Le ménagier de Paris: traité de morale et d'économie domestique composé vers 1393 par un bourgeois parisien*, edited by Jérôme Pichon, 2 vols (Lille: R. Lehoucq, 1846), II.127.

5. 'Lorenz gist sus le greil' ('Lawrence lay on the grill'); *La Vie de Saint Laurent: An Anglo-Norman Poem of the Twelfth Century*, edited by D.W. Russell, ANTS 34 (London: Anglo-Norman Text Society, 1976), v. 854.

6. *Middle English Dictionary*, edited by Hans Kunrath et al. (Ann Arbor, Michigan: University of Michigan Press, 2001), *s.v.v.* grille, n. 1 and 2.

7. In a feedback effect, vernacular words often appear in Latinized form in utilitarian texts in medieval Latin such as inventories, e.g., as *gridila***, *girdalium.*

8. *MED, s.v.* gridēre**.

9. *Rotuli Parliamentorum*, 4 vols (London: Record Commission, 1767–77), I.iv.24; *ib.* I.iv.241: 'Item, V Gredieryns de Ferre, pois' ensemble LXX lb' ['five iron gridirons with a total weight of 70 pounds').

10. Recipe in *The Forme of Cury*, edited by Samuel Pegge (London: J. Nichols, 1780), 98.

11. *Forme of Cury*, 107.

12. *A Noble Boke off Cookry*, edited by Robina Napier (London: Elliot Stock, 1882), 51.

13. *Calendar of Plea and Memoranda Rolls ... of the City of London ... 1437–1457*, edited by P.E. Jones (Cambridge: Cambridge University Press1954), 31, from 1440.

14. *The diary of Samuel Pepys: a new and complete transcription*, edited by Robert Latham and William Matthews (London: G. Bell, 1970–1983), 26 Sept., 1668, IX. 317: 'I had two grilled pigeons, very handsome, and good meat'. Cf., from 1672, Andrew Marvel, *Rehearsal Transpros'd*, in *The works of Andrew Marvell, esq: poetical, controversial, political, containing many original letters, poems, and tracts, never before printed. With a new life of the author* (London: H. Baldwin, 1776), II. 448: 'The ... boyling of men in caldrons, grilling them on grid-irons, [etc.] were but a small part of the felicities of Julian's Empire'.

15. 'To make stekys of venysoun or Beef'; *Two fifteenth-century cookery-books*, edited by Thomas Austin (London, N. Trübner & Co., 1888), 3; 'Take feyre moton of the buttes & kutt it in maner of stekes'; *Douce MS 55* in the same edition,

40: 'Take fayre Bef of þe quyschons & motoun of þe bottes, & kytte in þe maner of Stekys; þan take raw Percely & Oynonys smal y-scredde & 3olkys of Eyroun soþe hard … & lay hem on þe Stekys' ('Take fine beef from the rump and mutton from the haunch and cut them as steaks; then take well-shredded raw parsley and onions and the yolks of hard-boiled eggs … and put them on the steaks').

16. John Lydgate, *De Guileville's (G. de) Pilgrimage of the life of man* (London: Kegan Paul, Trench, Trübner, 1899–1904), 12802.

17. *King & Hermit,* in *Ten fifteenth-century comic poems,* edited by Melissa M. Furrow (New York: Garland Publishing, 1985), 262: 'Fyll þis eft and late vs lyke [*read* layke], And betwen rost vs a styke [*read* steyke]'.

18. John Palsgrave, *Lesclarcissement de la langue francoyse* (London: J. Haukyns, 1530), 275/2.

19. *An Icelandic-English Dictionary,* edited by Richard Cleasby, Gudmund Vigfuson, and William A. Craigie, 2nd ed. (Oxford: Clarendon, 1959) and *Norrøn Ordbok,* edited by Leiv Heggested, Finn Hødnebø, and Erik Simensen, 4th ed. (Oslo: Det norske samlaget, 1993), *s.v.v. steik et al.*

20. *Edda: Die Lieder des Codex Regius,* edited by Hans Kuhn, 4th ed. (Heidelberg: Winter, 1962), 186; *The Poetic Edda,* translated by Carolyne Larrington (Oxford: Oxford University Press, 1996), 162.

21. 'The Boroma', edited by Whitely Stokes, *Revue Celtique* 13 (1892), 32–125, at 46–47, par. 29.

22. *The Metrical Dindshenchas,* edited and translated by Edward Gwynn, 5 vols. (Dublin: Royal Irish Academy, 1903–35), III.388–389.

23. *Aislinge Meic Con Glinne,* edited by Kenneth H. Jackson (Dublin: Dublin Institute for Advanced Studies, 1990), 24; *Aislinge Meic Conglinne: The Vision of Mac Conglinne,* translated by Lahney Preston-Matto (Syracuse: Syracuse University Press, 2010), 35.

24. Shane McCleod, *The Beginning of Scandinavian Settlement in England: The Viking 'Great Army' and Early Settlers, c. 865–900* (Amsterdam: Brepols, 2014).

25. Chrétien de Troyes, *Le Chevalier au Lion (Yvain),* edited by Mario Roques (Paris: Champion, 1967), vv. 3450–64; English translation adapted from *The Knight with the Lion (Yvain),* translated by William Kibler, in *Chrétien de Troyes: Arthurian Romances* (London: Penguin, 1991), 338. At v. 4209 of the romance, *charbonee* is used of a slice taken from a cheek. Here, the cooking method for a slice of meat is referred back to the cut itself, although this is not a butchering scene but rather a battle with a giant!

26. *Dictionnaire de l'ancienne langue française,* edited by Frédéric Godefroy (Paris: F. Vieweg, 1881–1902), *s.v. lardé,* establishes that *larde* was used both of a larded roast and of a chop or steak taken from the flank.

Cheese

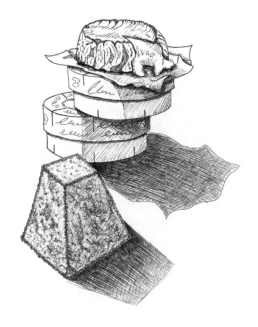

É mile Zola's recognition of major commercial food groups – fruit and vegetables, pork products, fish and sea-food, chicken and fowl, dairy goods – provides a historical guide to the old *Halles Centrales* of Paris but also to the organization of his novel based on the huge indoor food market, *Le Ventre de Paris* (The Belly of Paris, 1873). Specific behaviours, attitudes, and social values are associated with various food stalls and neighbouring shops, and are embodied in such figures as Lisa, the wife of the pork butcher (*charcutier*), Quenu, the fishmongers, *la belle Normande* and her sister, the poultry man Gavard.[1] Three other women, led by Mlle Saget, who might have been thought peripheral to events, play an increasingly important role in the latter part of the novel as their malicious gossip accelerates the undoing of the hero, Florent, also the victim of his own misguided republican aspirations.[2]

The setting for this gossip is a butter and cheese stall run by Mme Lecoeur. On a hot summer afternoon, the smells of the ripe, ripening and, indeed, over-ripe cheeses are likened to a variety of noxious odours, while the appearance of the cheeses and their varying skins and rinds are compared to a series of unfortunate or unpleasant natural phenomena. There is even an extended musical metaphor, creating effects of synesthesia, which has given rise to the characterization of the passage as a symphony of cheeses, akin to the colour organs developed during the eighteenth and nineteenth centuries. Zola prepares the reader for this scene by references early in the novel to the pestilential stench of ripened cheeses, one as early as the opening scenes, when Florent and his new acquaintance, the painter Claude, are strolling around Les Halles and meet 'la senteur pestilentielle des beurres et des fromages'. The eye – and nose – of Zola, no doubt once also a *flâneur*, were surely caught like those of his two characters.

He names some 20 cheeses, the majority native French sorts and all surely represented in Les Halles as the author knew them.[3] His list is strongly tilted in the direction of the most odoriferous soft-ripened sorts. In addition, we find Chester, Parmesan, firm Dutch cheeses, and others. The various cheeses offer a progression around rural France, with two emphases: six soft-ripened cheeses originate in Normandy, which is within convenient transport distance of Paris, and the three rounds of Brie from the Ile-de-France and especially Seine-et-Marne are singled out for a particularly unfavourable bit of virtuoso description. Perhaps they best symbolize the women. Since Florent's protectress, the widowed market gardener Mme François, is from Nanterre, west and a bit north of Paris, the toxic Bries seem fetched from the diametrically opposed side of the Parisian region.

Provinces also represented are, clockwise, Champagne, Lorraine, Lyonnais, Dauphiné, Auvergne, Aquitaine, Anjou, Orléannais, Maine. Only the drier cheeses such as Cantal and Chester escape the author's disapprobation.

The central image of the novel is Les Halles as a temple to consumption and the central theme in this third novel of the Rougon-Macquart series is once again the class war between *les gras* and *les maigres*, the fat and the thin, haves and have-nots. Les Halles monumentalize other elements of the novel, even the humble and not so humble cheeses. There is a degree of ironic rhetorical overkill, the lavish description matching fancied corruption, both moral and 'caseuistic'. The composite, violent image that emerges from the initial description of the cheeses, in anticipation of the later concentration on odour, is of an abandoned battlefield at night: rocky mountains, pale moon, cadavers, severed heads, wounds, abandoned gear (wheel, discus, axe), sulphur fumes, decomposition, and vermin but also vain medals neatly ranked in boxes. From this perspective, the Bries and Camemberts are whited sepulchres. The red marble veined in grey atop the display counter in the cheese shop suggests the colourful military dress of the day. Particularly in the colours describing the cheeses, transformation is stressed, one colour shading into or stained with another, again a symbol of societal change and not for the better. The *haute bourgeoisie* is tagged with a pathological condition due to over-eating, and the matching cheese is Roquefort. In another nod to synesthesia, Zola adopts a paratactic style with free-standing participial constructions, adjectival phrases, nominal appositions, like daubs of paint from an impressionist's brush or palette knife.

Two corporeal images, which bracket the first passage, are of unfinished torsos in a sculptor's studio and of the slow, laboured breathing of a sleeping man – perhaps napping after over-indulging from the cheese platter. Against this pompous monumentality we have the petty-mindedness of the gossips, not themselves to be counted among *les gras* but consumed with envy and greed like the cheeses with the formation of ammonia. The last cheese presented in the lacto-cacophony, a Géromé from Lorraine, is characterized by its slim, pretentious box and added aniseed flavor but is poisonous enough to kill flies on the wing.

Concentrating on the olfactory assault, Zola does not get into the specifics of cheese-making. A more technical vocabulary would appear in later novels such as *La bête humaine* (railways) and *Germinal* (mining). Where did he develop his sensitive nose? The description cannot have been due to the fastidiousness of the former resident of Provence, for the south has its own soft-ripened cheeses (but none mentioned here). Perhaps these are literary cheeses, intertextual in texture. Flaubert employs the awful quality of the local Neufchâtel as one more detail to damn the provincial Norman town of Yonville to which Madame Bovary moves ('C'est là que l'on fait les pires fromages de Neufchâtel de tout l'arrondissement', Part 2, Ch. 1). And why the correspondence (a key concept among near-contemporary poets such as Baudelaire) between cheese and gossip? Intertextuality may be matched with word-play. French *commérage* 'gossip' is a near-anagram of *fromage* (earlier *formage*, 'made in forms'). More assuredly it was the air-borne nature of gossip (cf. Vergil's *rumor*, here as *odor*), wafting its way like a foul stench, that would have prompted the metaphor. There is also the contrast between the original pure white milk and the resulting cheeses, with their often innocuous rinds and skins or the light mould so easily equated with bourgeois self-righteousness and hypocrisy. All the foodstuffs of Les Halles stand in contrast with the simple fresh omelette prepared by Mme François for Florent and Claude on their visit to Nanterre, a kind, natural otherworld to the maw and belly of Paris.

Zola's review of cheeses, in four sections, runs to about one page in modern editions of the novel and is to a considerable degree self-contained. The passage is reasonably well handled in Brian Nelson's English translation from 2007, but several corners have been cut, lexical difficulties are planed over, phrases such as 'decapitated heads' and scenes of 'rams' leading 'flocks' of goats are grating, and more than one lengthy phrase has been skimmed off.[4] Food-writer Mark Kurlansky has even less concern for technical terminology in a slipshod version of the novel from 2009. As a sample, a hat-trick sentence with three distinct kinds of error, back to back: lexical, syntactic, orthographic: 'At this time of day all the cheeses exhaled together in a cacophony of bad breath, from the heavy softness of the cooked preparations to the Cruyére and the Dutch cheeses to the sharp alkaline Olivet' ('Tous, à cette heure, donnaient à la fois. C'était une cacophonie de souffles infects, depuis les lourdeurs molles *des pâtes cuites, du gruyère* et du hollande, jusqu'aux pointes alcalines de l'olivet'; my italics).[5] A fresh – or perhaps lightly cured – translation of this *Chant de Maldodeur* is offered below.[6]

Around [the three women], the cheeses stank. On the two shelves of the stall, at the back, enormous blocks of butter lined up: butter from Brittany filled wicker baskets to the brim; butter from Normandy, wrapped in muslin, looked like roughed-out bellies over which a sculptor had thrown wet cloths; other blocks, already cut into and carved by broad-bladed knives into rocky peaks, full of valleys and fractures like collapsed summits gilded by the pallor of an autumn evening. Under the display counter of red marble veined with grey, baskets of eggs gave off the whiteness of chalk; and, in crates, on little racks of woven straw, *bondons* were placed end to end; *gournays*, lined up flat like medals, created darker patches, spotted with greenish tones. But it was above all on the counter that the cheeses piled up. There, next to one-pound rolls of butter, in leaves of Swiss chard, a huge *cantal* fanned out, looking as if it had been split with blows from an axe; then came a *chester*, the colour of gold, a *gruyère*, like a wheel fallen from some barbarian chariot, Dutch cheeses as round as severed heads smeared with dried blood, with the hardness of empty skulls that gave them name of 'death's heads'. A *parmesan*, in the midst of the heavy ambiance of the firm cheeses, added its touch of aromatic odour. Three *bries*, on round boards, had the melancholia of extinguished moons; two, quite dry, were full; the third, in its third quarter, oozed, voided itself of a white cream that spread in a pool, breaching the thin strips of wood with which a vain attempt had been made to contain it. *Port-saluts*, like the discuses of Antiquity, boldly displayed the printed names of their makers. A *romantour*, clothed in its silver paper, prompted dreams of a bar of nougat, of a sugary cheese, gone astray among these acrid fermentations. The *roqueforts*, as well, under bells of crystal, took on princely airs, their faces marbled and fat, shot through with veins of blue and yellow, as if beset by some shameful disease of the rich who have eaten too many truffles; while, on a platter next to them, goat cheeses, no bigger than a child's fist, hard and grayish, recalled the pebbles that bucks, leading their herds, rolled into the turns of stony paths. Then the stenches began: the *mont-d'ors*, bright yellow, stank with a mildish odour; the *troyes*, dense, bruised at the edges, with a slightly more potent acridity, added the fetid atmosphere of a dank cellar; the *camemberts*, with their whiff of game hung too long; the squares of the *neufchâtels*, the *limburgers*, the *marolles*, the *pont-l'évêques*, each adding its sharp and distinct note in a phrase harsh to the point of nausea; the *livarots*, stained in red, as hard on the throat as fumes of sulphur; lastly, then, over all the others, the *olivets*, wrapped in walnut leaves, like the animal carcasses peasants leave covered with branches at the edge of a field, smoking in the sun. The hot afternoon had softened the cheeses; the moulds of the crusts were melting, were being varnished with rich tones of red copper and verdigris, like poorly healed wounds; under the oak leaves a breath of air fluttered the skin of the *olivet*, which palpitated like a breast with the slow, gross breathing of a man asleep; a lively swarm had pierced a *livarot*, spawning through the gash a populace of worms. And, behind the scales, in its slender box, an anise-flavored *gérômé* spread such a stench of infection that flies had fallen dead around the box, on the red marble veined with grey. ...

The slanting sunlight entered under the pavilion, the cheeses stank more strongly. At that moment it was particularly the *marolles* that predominated; it threw off powerful blasts, a stink of unswept stable litter, against the blandness of the blocks of butter. Then, the wind seemed to turn; suddenly, the rales of the *limburger* reached the three women; sour and bitter, as if exhaled from the throats of the dying. ...

And, since the women were breathing a bit heavily, it was above all the *camembert* that they smelled. The *camembert*, with its scent of game, had overpowered the more muffled odours of the *marolles* and *limburger*. The cheese amplified its exhalations, smothered other smells under its halitosis-tainted effluvium. Yet, in the midst of this vigorous phrase, the *parmesan* at times sounded the slender line of a shepherd's pipe; while the *bries* added the mild fustiness of wet tambourines. Then there was the suffocating *reprise* of the *livarot*. And this symphony was sustained for a moment on a shrill note from the aniseed *géromé*, held like an organ peal. ...

[The women] remained standing, saying their goodbyes, in the ultimate bouquet of the cheeses. All of these were now sounding off at the same time. It was a cacophony of infected respirations, from the flat and flaccid weightiness of the firm cheeses, the *gruyère* and Dutch, to the alkaline notes of the *olivet*. There were muted snores from the *cantal*, the *chester*, the goat cheeses, comparable to a *largo* by basses, over which stood out the sour notes, sudden little whiffs of the *neufchâtels*, the *troyes*, and the *mont-d'ors*. Then the odours rose in *crescendo*, rolling one over the other, thickened with gusts from the *port-salut, limburger, géromé, marolles, livarot, pont-l'évêque*, all gradually coalescing and then expanding in a single explosion of malodorousness that spread and persisted in the midst of the over-all vibrancy, no longer as distinct smells but with the constant vertigo of nausea and the terrible force of asphyxiation. Still, it seemed that it was the malicious words of Mme Lecoeur and Mlle Saget that stank so high.

NOTES

1. This chapter first appeared as 'Zola and the Gorgons: Cheese and Gossip in Le Ventre de Paris', in *Petits Propos Culinaires* 96 (2012), 72–79. Recent critical studies of relevance include Kubilây Aktulum, 'Les métamorphoses de l'objet dans *Le Ventre de Paris* d'Émile Zola', *Süleyman Demirel Üniversitesi Fen-Edebiyat Fakültesi Sosyal Dergisi* 5 (2005), 343–58; Nina Hopkins Butlin, 'Opérations de description dans *Le Ventre de Paris* de Zola', *ALFA* 5 (1992), 87–107; Anna Gural-Migdal, 'Représentation utopique et ironie dans *Le Ventre de Paris*', *Cahiers Naturalistes* 74 (2000), 145–61; Philippe Jousset, 'Une Poétique de la 'Nature morte': Sur la pratique descriptive dans *Le Ventre de Paris*', *Cahiers Naturalistes* 44 (1998), 337–50; Dominique Julien, 'Le 'Ventre' de Paris: Pour une pathologie du symbolisme dans l'œuvre d'Émile Zola', *French Forum* 17 (1992), 281–99; Jean-Yves Mollier, 'Émile Zola dans le ventre de la ville: De la réalité à la fiction', *Cahiers Naturalistes* 44 (1998), 263–73; Marie Scarpa, '*Le Ventre de Paris* ou "le monde immonde" d'Émile Zola: Lecture ethnocritique', *Iris* 19 (2000), 45–55; Kate E. Tunstall, '"Crânement beau tout de même": Still Life and *Le Ventre de Paris*', *French Studies* 58 (2004), 177–87.

2. See Pauline Wahl Willis, 'Commestibles et commérages dans *Le Ventre de Paris*', *Excavatio: Émile Zola and Naturalism (Excavatio)* 14: 1–2 (2001), 63–72.

3. Cursory information on the cheeses is intentionally drawn from the somewhat dated *Guide du fromage* (Paris: Stock, 1971) by the *doyen* of French cheese, Pierre Androuët.

4. Émile Zola, *The Belly of Paris* = *Le Ventre de Paris*, trans. Brian Nelson (New York: Oxford University Press, 2007).

5. *The Belly of Paris*, trans. Mark Kurlansky (New York: Modern Library, 2009).

6. The translation is based on the edition of *Le Ventre de Paris* as it appears in Émile Zola, *Œuvres complètes*, ed. Henri Mitterand, vol. 5 (Paris: Nouveau Monde, 2002). The punning reference in *Chant de Maldodeur* is to the book of poems, *Les Chants de Maldoror* (1868–69), by le Comte de Lautréamont (Isidore Ducasse).

Scones & buns

*O*ED heads its entry for *scone* with the identifier 'Orig. Sc.' and provides this definition:

> A large round cake made of wheat or barley- meal baked on a griddle; one of the four quadrant-shaped pieces into which such a cake is often cut; more generally, a soft cake of barley or oat-meal, or wheat-flour, baked in single portions on a griddle or in an oven.

The Scottish connection seems borne out by the first recorded instance in Gavin Douglas's 1513 adaptation of Virgil's *Æneid*: 'The flour sconnis war sett in, by and by, Wyth wther mesis'. From a few decades later we read, again in Scots: 'Thai hed na breyd bot ry caikis and fustean skonnis maid of flour'.[1] It then comes as rather a surprise that the etymological note reads: 'Perh. a shortened adoption of MDu. *schoonbrot*, MLG *schonbrot* "fine bread"'. These are angular or triangular loaves and the latter term is claimed as the source of MSw. *skanroggä*, MDa. *skonroggen*, Icel. *skonrok* 'a biscuit'. To pause only briefly over this last trio, surely rye (Germ. *Roggen*) is involved here and then, since rye is the least valued of the cereals – the recourse of northerners – it makes an uncomfortable partner with fine quality, if indeed the *skan/skon* element seen above is related to Germ. *schön*. More relevant to present concerns, deriving *scone* from *schoonbrot* entails favouring the first adjectival element over the nominal referent for a semantic charge something like 'goodies'.[2] Further, such baked goods, as opposed to, say, rye biscuits, are an unlikely trade item and, while there was a substantial Flemish presence in medieval lowland Scotland, the continental connection does not convince.

Scottish Gaelic has the term *sgonn* (vars. *sguinn, sgoinn*) with a variety of meanings, most, however, correspondent in terms of rough shape and/or affective value. A non-exhaustive listing includes: short block of wood; shapeless mass; dolt, blockhead; large mouthful; huge, unshapely person; talkative person. More to the point, *sgonn* could mean a large slice of bread or meat, and *sgonn arain* was a common phrase for a block of bread.[3] It is scarcely plausible that a basic meaning of 'fine bread' could have been so leavened, to use a baker's term, that its meanings in Gaelic came to encompass blocks of wood, block-headed persons, mouthfuls, as well as loaves and slices of bread – in a material and linguistic environment where oats and barley would have been more common than wheat.

Recalling that Scottish Gaelic has its roots in Old Irish, the closest equivalent in Modern Irish, in the narrow sense of baked goods and in semantic rather than phonetic terms, would seem to be at some remove: *srubhán* (vars. *srathán, sreabhán*) 'cake, pancake'; cf. *srubhán crústálta coirce* 'crusted oatcake'.[4] This word has remote antecedents. The early Irish law texts, some dating from the seventh century, allow the assembly of a modest glossary of bread-related terms. Along with *bairgen inraic* (a standard loaf) and *bairgen banfhuini* 'woman's loaf' (half the size), we find *tortine* (< Latin *torta* 'loaf') for a small loaf or bun. Fergus Kelly, who has gleaned this terminology from the law tracts, continues:

> Another term for bun is *srúbán*, which is stated in legal commentary to be one eighth the size of a loaf. It seems likely that it was so called because it was shaped like a snout (*srúb*).[5]

But if this were not baked separately in the shape of a snout (standing up? lying flat?) but rather represented one of eight wedge-shaped pieces into which a loaf or cake were cut, its triangular form would certainly qualify as snout-like. Perhaps smaller cakes were baked in a triangular shape. *Srúbán* is a diminutive and the addition of the suffix causes lenition of the now intervocalic *-b-*. An anglicized form, *sroan*, which is found in medieval documents as a measure of oatmeal (1½ gallons, the reference is more likely to a snout- or funnel-shaped container than to an oatcake or slice thereof) gives some indication of the phonetic value of *srúbán*. From *sroan* 'slice of bread or cake' to *sgonn* 'scone' is no great step, but we must ask why Gaelic speakers would take it, when original Irish initial *sr-* continues to be well preserved in Scotland, albeit often realized as *str-*.[6] And, indeed, OIr. *srúb* appears in Scotland as *srub* 'spout' and as the verbal noun *srùban* meaning 'sucking, drawing in'. *Srubh* has the original meaning 'snout'. To complicate the picture (or at least our picture), we find *srubhag* as a 'cake baked before the fire' (cf. Irish *srúbán*, Manx *strauan* 'triangular cake').[7] Another issue to be addressed in seeking to establish or evaluate the possible influence of OIr. *srúb* on Sc. Gael. *sgonn* is the substantially wider semantic field that the latter covers in comparison with the former. But such a metaphorical expansion is not unprecedented.[8] However, the phonological development needed to support this hypothesis, *sr-* > *skr-* > *sg-*, is unprecedented and further speculation in this direction seems unwarranted. At a minimum, we have documentary proof of something very like a scone at a historical depth much greater than that imagined for loans from Dutch or German.

If we shift our focus from type of baked goods to their state, several other avenues of enquiry open. In his etymological dictionary (from 1896, it should be noted), MacBain has an entry for *sgonn* 'block of wood, blockhead,' with the example *sgonn-balaich* 'lump of a boy', and posits an early form – perhaps something like 'Common Celtic' in his mind – **skotsno* with the meaning 'section', the same root as generated Sc. Gael. *sgath* 'cut off' (among other meanings).[9] The current editors of *Lexique étymologique de l'irlandais ancien*, the successors to Vendryes, take us a step further, first in the entry *scoth-*, identified as a verbal root with the meaning 'cut, remove by cutting'.[10] *Scoth* as noun meant 'point, edge'. The derivative *scathan* was used of a moment in time, one excised from the temporal continuum. These and related verb forms, for example, *scaraid*, are most plausibly traced to an Indo-European root **skeu-*, itself derived from **sek-* 'cut'.[11] The *Manx Dictionary* has an entry for *skon* (168) with the cryptic meaning 'meat or drink got by intrusion', which might be understood as the share of the meal grudgingly 'cut out' for an uninvited guest. Another, perhaps less rigorous, dictionary of Manx equates *skon* with 'snack', which might similarly be construed as something cut out (literally or figuratively) from a larger amount or unit.[12]

The IE roots *(s)teu-*, *(s)teug-*, *(s)teuk-* 'strike' and, in one of the narrower senses, 'strike off a piece', are unlikely sources of *sgonn* but they do illustrate the semantic extension from 'cut' to 'that cut', that is, 'cutting, slice, piece'.[13] Reflexes here are Irish *tócht* 'piece, part', Old Norse *stukki*, OE *stucce*, German *Stück* with the same meaning. Irish *túag* 'axe' reflects the agent aspect of the root.[14] We might similarly adduce derivatives of the root *scoilt-* 'split, separate, divide'. For example, *scoiltech* was a collective noun for 'pieces, fragments' and *scoiltén* the unit piece.[15] We seem to be in the presence of a semantic field that encompasses a mass, its aptitude for subdivision, and the resulting sections.

It is just possible that *sgonn* is reflected in plural form in a poem from the sixteenth century on the unlikely topic of the carcass of a dead piglet. The editor thinks it a simple rhetorical exercise but one might speculate whether the piglet is not a rival poet (cf. the celebrated flyting between Dunbar and Kennedy). Two verses, standing, like most of the others, in apposition to the subject pig, read: 'Sgoinne rem sgoil / foille na frigh', which the editor translates (omitting our key term, opaque to him): '… to my school / smaller than mite';[16] Since most of the lines are paratactic, we cannot see *sgoinne* as 'pieces' qualified by the *foille* 'smaller' of the next line. Furthermore, most lines feature alliteration, so that *sgoinne* and *sgoil* are paired, at least in part, to satisfy this need. The preposition *re* meant 'before' in both the temporal and local senses, and was used with verbs meaning 'flee' and 'suffer defeat (before).'[17] Thus, with one of the attested meanings of *scol*, we might tentatively offer: '(mere) cuttings before my school (of bardic poetry)'. But this is highly speculative.

In Scotland, *sgonn* in the sense of 'block' seems also to have been used of the head, just as in informal English. This could account for such phrases as *sconer cap* for a Lowland bonnet, *do one's scone* 'lose one's head or temper'. In the case of Australian English *scone* 'head' we might look to Irish speakers as a source. As the word was more fully absorbed in Australian English and a precise original meaning lost, it is possible that the phrase 'to go [someone] scone-hot', in the sense of reprimand someone or lose one's temper at someone, suggested not only 'losing it' (to update to our own idiom) but also having a temper hot as freshly baked scones – not folk etymology but folk semantics.[18]

On balance, the etymology of *sgonn* must still be judged moot, given the absence of sure intermediate forms between Old and Middle Irish and the Scottish Gaelic of later centuries. The available evidence points toward a derivation from a word in the semantic field of cutting and sub-division: the loaf as a shaped part of the mass of dough or mix of barley or oat meal, the slice as part of the larger loaf or cake. At any event, the Celtic evidence does seem sufficient to divert our attention from unsupported claims of a continental Germanic origin for *scone* and encourage the further exploration of early medieval cereal culture in the British Isles. Thus it is doubly troublesome that the entry in the newly amalgamated *Dictionary of the Scots Language* should echo or anticipate the *OED* in identifying *scone* as 'appar. shortened f. MDu. *schoonbrot* "fine bread".'[19] Although this must remain a subjective impression, this writer's inquiry into such English words and phrases as *John Doe, malarkey, queer, sail, sog/soggy,* and *tinker*, which *OED* would refer to various Germanic languages (or pull a blank), suggests that, while the Norse and Dutch contributions to English vocabulary were well recognized by the first editors of the dictionary, Germanic was often adduced, with no attempt at explanation of the dynamics of lexical transfer, in cases where a better knowledge of the Celtic languages of Great Britain – seeing Celtic not as substratum but adstratum – would have yielded a more plausible and convincing etymological comment on the words in question.[20]

******

Bun is part of the everyday vocabulary for which we often think that the last word must already have been said. But, when we learn that the linguistic history of *bun* may be as variegated as the recipes gathered under this culinary term, the word takes on a bit of mystery, for some speakers perhaps enhanced by its monolithic monosyllabicity: *Bun*. Mary-Anne Boermans' recent article, 'Royal Chelsea Buns' (*PPC* 98), recalls one of the prestigious and traditional British buns to our attention and prompts the following reflections on the history of the word, which we might hope as clearly explainable as that of the Chelsea variants.

The *Oxford English Dictionary* has several separate entries for *bun* as a noun, with extended or additional meanings for some of them. These are 1) a hollow stem, esp. of an umbelliferous plant (now obsolete or dialectal) and the stalk or stalky part of flax or hemp; 2) a sort of cake (dating from 1370, but not found in Old English; 'the use differs greatly in different localities, but the word generally denotes in England a sweet cake {usually round} not too large to be held in the hand while being eaten', *OED*); 3) the tail of a hare (Scotland and northern dialects); plus a name given sportively to the squirrel and rabbit, and to a drunken condition, e.g. 'to get, have, tie a bun on'. *Bun* as part of a woman's hair styling is (curiously) listed under 2) above ('hair coiled at the back of the head in a shape suggesting a bun'). [21] Of these, *bun* as 'sweet cake' will be first addressed. Lightly edited for length, the *OED* commentary on etymology reads as follows:

> Etymology doubtful. The modern provincial French *bugne* is said … to be used at Lyons for a sort of fritter; the word is not recorded in Old French with this sense, but *bugne, beugne* (= modern *bigne*) occurs with the sense of 'swelling produced by a blow'; the diminutive *bugnete* is found in Old French with the sense of 'fritter' … It is conjectured that Old French *bugne*, originally 'swelling' may have had the unrecorded sense of 'puffed loaf' (= *bugnet*), and may have been adopted into English as *bun*. But the existence of this sense in Old French is at present hypothetical, and it is questionable whether such a derivation would account for the form of the English word. [22]

Before turning to additional Old French and related evidence, it will be useful to consult the French counterpart of the *OED* as historical dictionary, *Le Trésor de la langue française*, and its entry for *beignet* 'fritter' (see above). As 'pâte frite enveloppant quelque substance alimentaire (fruit, viande, etc.)', *beignet* does not appear in French until 1314.[23] From the middle of the following century we have this detail of local monastic management and food rents:

> Le vycaire de la chapelle de Sainct Romain doit a ung checun religieulx cin bysoles du lac de Genefve, l'uylle pour la frire, la moutarde et les bugnestes.[24]
> [The vicar of the chapel of Saint Romain owes to each and every monk five *bysoles* (an extinct freshwater fish, *Coregonus fera*) from Lake Geneva, oil for frying, mustard, and fritters.]

To be noted in passing is the vocalism of *bugnetes*, with *u* in the stem. More luxurious fare is served at a royal court, as depicted in *Le Roman de Fauvel*: 'Il y ot gauffres et oublees, … Pommes d'espices, darioles, Crespines, bignez et roissoles' ('There were waffles and crisps … spiced apples, flavoured pastries, crêpes, fritters, and rissoles').[25]

As to the etymology of the diminutive *beignet*, the *TLF* refers the reader to *beigne* with the meaning 'bump' (on the head) or, by extension, the blow that would create such a bump. Earlier forms are *buyne*, *bigne*, *beugne*. The dictionary proposes a non-Latin origin for the word, and would trace it back to Gaulish, one of the Celtic languages of continental Europe, citing a hypothetical Gaulish *bun(n)ia* 'trunk of a tree' and Celtic cognates from Great Britain (Welsh *bon*, Irish *bun*). The same root is allegedly realized in Provençal *bougno* 'tree trunk', and northern Italian *bugna* and Catalan *bonv* 'bump'. But it is difficult to reconcile the Gaulish term *bunda* 'ground, base, foundation', as it is now more accurately represented and explained (cf. Latin *fundus*), with the idea of a bump, although the extension from base to tree-trunk is not implausible. *Bunda* is otherwise represented in French dialect as *bonde* 'deepest part of a pond' and in Provençal as *bonda* 'swampy ground'.[26]

A more plausible source for French *beigne* and *beignet* is Frankish, the language of the Germanic Franks who invaded sub-Roman Gaul in the mid-fourth to sixth centuries and gave the country-to-be its name, France. We have no written records of Frankish, only the reconstructions of historical linguists, but Old High German, a cognate language, had a term *bungo* that was used of a pile or bunch of one thing or another (as well as more specifically of harvested cress and onions).[27] As an adjective, *bungo* meant 'thick, fat'. Adapted into Gallo-Romance as **beungue*, then recast as *beugne, beigne*, this term for a roughly spherical mass could plausibly have been extended to a small unit of baked goods or its dough and, figuratively, to a comparably shaped bump on the head.[28] But a word's origins do not determine its subsequent range of meanings over time and through space. Etymology is not destiny.

If we provisionally accept that the early associations of 'the bun word' in Germanic were with various kinds of globular masses, and only in Gallo-Romance with cranial swellings and the violence that produced them and, by extension and in the form of a diminutive, with baked goods, we may turn to the Anglo-French evidence and a scene from the popular medieval romance of *Floire and Blancheflor*, in a recension from the early thirteenth-century. The menu for a feast at an eastern palace is described, after due attention to the wines imbibed:

> Ne savriez riens porpenser
> Que la ne veïssiez porter:
> Grues et gentes et paons,
> Niules, oublees et buignez
> Et pastez de vis oiselez[29]
> [You couldn't think up anything that you would not have seen borne
> in there: cranes and wild geese and peacocks, puff pastries, snaps,
> and fritters, and pies stuffed with live young birds.]

Little noticed in this regard is the Anglo-French term *buignard* for a dolt or blockhead, which seems to complement the base term *buigne* with a deprecatory suffix -ard, for a meaning like 'bun- or dough-head' – unless this head is the object of multiple blows.[30]

Terms recognizably closer to early modern English *bun* appear in Middle English. But, accepting that a shift in vocalism from *ui* to *u* as not unusual, how is one to account for the reduction of the velar nasal sound represented by -gne- to the simple nasal -n? Firstly, words ending in this sound (represented in the International Phonetic Alphabet as ŋ) are not native to English (cf. the British pronunciation of *Charlemagne* and *Cologne*). Further, I suggest that this shift occurred through a process linguists called dissimulation and that the present form of *bun* distinguishes it from *bung*, the stopper for a cask (Middle English *bunge*). Some of the earliest written evidence in Middle English for *bun* is from a letter-book (a book in which correspondence is copied out, or in which letters or copies of letters are kept for reference) from 1441: 'All maner of brede that thei can make of whete … white loofe brede, wastell [a high quality, white, wheaten bread], bunnys, and all maner of whyte brede'.[31] In the late fifteenth century, uniformly shaped buns were brought to well-set tables wrapped in a linen cloth: 'Thow must square & proporcioun þy bred … þat no loof ne bunne be more þan oþer proporcionly … Þan ley … in myddes of þat towelle viij loves or bonnes'.[32] But we have no distinct recipe for buns from this early date. One is tempted to conclude that initially the term *bun* continued to refer to size and shape rather than to ingredients and composition and, if this were the case, would, for a time, have remained true to its origins as proposed here, as baked goods originating in a small, globular mass of dough.

Most of the lexical buns listed by the *OED* may now be brought under this same rubric (or cambric): the hare's tail, the hare or squirrel itself, and the lady's hair when coiled at the back of her head. *Bun* as a hollow plant stem or the stalk of flax or hemp, on the other hand, seems more likely a native English term (< Old English *bune*), ultimately traceable to the same Indo-European root as the hypothetical Gaulish *bunia* 'trunk of a tree', as seen above.

Bun began in archaic Germanic as an all-purpose designation referring to the shape and size of things, then in early French narrowed its application to baked and fried goods, initially most likely close to bread in composition. This overt and superficial designation gave way over time and through space to a generalized term with a wide range of implicit associations that called up memories of specific recipes and culinary processes, contents and occasions, textures and tastes, all around the British Isles. As a word, *bun* has yielded some secrets. The multiple recipes for buns, past and present, surely contain many more.

NOTES

1. Gavin Douglas, *The xiii bukes of Eneados of the famose poete Virgill*, VII.iii.15; *The Complaynt of Scotlande*, VI, 43. This note was first published as 'Scones, the *OED*, and the Celtic Element in English Vocabulary', *Notes & Queries* 52 (2005), 447–50, and is reproduced with the permission of the publishers.

2. Independently of this speculation, the preserved vocabulary of Old Norse has no word that would have been a plausible antecedent of *scone*. This said, we should bear in mind the documented dynamics of medieval and earlier technology transfer. While more Norse words found their way into Irish and Scottish than the other way around, Latin *furnus* generated Irish *forn*, which in turn was loaned as *sorn* into Faroese and Norwegian with the meaning 'drying kiln', as used with grains after harvest (when lenited, *f-* is without sound, as is *s-* under similar circumstances, so that the *s-* of *sorn* represents a kind of hypercorrection).

3. *The Illustrated Gaelic-English Dictionary*, 829; cf. *A Dictionary of the Gaelic Language*, II, 94. Welsh *sgonn* is identified as a twentieth-century loan from English; *Geiriadur Prifysgol Cymru: A Dictionary of the Welsh language*, 3245.

4. *Foclóir Gaedhilge agus Béarla: An Irish English Dictionary*, 1115.

5. Kelly, *Early Irish Farming*, 330.

6. Gillies, 'Scottish Gaelic', 161; similar development in Manx; see Broderick, *A Handbook of Late Spoken Manx*, 117–18.

7. *Illustrated Gaelic-English Dictionary*, 895; *The Manx Dictionary*, 176.

8. Some of the Scottish Gaelic meanings for *sgonn*, such as 'a garrulous person', may show the influence of a quite different root and words, whose reflexes in Modern Irish are *sconna-* (in compounds), meaning 'gushing, hasty'; cf. *sconna* 'a rush of talk', *sconnnach* 'rash, hasty', *sconnaire* 'reckless fellow, prater, dunce'. *Sconnaire* as 'an overgrown young person,' even if we see the image of a spurt of growth, does, however, recall the various 'lumpish' meanings of Sc. Gael. *sgonn*.

9. *An Etymological Dictionary of the Gaelic Language*, 287. See Thurneysen, *A Grammar of Old Irish*, par. 327, on examples of *sn* being reduced to *nn*. This goes some way toward increasing the plausibility of MacBain's derivation of *sgonn* from **skotsno*.

10. *Lexique étymologique de l'irlandais ancien (LEIA)*, S-52.
11. *Indogermanisches etymologisches Wörterbuch (IEW)*, I.954.
12. *Fockleyr Gaelg-Baarle [Manx-English Dictionary]*, at http://www.ceantar.org/Dicts/.
13. *IEW*, I.1032; *LIV: Lexikon der indogermanischen Verben*, 582, *s.v.* 1. **teuk* 'stossen, schlagen'.
14. *LEIA*, T-88; cf. the relationship between *scían* 'knife' and *scaraid* 'cuts'.
15. *Dictionary of the Irish Language (DIL)*, fasc. S, 99.
16. Quin, 'Truagh truagh an mhuc' [Poor little pig], 31, st. 52.
17. *DIL*, fasc. R, 22f.
18. *Scone* is not represented in *Dictionary of American Regional English*. One might have looked to Appalachia, but settlers of Scottish origin in the region were largely Ulster Scots, and not Gaelic-speakers.
19. *Dictionary of the Scottish Language*.
20. See, for example, the many lexical notes on the Celtic–English axis published by Andrew Breeze.
21. *OED*, *s.v. bun*, n. This second note first appeared in *Petits Propos Culinaires* 100 (2014), pp. 126–131.
22. *OED*, *s.v. bun*, n.².
23. *Trésor de la langue française (TLF)*, *s.v. beignet*.
24. Georges de Seyturiers, *Manuel administratif*, in *L'Histoire de l'abbaye de St. Claude*, II, 307.
25. Gervais du Bus, *Roman de Fauvel*, 157, v. 426. The translations of some of the names for baked goods, here and below, are only approximate.
26. *Dictionnaire de la langue gauloise*, 94, *s.v. bunda*.
27. *Althochdeutsches Wörterbuch*, *s.v. bugno*; *IEW*, I.127.
28. *TLF* doubts the possible spread of such a Germanic word to northern Italy but we must recall that Lombardic was also a Germanic dialect or language.
29. *Floire et Blancheflor*, Pelan (ed.), vv. 2948–53. Other manuscripts than that edited by Pelan replace fritters with *gibelés*, probably giblet pies, e.g., Robert d'Orbigny, *Le Conte de Floire et Blanchefleur*, v. 3201.
30. Adgar, *Le Gracial*, 269, l. 185.
31. *Calendar of Letter-Books*, 258, from 1441.
32. *John Russell's Boke of Nurture*, in *Early English Meals and Manners*, ll. 211–218.

Beehives & honey

In a recent note in *American Notes & Queries*, Marijane Osborn sought to confirm the solution to Riddle 17 of *The Exeter Book* as a beehive or, more precisely, a skep made of straw. The present contribution broadens the frame of reference beyond the Anglo-Saxon world by considering bee-keeping elsewhere in the British Isles, both in the Celtic realms and in the Danelaw. In particular, it addresses the two runic letters that accompany the poem in the manuscript and questions Osborn's proposal that the second of these, the L-rune, is a prompt for the word *leap*, 'basket' and thus complements the B-rune read as *beo*, 'bee.' Osborn's solution to this dimension of the riddle is reflected in the hypothetical OE *beoleap* that figures in her title, along with English *skep* and the explanatory German *Beinenkorb*, an unfortunate typographical error for *Bienenkorb*, but wryly consonant, as 'basket of bones', with the OE poetic lexis.[1]

Osborn agrees with Bierbaumer and Wannagat that the correct – or, perhaps, best-fitting – solution to the riddle is a beehive. But in contrast to their description of the object as a 'geflochtener Bienenkorb', which might be imaged as wickerwork (willow, heather), conceivably with an earthen or dung coating, she favors a lighter 'coiled-straw skep' (a term to which I return below). A clear and very useful account of the fabrication of such an object then follows. Citing the preeminent authority, Eva Crane, Osborn does not question the conclusion that the straw skep was introduced into Britain by the Angles and Saxons some time after 500 AD and spread westward during the subsequent centuries.[2]

Osborn provides a close translation of the riddle as it appears in Muir's edition, one not overly steered by the eventual solution.

Earlier proposed identities for this 'guardian of my flock' (*mundbora minre heorde*) include ballista, fortress, forge, inkwell, weapon chest.[3] Some points of detail: given the seried oppositions in the poem, I would see a more open contrast between the bees' daily movements in and out of the hive and their definitive return at dusk. Thus, *dægtidum* is explicitly daytime and *hwilum ... sweartum* a more covert phrasing for night. OE *wir*, the material that holds the hive together, unequivocally points toward drawn metal. Crane avers that the 'wires' are probably the long vegetative shoots of the blackberry. The bramble's resistance to decomposition as well as its flexibility make it suitable for skep-making but also, because of its durability and appearance (including the clouded mauve color of first-year shoots), make it teasingly appropriate to be called *wir* in the poem. Lastly, the statement *sped biþ þe mare / fylle minre*, which Osborn renders 'luck is the greater / with my fullness', might be improved if 'luck' were replaced by 'prosperity', which makes successful beekeeping a less random operation and underlines the economic worth of honey and beeswax.[4]

The implicit assumption behind Crane and Osborn is that the Anglo-Saxons brought elements of beekeeping culture with them from the Continent. But what of bees in Britain before the Anglo-Saxon invasion? Apparently unknown to Osborn and other scholars who have seen some kind of beehive in Riddle 17 is an early Irish law tract known as *Bechbretha* or *Bee-Laws*.[5] The basic tract, to which succeeding generations added multiple levels of glosses, is judged by one of its editors, Fergus Kelly, to have been composed about the middle of the seventh century, and, thus, considerably predates the first written references to bees and beekeeping in Old English writings. The basic concern here is property rights when bees swarm and may be guilty of 'grazing-trespass'. In this, 'the topic of bees is fitted, with some ingenuity, into the general framework provided by the law of neighbourhood'.[6] Linguistic evidence, including the absence of loans from Latin, Kelly contends, points to the presence of honeybees in Ireland long before the fifth or sixth centuries.[7] If the Celtic-speaking people who came to Ireland brought with them some knowledge of beekeeping, we might expect bees to have been kept in Britain as well as in continental Gaul. Whatever the exact nature of this Old British beekeeping, it would have had some influence on Anglo-Saxon practices, as these may have been imported from northern Europe.

Precise information on the type of beehive employed in early Ireland is lacking. Kelly and Charles-Edwards state that the usual Old Irish word was *lestar*, and point to a loan from British (cf. Welsh *llestr*, Cornish *lester*, Breton *lestr*; I use the synthetic 'British' form *lester* here, for the sake of convenience). The *Bee-Laws* make only a single reference to hives, and then in the plural, in reference to a group of hives or apiary.

> Mad súil rocháecha iss i suidiu áilid cocrann forsin lestrai n-uili; cip lestar día toth dib ar-tét a fíach.
>
> [If it be an eye which it has blinded, it is then that it [the injury] requires the casting of lots on all the hives; whichever of the hives it falls upon is forfeit for its [the bee's] offence.[8]]

In all the Celtic languages where it is attested, *lester* and cognates mean 'vessel', both as 'container for liquids' and as 'boat, ship'. A later term for hive is *coirceóg*. If this is indeed derived from *corca*, 'oats', it may point to hives made of oat straw.[9] Kelly speculates that *lestar* in Irish referred to heavier hives with wooden frames and later terminology to lighter units in straw, but there is no evidence for technological development that reflects such lexical change. *Lestar* derives from an Indo-European root *les-*, 'gather', and Pokorny suggests that the basic meaning of nominal forms would have been a 'basket for berry-picking' or something similar.[10] The extension in meaning to 'boat, ship' may be hypochoristic, as in the case of *tub* in English. In the light of semantics and etymology, *lestar*, then, seems less likely to have been a heavy, frame-based hive, and the basket image seems secure. At a minimum, there is good reason to believe that British farmers were speaking of the beehive as *lester* when the Anglo-Saxons arrived.

The Old French term for a hive was *ruche*. This is traced to a Gaulish word meaning 'bark' and has cognates with this same meaning in Irish *rúsc*, Welsh *rhisgl*, Cornish *rusc*, and Breton *rusk* and *ruskl*, although Breton *ruskenn* (for a single object) also has the meaning 'beehive', doubtless under influence from neighboring French.[11] French historians of apiculture believe that hives made of cork from the oak were supplanted by the woven straw hives of the Franks, who would not have known this species of oak. The traditional name, however, lived on as *ruche*.[12] We have no evidence of *rúsc* being used in Ireland for a hive, nor of any kind of bark as a chief constituent, although one can imagine weaving or plaiting such a container. Even with thin strips of bark, however, it would have been difficult to achieve the desired degree of weatherproofing. With so much of Middle English vocabulary influenced by Anglo-Norman French, we might look for a loan of *ruche*, but only a single instance appears, a Latinized form in a Latin text, and we might disagree with the editors of the *Middle English Dictionary* as to whether this instance really qualifies as English.[13] Although it is always imprudent to argue from silence, we may speculate that the English terminology for beehives – whatever this might have been exactly – was firmly enough established that it resisted French imports. This, in turn, suggests that French and English beekeeping practices were sufficiently similar that the Anglo-Normans were not seen as introducing any new techniques, techniques that would have facilitated the introduction of new vocabulary. But we stray from the central object of our concern, the Anglo-Saxon hive.

Riddle 17 quite naturally uses no word for hive, and it would be foolhardy to suggest that the absence in the poem of any word with initial *l* is yet another inverse clue. But it is similarly the case that no word for 'hive' is found in the Old English corpus, and the *beohyf* proposed by Tigges in his 'Solutions' is his own coinage.[14] Only the paraphrase 'little huts' (*exigua tuguria*) occurs in Aldhelm's *De Virginitate* in a metaphorical allusion to bees and hives. Osborn defers discussion of *skep* as 'hive' to her endnotes, where she cites Onions to the effect that the OE word *sceppe*, 'basket', 'entered the language late in the Anglo-Saxon period, and its attested use to designate a hive does not occur until the fifteenth century'.[15] Here it is of interest to be precise as to the source of this loan. The lexicographers of the *Middle English Dictionary* trace *skep* to Old Norse *skeppa*, 'basket, bushel'. The word also appears in the Latinized forms *sceppa, (e) scheppa, eskeppa*, etc. Yet, as Osborn concludes, *skep* must be ruled out as a candidate for the OE term for 'hive' until the period after the Scandinavian invasions and, most likely, the emergence of Norse-inflected English speech in the Danelaw. Then, whether solely because of the resemblance of hives to inverted baskets or partly because Anglo-Norse **skep* seemed to have the same association with *skip* 'ship' (despite differing etymologies) that was available in British *lester* as both kinds of 'vessel', a lexical overlay or a calque seems to have occurred. Since the Norse, for reasons of climate, are unlikely to have introduced any significant innovation in the area of beekeeping, it seems more probable that, when assimilating the apiary culture of Britain, they replaced the evolved form of Celtic *lester*, which could have suggested nothing to them (unlike other English words that had Norse cognates), with a term from Norse that simply captured the visual impact of the straw hives.

But back to Riddle 17. Under these circumstances and in the absence of any evidence that OE *leap*, 'basket' was ever used for beehives, it seems possible, in the conjunction of the L- and B-runes in the context of the riddle, that the second clue points to the currency of a substratum British term *lester* in OE in the sense of 'coiled-straw hive'. The juxtaposition of the two 'initials' would then be congruent with other binomialisms, oppositions, and complementarities in the poem – British hive, Anglo-Saxon bee.[16]

******

A basic apiarian vocabulary consisting of *bee, comb, hive, honey,* and *swarm* is represented in Old English (*béo, comb, hunig, hýf,* and *swearm*, respectively) and survives intact in Middle English and beyond.[17] However, not much is known about Anglo-Saxon beekeeping – for example, there is no information available about the material and construction of early hives, the care of bees, or the recovery and processing of honey. Rather, bees appear in similes or are sources of symbolism and figuration, as in the *Paris Psalter*: 'Þá hí me ymbsealdon samod anlice swa beon bitere'.[18] This is not the case in Ireland, where the archaic *Bech Bretha* (Bee-Laws), as edited and analysed by Fergus Kelly and Thomas Charles-Edwards, has provided a great deal of relevant information on early medieval beekeeping.

Although reference to 'first attestations' in Middle English of a native vocabulary derived from Old English is a bit of a misnomer, it is of continuing interest to note instances of the emergence of the early modern lexis and, more importantly, to locate instances where a set of apiarian vocabulary is used together. Little noticed in this regard and largely unreflected in the *Middle English Dictionary* and the *Oxford English Dictionary* is *Le Tretiz* of Walter of Bibbesworth from about 1275. This household manual for the instruction of English-speaking housewives wishing to learn French has sections on wild and domestic animals, dressing flax, spinning thread, baking, brewing, and, toward the end of the tract, a passage titled 'Ore pur attirer bel la mesoun' ('Now [the French] for decorating the house [for a feast]').[19] The French verse has interlinear glosses in English. Walter mentions putting an old (straw?) beehive (not the ladle; he puns on the French words *rouche* and *louche*) on the fire under the cooking pots and, at the close of his kitchen scene, returns to the French word *rouche*, earlier glossed as *hivve* (l. 1037). In the following, interlinear English glosses (in italics) appear in the right margin:

Mes a la vile rouche redirroms,	
Ou plus aprendre i pouns.	
La rouche server deit des ees,	*bees*
Dount nous veom voler les dees	*swarmes*
E un par sei singulerement	
An hony bee esproprement,	
E proprement un dé d(e)s ees	
En engleis est *a suarme of bees*.	
E c'est une brecche de mel nomé	*honny come*
Ki en la rouche funt les ees de gré.[20]	

This note exploits the juxtaposition of French and English vocabulary in a reconsideration of the etymologies of several of these words and in providing an enhanced understanding of their history. First, the French vocabulary merits consideration. The greatly reduced form *ee*, from Latin *apis* 'bee', has been replaced in modern French by *abeille*, which is judged to have been borrowed from the Provençal *abelha*, which, in turn, reflects Latin *apicula*. *Le Tretiz* is the only source for *dees* as 'swarms'. Since no other etymology offers itself, it seems justified to accept that this is an abbreviated and compressed form of *essaim d'ees* ('swarm of bees'), with the first element deriving from the Latin *examen* in the sense of 'something expelled'.[21] *Rouche* is more interesting in that it reflects Gaulish *rusca*, 'bark'.[22] It is believed that these Celtic hives were built of cork and that this construction practice continued during the Gallo-Roman period. Centuries later, the word was used to denote the beehives of coiled oat straw introduced by the Franks, as no cork oaks grew in their homeland. This Celtic origin for *ruche* invites the speculation that Walter's *brecche de mel* may be traced to the Gallo-Latin **brisca* 'honey comb'.[23] Modern French has replaced this with *gâteau de miel* or *rayon de miel*, perhaps because of its homonymity and thus possible confusion with *brèche* 'gap, opening, breach'; the English word *comb* may be thought to share in a comparable ambiguity.

Walter's passage can then be translated as follows, with the additional guarantee of accuracy offered by the English glosses:

> But let us return to the old hive, about which we can learn even more. The hive is there to serve the bees, swarms of which we see flying about. One on its own is properly [called] *an hony bee*, and a swarm of bees is correctly [called] in English *a suarme of bees*. And what the bees gladly make in the hive is called a honeycomb.

Next to be examined are the Middle English glosses, in the order of their appearance in Walter's text. Of these, *hivve* is perhaps the most interesting, since Old English *hýf* is without cognates in continental Germanic. Previous scholarship has called attention to Old Norse *húfr* 'hull', proposing that the term for the hive, whether a cognate or a loanword, was based on the image of an overturned or careened ship. Before exploring this possibility, it should be noted that the British or Late Brittonic term for *beehive* likely encountered by the invading Anglo-Saxons was **lester*, with a basic meaning 'vessel', although not necessarily a marine one.[24] In the late Middle English period, *skep* was also used of 'beehive'. Old English *sceppe* 'basket' is thought to be a loanword from Old Norse *skep* 'basket, container' and has a superficial similarity to *skip* 'ship, vessel'. Thus, it would seem that in the term for 'hive', a basic dual metaphor of vessel (as both ship and container) persisted through a succession of languages. In summary, the Celtic *lester* ('vessel, hive') was supplanted by Old English *hýf* (Old Norse *húfr* 'hull'), which was then joined by Middle English *scep* 'basket, hive' (in Old Norse, *skep* 'basket'; cf. *skip* 'ship'). In modern English parlance, both *hive* and *skep* are used, the former for constructions with removable frames, the latter for traditional coiled-straw units that cannot be dismantled. The skep's construction poses difficulty both with regard to inspection (e.g., by government health agencies) and to the recovery of honey and wax; in the future, the skep is likely to be the sole preserve of hobbyists. What is interesting for our understanding of cultural interactions is that it is the hive, as a cultural construct in both French and English, that seems to have been the object of material and lexical transfer, with the Gaulish term percolating up into Gallo-Romance and the Norse metaphor being introduced to Old English in the course of population movements.

The terms used for the product of the hive – the honeycomb – are also of interest. The considerable historical depth of the word *honey-comb*, continuously in evidence from the Old English period, invites a reconsideration of the etymology of the compound. The *OED* judges it to be a simple joining of *honey* and *comb*, the latter in its most common meaning – that is, a comb for the hair, for dressing wool or flax, and so on – characterized by its regular teeth. The editors continue:

> This use [the compound of *honey* and *comb*] seems to be confined to English. It does not appear to originate in any likeness of a single

plate or cake with its cells to a comb for the hair, but either in the fact that the arrangement of the whole of the plates hanging parallel to each other from the roof of the hive suggests a comb with its teeth, or because each plate or 'comb' forms a ridge, and the whole a series of parallel ridges, like roofs of houses or ridges of hills rising beyond each other.[25]

This note suggests that the solution to this apparent problem may be a good deal simpler. The Old High German term for *honeycomb* was *waba*, *wabo*, which is related to the verb *weban* 'to weave, plait, spin' and is derived from the Indo-European root **uebh-* with these same meanings.[26] Under the effects of folk etymology and a perception of the comparable regularity of a comb's teeth and a honeycomb's cells, an original Old English compound **hunig-waba* experienced a shift in the semantic and phonological interstice of the phrase: the [g] sound moved toward the second element. Then a semantic realignment of this second element along the lines of the known word *comb* occurred, since **waba* no longer had – if it ever had – independent status in Old English. In light of our understanding of the Anglo-Saxon hive, which was a unitary structure of coiled straw and did not have removable frames, *comb* in this context may also have seemed consonant with the means of recovering the honey from the hive. Pressing the honey from the honeycomb may have seemed a process comparable to carding wool or flax: the honey was 'combed' out from the regularly structured comb.[27] *Hunigcamb* and *hyfe* are linked in the Old English adaptation of the *Regularis Concordia.*[28]

This line of thought leads us to review the juxtaposition of *hyfa* and *hunigbinna* in an Anglo-Saxon legal tract enumerating the tools and utensils that should be found on a well-stocked estate. Editor F. Liebermann translated both as *Bienenkörbe*, or 'beehives', but the focus in the latter term on the produce of the hive, rather than on the producers, invites the question of whether the basic meaning of *binn* ('bin, manger') is not here extended to some kind of honey extraction box).[29]

This note's last consideration is of the word *honeybee* itself. The *Oxford English Dictionary*'s entry for *honeybee* offers a quotation from

1566 as the first instance of this word, which we may analyse as a basic term with a complement. The compound can hardly be seen as a neologism or an effort to shore up an eroding word, as French *abeille* replaced *ee*, but rather as an effort toward dissimulation. *Bumblebee*, for example, is similarly first noted from the middle decades of the same century.[30] But Walter's phrase 'an hony bee' illustrates that the former phrasing is older by two and a half centuries.[31]

Cambridge MS Gg. 1.1 of *Le Tretiz* from the early fourteenth century has the advantage of gathering some of the earliest post-Conquest instances of beekeeping terminology in French and English into a neat, if limited, set. No single modern lexicographical work gives a full picture of the development of the French and English apiarian vocabularies, which are relatively straightforward, with the exception of English *hive*.[32] This note has explored the etymologies of some of this vocabulary, noted some additional early attestations, and enriched scholarly understanding of some terms. In light of the Gaulish influence on French and comparable Norse influence on English, the set retains our interest because of the apparent total lack of influence of Anglo-Norman French on the Middle English terminology. This suggests that the Norman Conquest entailed no technological innovations in beekeeping. Inevitably, perhaps, what intrigues us most in *Le Tretiz* is what the scullion was doing with the old hives on the kitchen fire. But, as illustrated by Walter's 'snapshot' in this same passage of a haggis – assembled from offal, grain, herbs, and stomach membrane – being removed from the pot, little went to waste in a medieval household.

NOTES

1. See Osborn for a full listing of earlier scholarship on the riddle. This note was first published as 'Exeter Book Riddle 17 and the L-Rune: British *lester 'vessel, oat-straw hive'?', *American Notes & Queries (ANQ)* 19: 2 (2006), 4–9, and is reproduced with the permission of the publisher.

2. Eva Crane, *The World History of Beekeeping and Honey Hunting*, 251–52.

3. For a full list of proposed solutions, see Williamson, 173.

4. With the slight adjustments proposed above to Osborn's translation, the poem in English would read: 'I am guardian of my flock, a protector made fast with wires, filled within with noble treasures. By day I often spit spear-terror; prosperity is the greater with my fullness. The lord beholds how out of my belly fly battle-darts. At dark times I begin to swallow shining battle-weapons, fierce points, horrible poison-spears. My insides are useful, a shining wombhoard, precious to the proud; men remember what goes through my mouth.'

5. *Bechbretha: An Old Irish Law-Tract on Bee-Keeping*, eds Kelly and Charles-Edwards, 24.

6. Kelly and Charles-Edwards, 41.

7. Eva Crane and Penelope Walker give a summary of other references to bees and beekeeping in early Irish literature, mainly in hagiographical accounts.

8. Kelly and Charles-Edwards, 68, par. 30.

9. Kelly and Charles-Edwards, 44f.

10. *Indogermanisches etymologisches Wörterbuch (IEW)*, I.680.

11. See *Lexique étymologique de l'irlandais ancien*; the information is reiterated in *Dictionnaire de la langue gauloise (DLG)*, 264. The entry for Gaulish *rusca* also provides evidence for personal and place names with this element. The compiler Delamarre believes that the presence of reflexes of *rusca* as 'bark' in areas without a Celtic substratum, such as Sicily, Sardinia, Calabria, points to a pre-Indo-European word. This may well be the case, but it is not directly relevant to the matter of *rusca* as 'bark container' being extended in the Gallo-Romance area to apiculture.

12. *Trésor de la langue française*, s. v. ruche.

13. *Middle English Dictionary (MED)*, s. v. rush, citing the manuscript of the Court Rolls of Great Amwell, Hertfordshire, London, British Library, Additional Roll 66727.

14. Tigges, 73.

15. This is confirmed by the *Dictionary of Old English*, which records two instances of *sceppe* as a unit of measure in charters associated with Bury Saint Edmunds, and *MED, s.v. skeppe*, with the numerous examples beginning in about 1325.

16. In reference to the last line of the poem, which Osborn renders 'men remember what goes through my mouth', she makes the stimulating but somewhat puzzling remark that '[t]his line may also allude to the often fierce honey of rhetoric' (11). The allusion is, I believe, rather more pointed, and we may recall such clichés as 'honey-tongued flattery' and 'stinging satire', aspects of the archaic conception of the poet as arbiter of praise and blame.

17. See, as the most authoritative work on this subject, Crane. This second note

was first published as 'An Early Set of Bee-Keeping Words in Anglo-Norman French and Middle English', *ANQ* 22: 2 (2009), 8–13, and is reproduced with the permission of the publisher.

18. *Paris Psalter*, ed. Krapp, Psalm 117, v. 12. This phrase translates the Vulgate's 'circumdederunt me quasi apes' ('They compassed me about like bees'). For apiarian motifs in the medieval Old English riddle tradition, see Osborn and the companion note which is the first half of this chapter.

19. Walter of Bibbesworth (1990), 26.

20. Walter of Bibbesworth, vv. 1043–52.

21. *Französisches etymologisches Wörterbuch* (*FEW*), Vol. 25. 11–13 and n3. If the queen bee were also figured as a 'goddess', one could imagine some connection with the homonym *déesse*.

22. *DLG*, 264; *FEW* 10.582, *s.v. rusca*.

23. *FEW*, I. 535, *s.v. brisca*.

24. See the previous note in this chapter on hives.

25. *OED*, *s.v. honeycomb*.

26. *IEW*, 1.1114–15, *s.v. uebh-*.

27. *Honibike* is also found in Middle English as 'honeycomb' and for 'a nest of wild bees'. For the second element, both the Old Norse *bi* and Old English *byc, buc* 'belly' have been proposed.

28. *Regularis concordia*, section 6, line 66.

29. *Die Gesetze der Angelsachsen*, I, 455.

30. 'I bomme, as a bombyll bee dothe', Palsgrave, 460.

31. Fyler, 158–59.

32. *MED* notes most of the English glosses to this section of Walter's treatise, but not *biselet* (l. 1032) as a small tablecloth of fine cotton or linen (see *MED*, *s.v. bis, bisse*) or the variant spelling *szhikinston* (v. 1040) for sleekstone (*MED*, *s.v. slikeston*).

Oats, brose & frumenty

The *Dictionary of the Scots Language* provides a familiar definition of *brose* as 'oatmeal with boiling water added'. The first attested use in Scots is from Urquhart's *Rabelais* (1653). Somewhat surprisingly, the dictionary also states a possible etymology but will not confirm it ('not a normal variant of *bruis[e]*') and summarizes with the statement 'of obscure origin'. Attested somewhat earlier (1515), *bruise* is, in turn, defined simply as 'broth' and variant spellings are listed as *bruise, browis, brwis(e, brwes, brewis,* and *broois*. Here we are on better-known etymological ground; parallel and source forms are Middle English *browes(se, -yce, brouwys* and Anglo-French *bruet, bru, brué; broé, broué, brouhei, browet, bruoy; bré, breo, breof, bro, brof* all 'broth, soup'.[1] These Anglo-French and underlying Norman French terms are allied with the common Old French form *breu* 'soup' completed by the diminutive suffix *-et*. The medieval word has survived only in some modern regional dialects or patois of French.

A more distant origin for all these forms, English and French, is found in a Germanic *brod* 'soup' (cf. Old High German *brod, prod*, Old Norse *broð*) that was also adopted into Late Latin (cf. *brodium* 'bouillon', *brodettum* 'soup, bouillon', *brodialis* 'soup-like [of a liquid])', later evident in Italian *brodo* 'liquid food'.[2] However, interesting for the later intersection of native English *broth* (< Old English *broþ)* and Anglo-French *bruet* in the early Middle English and early Scots period, this is of little help in illuminating the Scots use of *brose* in terms of its distinctive vocalism vis-à-vis *bruise* and of its specific referents in oatmeal and boiling water.

Another avenue of approach would be to consider possible antecedents in Scottish Gaelic or at least adstratal effects from that source. Old Irish had the forms *broth* 'corn, grain' (thought derived from Norse) and *brothchán* 'broth, gruel, pottage, soup', although the latter is more likely related to another *broth* meaning 'meat, flesh'. Dwelly and earlier dictionaries of Scottish Gaelic list *brot* as an archaic term for 'grain, corn' (as well as noting homonyms meaning 'flesh', 'fire', etc.), in addition to *brot* 'broth'.[3] The first of these, if ever truly in common use, would have been pronounced /broh/. If it were granted that this *brot* contributed to the semantic narrowing that resulted in the close association between *brose* and oats, it could equally well be seen as having coloured the relevant vocalism, leading to the present distinction between Scots *brose* and *bruise*. Until fresh evidence appears, Scots *brose* is, however, best seen, along with *bruise*, as outlying collateral derivatives of French *brouet* and Middle English *browes*.

Here it will be appropriate to consider the collocation (and collation) *Atholl brose*, the mixture of oat water, whisky, cream and honey. Folklore would trace the name to the first Earl of Atholl, who is reputed to have befuddled Highland rebels in 1475 by filling a well with the intoxicating mixture. However reluctant one may be to quash a good story, the truth is that there existed in Old Irish a verbal compound *athól*, which is not found in recorded Scottish Gaelic but which meant 'drinking, carousing'.[4] It consists of the verbal noun *ól* 'drinking' (in its most general sense) plus the prepositional prefix *ad-, ath*, used in the formation of compound nouns. This evidence seems sufficient to justify the speculation that early Scottish Gaelic had an expression **brot athóla* (or *brot athóil*, with the second element displaying a variant genitive singular form) with the meaning 'grain (steeped) for carousing', more exactly an oat-based drink containing, *inter alia*, alcohol. Yet, on balance, the *Atholl brose/*brot athóla* correspondence is perhaps best seen as an entertaining coincidence, since, for an adoption of this unattested Gaelic phrase into Scots, several undocumented processes would have had to occur: 1) a place name *Atholl* was substituted for the Gaelic verbal noun and the sequence of elements of the phrase reversed, 2) the vocalism of Gaelic *brot* was retained, but, 3) as outlined above, the overall phonological contours of the word were determined by Scots *bruise* and related.

To summarize from a slightly different perspective, three cognate Germanic word forms, related to cereals or grains, baked goods, and gruels, soups, etc., were in play in the development of Scots *brose*: 1) Old English *broþ*, preserved in Middle and Modern English as *broth*; 2) common Germanic (or Frankish) *brod* 'soup', the ancestor of Old French and Anglo-French *breu* and the diminutive *brouet* 'broth'; and 3) perhaps Old Norse *broð*, at the origin of Old Irish *brot* in the sense of grain and grain products. Forms 1 and 2 coalesced in Scots *bruise*, while the Irish term (irrespective of the folklore-coloured name *Atholl brose*) may have contributed to the development of the simplex *brose* 'oatmeal and boiling water'.

******

To stay with oats and oatmeal, some of the semantic and phonological overlapping met in *brose* and *bruise* is evident in the Scots term *spurtle* (var. *spurtill*). Two oats-related instruments are so designated, perhaps with a temporal and geographical distribution not easy to trace: 1) 'a flat implement used for turning oatcakes', 2) 'a wooden stick for stirring porridge' (*OED*, which also notes the northern English variant *spartle*).

While one might be ready to entertain a lexical derivation of *spurtle* from Latin *spatula* (disregarding the phonological difficulty of the intrusive epenthetic *-r-*), the latter tool is far in function from a stirrer, although *spatula* was so used in Latin in connection with mixing medications. Middle English *spatyl*, *spattle*, *spatule* are earlier attested than comparable Middle French forms and seem to derive directly from Latin.[5] Scots *spurtle* in the sense of 'stirrer', I contend, has a wholly different early history. Old Norse had a word for 'sprout, twig, stick, rod': *sproti*.[6] A process of adaptation into Scots would involved the following: 1) metathesis of the *-r-* from the initial consonant cluster *spr-* to a post-vocalic position; 2) (concurrent?) lowering of the vowel from *-r-* to *-r-*; 3) alignment of the word ending with the ubiquitous English and Scots instrument prefix *-le* (cf. *ladle*, *treadle*, with their origin in verbs, *thimble*, *handle*, in nouns). This Scots *spurtle* may well have attracted some of the semantic content of words for 'spatula' so that it, too, on occasion came to designate a flipper as well as a stirrer of oatmeal dishes.

Yet another Scottish and northern English pot-stirrer is the *thivel*. The *OED* calls attention to the widely varying vocalism (varieties of *a, e, i, o*) and gives as first attestations Middle English *thyvelle, thyvil, thivel*.[7] According to this reference work, the term is 'of obscure origin and history'. In the course of a summary of earlier scholarship devoted to *thivel* and its northern distribution in Britain, the *OED* states, in a phrasing reminiscent of the smug editorialism of an earlier lexicographical age:

> [T]his localization suggests a Norse origin, and it has been referred to Old Icelandic *þefja* / θɛvja / ; but this is a very rare word of doubtful standing, and in any case meant 'to thicken by beating or stamping' rather than 'to stir'. The actual Old Norse name for a stirring-stick was *þvara*, between which and *thivel* there is of course no connection.

Here the dictionary is in error. Old Norse did, indeed, have a specific verb for fulling and thickening, but this is *þæfa* (cf. modern Danish *tæve* 'to beat, stamp'). A clearly related verb, *þevja*, has been reconstructed on the basis of its occurrence in a participial form in the Icelandic *Eyrbyggja saga*, in which two Icelanders, crew-mates on a Norwegian ship, squabble over access to a cooking pot when the ship is pulled up on shore. Of the one, Arinbjǫrn, is stated: *hann hafði þá eigi þafðan sinn graut* ('he had not yet cooked his porridge thick enough' and there is explicit reference to stirring (Old Norse *hræra*).[8] The other man, Þorleifr *kimbi*, responsible for cooking a meal for the remainder of the crew, is impatient and dumps out Arinbjǫrn's porridge, for which he receives a crack on the head with the hot and dripping pot-stick, *þvara* (cf. the *OED* statement above). The context is clearly one of cooking and stirring porridge to promote water absorption and thicken the consistency. From the verb *þæfa*, a linguistically regular nominal derivation would be **þefill* 'pot stick' (cf. ON *ketill* 'kettle', also mentioned in the anecdote). In this formation the term references the purpose of the instrument: to thicken through stirring over heat, while in the case of *spurtle* it is the material of fabrication and shape (< ON *sproti* 'wooden rod') that form the basis for the name. With allowance for the inevitable phonological changes that accompany the adoption of a foreign word, Norse *þefill* offers a convincing match with the commonest Scots forms, *theevil, theevle*. *Þefill* could have figured in the Old Norwegian or Old Danish that was carried to Britain, while Icelandic *þvara* would represent the regional, insular term.

In conclusion, an informed guess suggests that more oat-related words in early Scots await adequate explanation. In reviewing the interplay of Celtic and Germanic languages in early Scotland in the area of cereal crops and food, and in particular, the loans from Norse, it is of interest to note at least one technological transfer from Celtic to Norse that likely occurred in the Highlands and Islands: Old Irish *sorn* 'grain-drying kiln' (< Latin *furnus*) later appears in some south-western Norwegian dialects.[9]

******

William Woys Weaver's recent article, 'The Lughnasa Platter: The Celtic Origins of Christmas Frumenty', invites us to consider the harvest festivals of pre-Roman Gaul and how the year's crops might have been incorporated and served on ritual or festive tableware such as the large first-century AD platter of Samian ware found in northern Africa but likely manufactured in southern Gaul.[10] Weaver suggests that frumenty, a potage made of boiled hulled wheat mixed with animal broth or milk, might have figured in such festivals dedicated to the divine figures that decorate the rim of the platter. His speculations raise the interesting question of which other elements of continental Celtic cuisine might have been absorbed into Gallo-Roman culture, survived into medieval French cooking and dining, and ultimately have been brought to Britain with the infusion of French language and French cooking that followed the Conquest.

Weaver notes that the name frumenty is to be traced not to a Gaulish word but to Latin *frūmentum* 'wheat'.[11] Before exploring the fragmentary Gaulish evidence, let us follow *frūmentum* forward to early pre-modern times in France and Britain. As it happens, the first written evidence for the dish comes not from France itself but from Britain. In the late thirteenth-century, Walter of Bibbesworth wrote a treatise on the French vocabulary required to effectively manage a country estate. His closing section is devoted to the arrangements for a feast in the lord's hall.[12] Bread, wine and beer are the staples. The first course features a boar's head, with the snout decorated. Then follows a course of game (*venesoun*) with *formenté*. This is only the beginning, and cranes, peacocks, swans, and wild geese follow. For Walter's full text, see Andrew Dalby's recent translation.[13] Other Anglo-French texts also associate frumenty with game, mutton, and porpoise (considered a fish during Lent).[14] This may represent the niche it occupied in a full-scale banquet menu.[15] However, one can easily imagine it served in other, less formal contexts. The association with game supports Weaver's linking of frumenty with the cereal harvest and hunting season but not his imagined scenario of pork, ham, and sausages being served with Gaulish frumenty.

The Norman-French term *frumentee* was absorbed into Middle English, which began to find written expression around 1300. In the so-called alliterative *Morte Arthure* (Death of King Arthur), from about 1400, we find 'Flesch fluriste of fermysone with frumentee noble' ('venison fattened up in the season closed to hunting, with fine frumenty').[16] Medieval recipes focus on the care needed with the cracked wheat and milk and there is no mention of fruits that might be added. An often-cited recipe in Middle English from 1381 begins: 'For to make Furmenty. Nym clene Wete and bray it in a morter wel that the holys gon al of and seyt yt til it breste … nym fayre fresch broth and swete mylk of Almandys or swete mylk of kyne and temper yt al … messe yt forthe wyth fat venyson and fresh moton'.[17] Here, too, the pairing with game continues, although instances of the term cited in the *Oxford English Dictionary* suggest that this lessened over time, until the dish was gradually eclipsed in the late nineteenth century. Frumenty plays a key role in the plot of Thomas Hardy's *The Mayor of Casterbridge*, part of the Wessex period atmosphere. In France, too, *fromentée* continued to be served as a rustic dish into the nineteenth century.[18]

Now, to turn now our culinary telescope in the opposite direction, what more can we learn of cookery in Gaul? A comprehensive statement on the contribution of Gaulish, via Gallo-Latin, to the French language is problematic. Given the multiple parallels between Gaulish and Latin vocabulary, it is often difficult to state unequivocally that a French word is of Celtic origin. The historical evidence of Gaulish is restricted to epigraphical texts (charms, curses) employing a circumscribed choice of words in a variety of alphabets, plus numerous personal and place names. While new finds of inscriptions continue to be made and the most difficult texts are now yielding their secrets, major additions to the Gaulish corpus seem unlikely. Some etymological triangulation is possible, when Irish, Welsh, or Breton words bear a sufficient similarity to a recorded Gallo-Romance word to authorize the reconstruction of a Gaulish term. Many French or Provençal words of putative Gaulish origin are attested only from rural dialects, e.g., Gaulish *buta* 'hut, simple dwelling place' but *boye* 'sheep shed' in nineteenth-century French rural dialects.[19] Since the golden age of the compilation of French dialect glossaries and word-lists is now past, thanks to technological advances and the spread of standard French, little new evidence can be expected from this quarter.

Nonetheless, the last decades of scholarly effort devoted to the vocabulary of Gaulish have resulted in the identification of about 170 words that can be reasonably posited as at the origin of French words, standard, dialectal, and archaic. The names of domestic animals have been preserved, e.g., *banuos* 'young pig', *bo* 'cow', *caerac-* 'lamb', *damos* 'deer', *oxso-* 'ox', but none for the meat served as food. Tree and plant names are similarly restricted. While we recognize English apple in Gaulish *aballo-* (although there is no direct filiation), French has *pomme*. Gaulish *cnoua-* 'nut' has a faint resemblance to French *noix* but the immediate source for the latter is Latin *nux*. Gaulish *cularon* 'cucumber, gourd' survives as *culara*, a dialect term in the French Dauphiné, but standard French *courge* (whence *courgette* 'zucchini') is drawn from Latin *cucurbita*. Nor, apparently, were other Gaulish terms such as *bracis* 'malt', *curmi* 'beer', *mesgos* 'whey' preserved in the Latin of Gaul. Gaulish *ceruesa* is, however, reflected in Spanish *cerveza* and Italian *cervògia*, while French *cervoise* is an outmoded term for barley beer. Gaulish *medu* 'mead' shares with the English word a descent from the Indo-European source of many European languages but did not leave a mark on French, where *hydromel*, modelled on Greek, is the standard term.

The Gaulish contribution to the vocabulary of French food culture must then be judged minimal. This does not, of course, preclude the existence of a Celtic dish of cracked wheat boiled in milk, flavoured with fruit, and served on platters decorated with grapes, figs, and hares, but in later Gallo-Romance it came to be called by the name already assigned in Latin culture. Put more bluntly, there is no compelling evidence for the filiation implicit in Weaver's sub-title, 'The Celtic Origins of Christmas Frumenty'.

This said, there is interesting evidence for the centrality of pottages and gruels in the cuisine of the early Celts. The word *iutta* and lexical root *iutu-* are found in several tribal and personal names, perhaps as an element reinforcing the image of a people having ample food (Delamarre, 194). Asterix had a historical compatriot in Ioturix, the 'Gruel King'. *Iutta* was adopted in Late Latin as *iotta*, a term referencing a soup or gruel cooked with milk. This is, evidently, far from frumenty and Latin *frūmentum*, and left no known trace in French, but does have interesting cognates, nearby and farther afield: Old Welsh, Old Cornish, and Old Breton *iot*, Old Irish *íth*, gruels made of cereal or pulse, Latin *iūs* 'soup, broth', Sanskrit *yūs* 'meat soup', and Lithuanian *jūšė* 'fish soup'.

Other evidence suggests that the Gauls, once conquered by Caesar, quickly turned to Latin as a communications medium that assured social advancement, as is paralleled in the later histories of speakers of the Celtic languages in the British Isles. Cuisine and culinary vocabulary may have been early victims to this upwardly mobile striving. Thus, tracing English frumenty to Gaulish ritual platters and moving between material culture and language may involve more than one slip 'twixt cup and lip.

NOTES

1. *Middle English Dictionary* (*MED*), s.v. *browes*; *Anglo-Norman Dictionary*, s.v. *bruet*. This note first appeared as '*Brose, Atholl brose, spurtle*, and *thivel*', *Scottish Language* 31–32 (2012–2013), 59–63, and is reproduced with the permission of the editor.

2. *Trésor de la langue française* (*TLF*), s.v. *brouet*.

3. *Dictionary of the Irish Language*, s.vv.. *broth, brothán*; *An Illustrated Gaelic-English Dictionary*, s.v. *brot*.

4. *Dictionary of the Irish Language*, s.v. *athól*.

5. *TLF*, s.v. *spatule*.

6. *An Icelandic-English Dictionary*, *Norrøn Ordbok*, s.v. *sproti*.

7. See also *MED*.

8. *Eyrbyggja saga*, ch. 39.

9. *Altnordisches etymologisches Wörterbuch*, s. v.v. *sorn, sornhus*.

10. William Woys Weaver, 'The Lughnasa Platter: The Celtic Origins of Christmas Frumenty', *Petits Propos Culinaires* 96 (2012), 53–58. This note on frumenty appeared in *Petits Propos Culinaires* 97 (2012), 13–17.

11. Weaver also mentions sops of bread that may have been used with the platter and frumenty. These he associates with the Gaulish term *embrekta*, but *embrecton* is currently understood as referring to fermented drinks (cf. *bracis* 'malt'); Xavier Delamarre, *Dictionnaire de la langue gauloise: une approche linguistique du vieux-celtique continental*, 2nd ed. (Paris: Errance, 2003), 162.

12. Walter de Bibbesworth, *Le Tretiz*, ed. William Rothwell (Aberystwyth: Anglo-Norman Online Hub, 2009), vv. 1105–1135.

13. *The Treatise of Walter of Bibbesworth*, trans. Andrew Dalby (Totnes: Prospect Books, 2012).

14. Examples are listed in the *Anglo-Norman Dictionary*, eds. William Rothwell et al., 2nd ed. (Aberystwyth: Modern Humanities Research Association, 2005), s.v. *frumenté*, now also accessible at The Anglo-Norman Online Hub. All these are from utilitarian texts such as cookbooks and we have no narrative scene with the dish being served. We may be surprised to see game at the head of the menu. Placement aside, game may have been prized at banquets as the product of aristocratic sport. By beginning with game, then proceding to exotic dishes with imported spices, medieval diners were also replicating the history of human culture as they may have understood it, from the open, savage wilderness to the language, law, and social order of the structured noble hall. But this, as is said, is mere speculation.

15. Sample menus in *The Good Wife's Guide (Le ménagier de Paris): A Medieval Household Book*, trans. Gina L. Greco and Christine M. Rose (Ithaca: Cornell University Press, 2009). 312.

16. *King Arthur's Death: The Middle English Stanzaic Morte Arthur and Alliterative Morte Arthure*, ed. Larry Dean Benson (Indianapolis, Bobbs-Merrill, 1974), v. 180. See, too, *Wynnere and Wastoure*, ed. S. Trigg, (London: Early English Texts Society, 1990), vv. 334–35: 'Venyson with the frumentee / and fesanttes full riche / Baken mete therby the burde sett'.

17. *The Forme of Cury*, ed. Samuel Pegge (London, J. Nichols, 1780), 91.
18. George Sand, *Le Meunier d'Angibault* (Brussels: Cans et compagnie, 1845), 57.
19. The increasingly negative connotations of the term – slipping from house to byre – have a milestone in late thirteenth-century poor laws from the Belgian town of Tournai, in which *bute* is a synonym for 'public house' – a locale where the poor should NOT be spending their alms; see William Sayers, 'Gaulish in French Lexis and Lexicography: The Case of *buta* "hut, small dwelling"', *French Studies Bulletin* 34 (2013), 1–3.

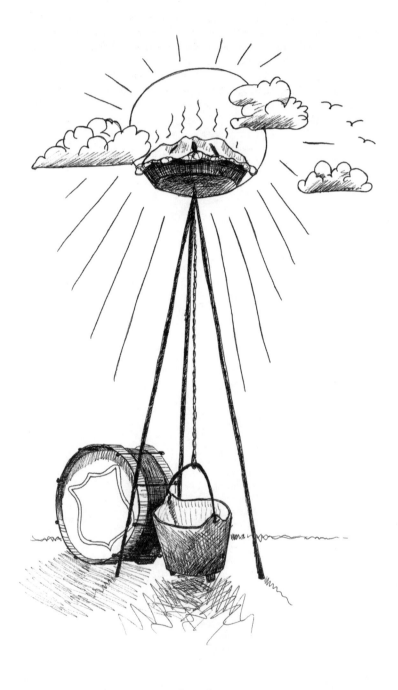

Strawberry & pie in the sky

Although the more conservative and cautious of modern lexicographical works admit of no sure etymology for *strawberry*, a number of popular explanations are current for a term long thought unrepresented in other western European languages: 1) the name refers to the *straw* mulch put under plants to improve drainage and prevent the fruit from rotting; 2) strawberries grow chiefly in grassy places and in hayfields; 3) the yellow achenes or ovaries present on the 'fruit' are *straw*-colored; 4) the extension of runners gives the impression of a plant *strewn* along the ground or propagating itself thereby; 5) the current form is derived from an earlier **strayberry*.[1]

Two little observed basic facts in the histories of this name and of strawberries and human culture are 1) that the English word is attested from the Old English period and 2) that the strawberry as is commonly known, *Fragaria x ananassa* or Garden Strawberry, is a cultivar dating from only the eighteenth century.[2] In short, the Old English name would have referred to the Woodland Strawberry, *Fragaria vesca* (also known as the Wild, European, or Alpine strawberry). Modern cultivation techniques such as mulching with straw are unlikely to have been practised in the medieval period, always assuming that some plants were transferred from the wild to gardens. The relative size and weight of the wild berries, entailing that they were unlikely to be in contact with the earth, would also make straw superfluous. Since the achenes of *Fragaria vesca* are less prominent than on the domesticated variety and can hardly be qualified as 'straw-colored', this explanation of the name is similarly invalidated. Grassy places or hayfields are emphatically not common habitats. Lastly, *Fragaria vesca* rarely produces runners, instead forming multiple crowns in a cluster.

The purported link with English *strew*, based on the phenomenon of runners 'scattering' the plant, is then also to be discounted in explaining the name.[3]

Strēawbergan and related forms are well attested in Old English, with more than twenty instances.[4] The early Germanic languages, with which the Old English word might be most aptly compared, stress the configuration of the plant and its proximity to the soil: Old Saxon *erthberi* 'earth-berry', Old High German *ertberi*, Old Swedish *iordhbær*. Yet, in Old English, the comparable *eorðbergan* is found only a single time. Since at least the possibility of an Old English form loaned from, or calqued by the Anglo-Saxons on, a Late British (or Brittonic) form should be entertained, it will be prudent to note attested Celtic forms. Old Irish *sub* references the sweetness of the berries, as do Welsh *mefusen* (ultimately traceable to *mêl* 'honey'), *syfien*, and Breton *sivenn*. These forms are all at appreciable distance from Old English *strēawbergan*. Nor can English *strawberry* be referred to Latin *fragum*, this too a word that has not been successfully etymologized.

Another approach, if we were to stay momentarily with the notion of 'strewn berry', is to consider the actual means of propagation of the Woodland Strawberry. Its usual habitat is trails and roadsides, embankments, hillsides, stone and gravel-laid paths and roads, meadows, young woodlands, sparse forest, woodland edges and clearings. With such a distribution, one might say that *Fragaria vesca*, even if wild, was almost destined to come to human attention. As noted above, the plant is not primarily propagated by the formation of runners. Ripened berries are, however, consumed by a variety of animals and birds, and the achenes are then spread far from the original plant. This accounts for the presence of wild strawberry plants even in locations where they do not receive sufficient light to form fruit. Although propagation through consumption by animals and birds is not exclusive to the strawberry, this would seem to offer a more justified connection with *strew* than the non-existent runners.

Old English *strewian*, *strewian* 'to strew' has a short vowel/diphthong, while that of *strēa(w)* is long. Furthermore, *strēawbergan* is the clearly dominant form in Old English.[5] It would seem incontrovertible that the *straw-* of *strawberry* does indeed refer primarily to straw and not to strewing. Yet the word *straw* itself deserves closer scrutiny. Old English *strēaw* has a host of Germanic cognates. The archaic signification of Common Germanic **strawa*, **strawam* was 'that (to be) strewn', as floor covering, litter, bedding, etc.[6] The later designation of the dried stalks of cereals as *straw* represents a transfer from a manner of use to the dried organic byproduct so used.

The most plausible origin for *strawberry* in its earliest reference to the Woodland Strawberry is as a name for plants growing at ground level (like straw spread as litter) irregularly distributed as the result of the spread of achenes by birds and animals – two interrelated senses of being strewn.[7] So reading the initial element of the compound then returns English *strawberry* to the Germanic fold as a variant on the 'earth-berry' designation.

******

Browsing the Web will reveal that the phrase *pie in the sky* has now taken on an existence independent of the song 'The Preacher and the Slave', by Joe Hill of the Industrial Workers of the World (IWW), the 'Wobblies'. It has lost its cutting humor, atheist cynicism, and, devoid of context, its social and economic relevance. In isolation, with an infantile monosyllabic rhyme and reference to dessert food, it now seems the equivalent of serendipitous gratification.[8] But the Web also offers a corrective. Michael Quinion's *World Wide Words* has a succinct January 2001 posting on the origin of the phrase. Hill's song dates to 1911 and was the labor organization's response to the proselytizing efforts of the Salvation Army to save working-class souls and provide some material relief to the thousands of migratory, casual, or unemployed laborers who gathered in North American cities, relief that Hill was loath to acknowledge because of ideological differences.[9]

Targeting the Salvation Army's hymn 'In the Sweet Bye and Bye', Hill wrote:

Long-haired preachers come out every night,
Try to tell you what's wrong and what's right;
But when asked how 'bout something to eat
They answer with voices so sweet.
   Chorus:
You will eat, bye and bye,
In that glorious land above the sky;
Work and pray, live on hay,
You'll get pie in the sky when you die.

Quinion concludes:

> By 1911, other expressions using *pie* had already been around for some
> time, such as *nice as pie* and *easy as pie* and it had begun to be used
> for a bribe or political patronage (of rewards being distributed like
> slices of pie) so *pie* was already in the air, so to speak.

Without refuting Quinion's observation and neat kicker,[10] this note
seeks to push the origin of the phrase to a time and place beyond
early twentieth-century America.

Hill was born in Gävle, Sweden, in 1879 as Joel Häggland,
although he later traveled in the United States under the names
Joseph Hillström and Joe Hill. Hill received some musical training
in the family home; then in 1902, like so many other Swedes of his
generation and before, he emigrated to the United States. How much
of the traditions of Swedish popular song did he bring with him, and
to which features of emigrant culture would he have been exposed?

Perhaps ultimately deriving from the 'land flowing with milk and
honey' promised in the Bible (Josh. 5:6), the Latin and vernacular
literatures of medieval Europe exploited a motif known in English
as the Land of Cockaigne. Here all physical reality is edible, as if by
a variant on Midas' touch everything has been turned not golden
but golden-brown, ready to eat – the first fast-food world. In some
treatments, such as the eleventh-century Irish *Vision of Mac Con
Glinne*, the author's intent seems to be to satirize monks living 'too

high on the hog'.[11] Elsewhere, sloth, greed, and gullibility are the targets. A Middle English version also appeared in Ireland in about 1300, satirizing the vices of monastic life: 'Fur in see bi west Spayngne Is a lond ihote Cokaygne … Þo3 paradis be miri and bri3t, Cokaygn is of fairir si3t … Al of pasteiis beþ þe walles, Of fleis, of fisse and rich met … Fluren cakes beþ þe schingles alle Of cherche … and halle'.[12] The sixteenth-century German poet and songwriter Hans Sachs, now best known from Wagner's opera *Die Meistersinger von Nürnberg*, devoted a poem to the motif under the title 'Das Schlaweraffen Landt'.[13] Houses and fences are made of cake and sausage, the wells are full of wine, the swimming fish are already boiled, salted, roasted or baked. And in the sky are roast chickens, geese, and pigeons. They fly directly into the mouths of those too lazy to catch them ('Auch fliegen umb … Gebraten Hüner, Genss und Tauben Wer sie nicht facht, und ist so faul Dem fliegen sie selbst inn das maul'). As well, roasted pigs run about Schlaraffenland, each with a knife in its back, so that a slice can readily be cut off and the knife put back.[14]

Sachs' poem was adapted by other comic authors. Motifs appear in the work of the seventeenth-century German writer Christian Weise, whose *Die drei ärgsten Erznarren in der ganzen Welt* ('The three most outrageous archfools in the whole world') was published in a Swedish translation in 1769. Here in the context of a narrator's naive enlistment in the French army for a campaign in Germany we find the lines 'Jag … mente, at jag skulle komma til Slaraffenland, hwarest stekta dufwor skulle flyga mig i munnen' ('I thought that I would come to Slaraffenland, where roast pigeons would fly into my mouth').[15]

By 1903 the Schlaraffenland motif was sufficiently well established in popular Swedish tradition that an author could write: 'Om jag bara ställde mig att gapa som en schlaraff, skulle det nog komma något flygande in i munnen på mig' ('If I just stood there gaping like a *schlaraff*, something would likely come flying into my mouth').[16] In an emigrant song entitled 'Bröder, vi har långt att gå' ('Brother, we have a long way to go') we find the lines:

Höns och änder regna ner
Stekta gäss och ännu fler
Flyga in på bordet
Med kniv och gaffel i låret.[17]
[Chickens and ducks rain down,
roast geese and even more
fly onto the table
with knife and fork in their thighs.]

Or should we say drumsticks?

Of course, Swedes were not alone in their hopes for, and disappointments from, the New World. The celebrated Norwegian violinist Ole Bull sought to establish an immigrant utopia in Potter County, Pennsylvania, in 1852, but the colony, popularly called Oleana, fell prey to land speculators and failed. A year later a comic song in Norwegian appeared from the pen of Ditmar Meidell, editor of *Krydseren*, satirizing the ill-founded hopes of his emigrant countrymen. Like Hill's title, the opening lines refer to the slave-like lives of laborers but here in Europe, not America. The lines most relevant for present concerns, which Hill would have no difficulty understanding, read:

Aa Laxene dem springer saa lystig i Bække,
dem hopper selv i Gryden aa roper: dem ska' dække!
Aa brunstegte Griser de løber om saa flinke
aa forespør sig høfligt, om Nogen vil ha' Skinke. ...
Fra Skyerne det regner med Kolerakaker,
Aa Gubevare Dere vel for dejlige Saker![18]
[And the salmon, they leap like mad in the rivers,
and hop into the kettles, and cry out for a cover!
And little roasted piggies rush about the streets,
politely inquiring if you wish for ham. ...
And cakes fairly rain from the skies above you.
Good Lord, what wondrous tidbits!]

As the song 'Big Rock Candy Mountain', dating from the 1920s, illustrates, the utopian theme was widespread in popular American culture and would have been acutely known to those for whom its promise remained unfulfilled. Here, the hobo world is portrayed, and the menu is appropriate: 'cigarette trees ... a lake of stew and gingerale too.'[19] Hill's stand is that the dream of the New World is not a simple fraud but that its realization, a workers' paradise, has been thwarted by capitalism. The church emasculates the nascent labor movement with the promise that workers' rewards will come not in a better world in the here and now but in a transcendent heavenly world. Perhaps it is only coincidence that the anti-clericalism of Hill's 'The Preacher and the Slave' seems to echo the distant medieval origins of some of the Cockaigne poems. And for those of us interested in intertextuality, it must also be only coincidental that the 1925 song by Alfred Hayes, 'I Dreamed I Saw Joe Hill Last Night' (popularized by Paul Robeson and Joan Baez), should employ the same literary convention of the dream vision as the *Vision of Mac Con Glinne*.

We are not authorized to see in the Swedish reflex of the Cockaigne motif the single source for Hill's metaphor. But the step from the emigrant Swede's flying roast squabs to the Wobblies' pie in the sky, compressing the promise of Christian heaven into one dismissive phrase, is not a long one. Hill's trial in Utah on a murder charge does not meet current legal standards for fairness. He was convicted and executed in 1915. Since then, evidence pointing to some prior petty criminality on Hill's part has also come to light. Historians and labor hagiographers will continue to debate the songwriter, while his *pie in the sky* pursues its now independent life.

To close on a personal note, my father traveled the roads and rails of Canada and the United States in the 1920s, and it was from him some years later that I first heard of *pie in the sky*. While never a churchgoer as an adult – he claimed that having been twice a Sunday as a child dispensed him from further attendance – he retained a more positive memory than Hill of the Salvation Army's hostels and kitchens, if not its sermons, and when he died in the mid-1980s, his modest will provided for a few last nickels on the Sally Ann drum.[20]

NOTES

1. Liberman, the most recent scholar to have reviewed this evidence and earlier studies, favors the equation *strawberry = grassberry* (81). This explanation was first advanced by Bender. Weekley, in *An Etymological Dictionary of Modern English,* sees an origin in the straw used to cover plants or in the straw-colored achenes. The *Oxford English Dictionary* suggests either the straw-colored achenes or the runners, while *The Oxford Dictionary of English Etymology* refers only to an uncertain origin. Collin noted the presence of *stråbär* in some Swedish dialects, although this may reflect the common practice of collecting ripened wild strawberries (*smultron*) on straws. This note was first published as 'The Etymology of *strawberry*', *Moderna språk* 103.2 (2009), 15–18, and is reprinted with the permission of the editors.

2. The earliest instance is found in the vocabulary traditionally attributed to Ælfric; *Anglo-Saxon and Old English Vocabularies,* 136, 14. The berry name has remained in continuous use in English, unaffected by Anglo-French. See *Middle English Dictionary, s.v. strauberie.* For the modern cultivar, see Clarke and Converse.

3. See '*Fragaria vesca* L'.

4. *Dictionary of Old English, Old English Corpus, s.vv. streaberige, streawberige, streowberige, streuberige.*

5. Campbell, 328, n. 10.

6. *Deutsches etymologisches Wörterbuch, s.v. strawa.*

7. This development was proposed by Bloomfield, 433–434, who did not, however, recognize its exclusive relevance to the Woodland Strawberry.

8. The titles of two recent films employ the phrase (*Pie in the Sky,* dir. Bryan Gordon, 1996, and *Pie in the Sky: The Brigid Berlin Story,* dir. Shelly Dunn Fremont and Vincent Fremont, 2000), one with some historical awareness, and a variety of commercial enterprises have appropriated it. Its resonance, however, continues for social and literary historians, e.g., Feied. This note was first published as 'Joe Hill's 'Pie in the Sky' and Swedish Reflexes of the Land of Cockaigne', *American Speech* 77 (2002), 331–36, and is reproduced with the permission of the publishers.

9. The song first appeared in the 6 July 1911, *Industrial Worker* edition of the IWW songbook, but it was not credited to Hill until the fifth edition, issued on 6 March 1913 (see Fowke and Glazer, 157). The music appears more recently in *Songs to Fan the Flames of Discontent,* and the complete lyrics and an audio file of the song performed by Utah Phillips are available on the Web (Killebrew).

10. Hill's final chorus, now in the songwriter's voice, with its concrete reference to food, somewhat undercuts Quinion's claim to a metaphorical loan:
    > You will eat, bye and bye,
    > When you've learned how to cook and to fry.
    > Chop some wood, 'twill do you good,
    > And you'll eat in the sweet bye and bye.

11. Sayers (1994).

12. Heuser, 145–50; cited in the *Middle English Dictionary, s.v. cokaigne.*

13. Sachs, 1: 124–27. This is not the place for a review of the disputed origins of

Cockaigne and *Schlaueraffenland*, but the former may be related to Latin and Romance words for 'cooking' and the latter to a term for 'lazy person' plus the German word for 'ape'.

14. For a fuller discussion, see Richter.

15. Weise, 48; this work is not held by North American libraries, and I am grateful to Cecilia Bäckstrand of the Royal Library, Stockholm, for providing a copy of the relevant passage.

16. Huch, 35, cited in *Ordbok öfver svenska språket*, s.v. *schlaraff.*

17. Brodin, 21; a variant version, under the title 'Bröder, wi bor långt ifrån' ('Brother, we live far away'), appears in Lantz and Jonsson, 18–19: punch and wine fill the streams and lakes, the mountains are of gold, the ground of sugar, and the trees filled with willing girls – Lutheranism meets the Koran. My thanks to Ingrid Åkesson of Svenskt Visarkiv for information on these songs.

18. Blegan and Ruud, 187–98; Ruud's translation is accurate but flat and now rather dated. Folksinger Pete Seeger popularized a version in English in the 1950s under the title 'Oleana'.

19. The song is attributed to Harry 'Haywire Mac' McClintock and exists in several versions. Coming to my attention after the acceptance of this note for publication is Rammel. After treating several of the concerns in this note, his book concentrates on McClintock. Neither Hill nor 'Pie in the Sky' is mentioned.

20. *Sally Ann* is an informal British term for 'Salvation Army'. According to the *OED*, *Sally Ann* is first recorded in *American Speech* (2 [1927]: 387) in Charlie Samolar's 'The Argot of the Vagabond' (385–92). The phrase, although not with its full historical import, has returned to the continent of its origins and appears with the meaning 'unjustified hope, wishful thinking' in Scotsman Ian Rankin's *Resurrection Men*, a novel in the Inspector Rebus series set in Edinburgh.

Bibliography

Adgar, *Le Gracial*, edited by P. Kunstmann (Ottawa: University of Ottawa, 1982).

Kubilây Aktulum, 'Les métamorphoses de l'objet dans *Le Ventre de Paris* d'Émile Zola', *Süleyman Demirel Üniversitesi Fen-Edebiyat Fakültesi Sosyal Dergisi* 5 (2005), 343–58.

Aldhelm, *De Laudibus Virginitatis*, in *Patrologia Latina Cursus Completus, Series Latina*, edited by J.-P. Migne, Vol. 89 (Paris: Migne, 1850).

Neil R. Aldridge, 'The Trinitarian Priory of Motynden at Headcorn', *Archaeologia Cantiana: Being Contributions to the History and Archaeology of Kent* 115 (1995), 177–212.

Altfranzösisches Wörterbuch, compiled by Adolf Tobler and Erhard Lommatzsch (Stuttgart: F. Steiner, 1925–2001).

Althochdeutsches Wörterbuch, compiled by Gerhard Köbler (2013), http://www.koeblergerhard.de/ahdwbhin.html.

Altnordisches etymologisches Wörterbuch, compiled by Jan de Vries, 3rd ed. (Leiden: Brill, 1977).

Altsächsisches Wörterbuch, compiled by Gerhard Köbler (2014), http://www.koeblergerhard.de/aswbhinw.html

American Heritage Dictionary (Boston: Houghton Mifflin, 2011).

Ancrene Wisse: A Corrected Edition of the Text in Cambridge, Corpus Christi College, MS 40 …, edited by Bella Millett et al. (Oxford: Oxford University Press, 2005).

Pierre Androuët, *Guide du fromage* (Paris: Stock, 1971).

Anglo-Norman Dictionary, edited by William Rothwell et al., 2nd ed. (London: Modern Humanities Research Association, 1992), Anglo-Norman On-Line Hub,<http://www.anglo-norman.net.

Anglo-Saxon and Old English Vocabularies, edited by Thomas Wright and Richard Paul Wülcker (London: Trübner & Co., 1884).

An Anglo-Saxon Dictionary, edited by Joseph Bosworth and T. Northcote Toller (Oxford: Clarendon, 1898).

Nathan Bailey, *Dictionarium domesticum* (London: C. Hitch, 1736).

Peter Bakker, '"The Language of the Coast Tribes is Half Basque": A Basque-American Indian Pidgin in Use between Europeans and Native

Americans in North America, ca. 1540–ca. 1640', *Anthropological Linguistics* 31 (1989), 117–47.

The Barnhart Concise Dictionary of Etymology, compiled by Robert K. Barnhart (New York: Harper Collins, 1995).

James H. Barrett, 'Fish Trade in Norse Orkney and Caithness: A Zoo-archaeological Approach', *Antiquity* 71 (1997), 616–38.

La Bataille de Caresme et de Charnage, edited by Grégoire Lozinski (Paris: H. Champion, 1933).

Bech Bretha: An Old Irish Law Tract on Bee-Keeping, edited and translated by Fergus Kelly and Thomas Charles-Edwards (Dublin: Dublin Institute for Advanced Studies, 1983).

Harold H. Bender, 'English *strawberry*', *The American Journal of Philology* 55 (1934), 71–74.

Benedeit, *The Anglo-Norman Voyage of St. Brendan*, edited by Ian Short and Brian Merrilees (Manchester: Manchester University Press, 1979).

Peter Bierbaumer and Elke Wannagat, 'Ein neuer Lösungsvorschlag für ein altenglisches Rätsel (Krapp-Dobbie 17)', *Anglia* 99 (1981), 379–82.

The Black Book of Kincardineshire, containing lists of the covenanters confined in Dunnottar Castle, in 1685, edited by James Anderson (Stonehaven: W. Johnston, 1843).

Theodore C. Blegan and Martin B. Ruud, *Norwegian Emigrant Songs and Ballads* (London: Oxford University Press, 1936).

Leonard Bloomfield, *Language* (New York: Henry Holt, 1933).

Thomas Blount, *Glossographia, or a dictionary interpreting such hard words … as are now used* (London: Thomas Newcomb, 1656; repr. Menston, Yorks.: Scolar Press, 1969).

George Broderick, *A Handbook of Late Spoken Manx* (Tübingen: M. Niemeyer, 1984–86).

Knut Brodin, *Emigrantvisor och andra visor* (Stockholm: Ahlén, 1938).

Horace Bushnell, *Sermons for the New Life* (New York: Scribner, Armstrong and Co., 1858).

Nina Hopkins Butlin, 'Opérations de description dans *Le Ventre de Paris* de Zola', *ALFA* 5 (1992), 87–107.

Calendar of Letter-Books Preserved among the Archives of the Corporation of the City of London at the Guildhall, edited by Reginald R. Sharpe, vol. 10 (London: J. E. Francis, 1911).

Calliope's Classroom: Studies in Didactic Poetry from Antiquity to the Renaissance, edited by M. Annette Harder et al. (Paris and Dudley, Mass., Peeters, 2006).

Angus Campbell, *Old English Grammar* (Oxford: Clarendon Press; New York: Oxford University Press, 1959).

D. A. Carpenter, 'The Household Rolls of King Henry III of England (1216–72)', *Historical Research* 80.207 (2007), 22–46.

J. Harold Clarke and Richard H. Converse, 'Strawberry', *AccessScience@ McGraw-Hill*. http://www.accessscience.com.proxy.library.cornell.edu, DOI 10.1036/1097–8542.659200.

Carl S. R. Collin, 'Eng. *strawberry*', *Moderna språk* 32 (1938), 76–79.

Samuel Colvil, *The Whiggs supplication, or, the Scotch Hudibras* (London [s.n.], 1681).

The Complaynt of Scotlande [attributed to Robert Wedderburn], edited by A. M. Stewart (Edinburgh: Scottish Text Society, 1979).

A Comprehensive Etymological Dictionary of the English Language, compiled by Ernst Klein (Amsterdam and New York: Elsevier Publishing Company, 1971).

A Concise Etymological Dictionary of the English Language, compiled by Walter W. Skeat (Oxford: Clarendon Press, 1961).

John Considine, 'PENDUGUM: John Skelton and the Case of the Anachronistic Penguin', *Neuphilologische Mitteilungen* 100 (1999), 187–89.

The Cook's and Confectioner's Dictionary or, the accomplish'd housewife's companion, edited by John Nott (London: C. Rivington, 1723).

Eva Crane, *The World History of Beekeeping and Honey Hunting* (London: Duckworth, 1999).

Eva Crane and Penelope Walker, 'Irish Beekeeping in the Past', *Apimondia* (21–26 Aug. 2005), <http://www.apimondia2005.com/historyof-irishbeekeeping/irishbeekeepinginthepast.html>.

Le Cuisiner françois, edited and translated by Jean-Louis Flandrin, and Philip and Mary Hyman (Paris: Montalba, 1983).

Christopher K. Currie, 'Southwick Priory Fishponds: Excavations 1987', *Proceedings of the Hampshire Field Club and Archaeological Society* 46 (1991), 53–72.

Curye on Inglysch: English Culinary Manuscripts of the Fourteenth Century, edited by Constance B. Hieatt and Sharon Butler (London: Oxford University Press, 1985).

Alan Davidson, *The Penguin Companion to Food* (Oxford: Penguin, 1999).

The Deeds of the Normans in Ireland: La Geste des Engleis en Yrlande, edited by Evelyn Mullaly (Dublin: Four Courts, 2002).

Thomas Dekker and Thomas Middleton, *The Honest Whore* (London: J. Hodgets, 1604).

R. B. Delderfield, 'The Origins of Ancient Woodland and a Fish-pond in Pound Wood, Thundersley, Essex', *Essex Archaeology and History: Transactions of the Essex Archaeological Society* 17 (1996), 322–24.

Deutsches etymologisches Wörterbuch, compiled by Gerhard Köbler (1995), http://www.koeblergerhard.de/derwbhin.html.

Deutsches Wörterbuch, compiled by Jacob and Wilhelm Grimm (München: Deutscher Taschenbuch Verlag, 1984).

Diccionario critico etimológico castellano e hispánico, compiled by Joan Corominas and José A. Pascual (Madrid: Gredos, 1980–91).

Diccionario Vasco-Castellano, compiled by Plácido Múgica Berrondo (Bilbao: Mensajero, 1981).

Dictionary of American Regional English, edited by Frederic G. Cassidy (Cambridge, Mass., Harvard University Press, 1985–2012).

Dictionary of Medieval Latin from British Sources, edited by R. E. Latham et al. (London: Oxford University Press, 1975–2013).

Dictionary of Old English, edited by Antonette diPaolo Healey et al. (Toronto: University of Toronto Press, 1986–).

Dictionary of Old English Corpus, edited by Antonette diPaolo Healey (Ann Arbor: University of Michigan Press, 1998).

A Dictionary of the Gaelic Language, compiled by Norman MacLeod (London: Henry G. Bohn, 1845).

Dictionary of the Irish Language, edited by E. G. Quin (Dublin: Royal Irish Academy, 1913–76).

Dictionary of the Scots Language – Dictionar o the Scots Leid (2005), http://www.dsl.ac.uk.

Dictionnaire de l'ancienne langue française, compiled by Frédéric Godefroy (Paris: F. Vieweg, 1881–1902).

Dictionnaire de la langue gauloise: une approche linguistique du vieux-celtique continental, compiled by Xavier Delamarre, 2nd ed. (Paris: Editions Errance, 2003).

Dictionnaire étymologique de l'ancien français, compiled by Kurt Baldinger et al. (Québec: Presses de l'Université Laval; Tübingen: Niemeyer; Paris: Klincksieck, 1974–).

Gavin Douglas, *The xiii bukes of Eneados of the famose poete Virgill* (London,: William Copeland, 1553).

John Dryden, *All for love; or, The world well lost* (London: T. Warren, 1696).

The Early English Carols, edited by Richard Leighton Greene (Oxford: Clarendon, 1935).

Richard Eden, *The decades of the newe worlde or west India* (London: William Powell, 1555, repr. 1885).

Geoff Egan, 'Le mobilier et le décor de la maison médiévale à Londres', in *Cadre de vie et manières d'habiter (XIIe–XVIe siècle)*, edited by Danièle Alexandre-Bidon, Françoise Piponnier, and Jean-Michel Poisson (Caen: Publications du CRAHM, 2006), 221–228.

Miren Egaña Goya, 'Basque Toponymy in Canada', *Onomastica Canadiana* 74 (1992), 53–74.

Alexander John Ellis, *On Early English Pronunciation* (London: Asher and Co., 1889).

Encyclopedia of Newfoundland and Labrador, edited by Joseph Roberts Smallwood and Robert D. W. Pitt (St. John's, Nfld: Newfoundland Book Publishers, 1981–94).

English Dialect Dictionary, compiled by Joseph Wright (New York: H. Frowde, 1898–1905).

An Etymological Dictionary of Modern English, compiled by Ernest Weekley (New York: Dover Publications, 1921).

An Etymological Dictionary of the Gaelic Language, compiled by Alexander MacBain (Stirling: L E. Mackay, 1911).

An Etymological Dictionary of the Norn Language in Shetland, compiled by Jakob Jakobsen (London: D. Nutt, Copenhagen: V. Prior, 1828–32).

Etymologisches Wörterbuch der deutschen Sprache, compiled by Friedrich Kluge and Elmar Seebold (Berlin, New York: W. de Gruyter, 1989).

Eyrbyggja saga, edited by Einar Ól. Sveinsson and Mattias Þórðarson (Reykjavík: Hið íslenzka fornritafélag, 1935).

Frederick Feied, *No Pie in the Sky: The Hobo as American Cultural Hero in the Works of Jack London, John Dos Passos, and Jack Kerouac* (New York: Citadel, 1964).

Femina, edited by W. Wright (London: Roxburghe Club, 1909).

Femina: Trinity College, Cambridge MS B 14.40, edited by William Rothwell (The Anglo-Norman On-Line Hub, 2005), <http://www.anglo-norman. net/texts/femina.pdf>.

Floire et Blancheflor, edited by Margaret Pelan (Paris: Les Belles Lettres, 1956).

Fockleyr Gaelg-Baarle [*Manx-English Dictionary*], compiled by Phil Kelly, http://www.ceantar.org/Dicts/.

Foclóir Gaedhilge agus Béarla: An Irish English Dictionary, compiled by Patrick S. Dinneen (Dublin: Irish Texts Society, 1927).

Giles Foden, *Turbulence* (New York: Knopf, 2010).

The Forme of Cury, edited by Samuel Pegge (London, J. Nichols, 1780).

Edith Fowke and Joe Glazer, *Songs of Work and Protest* (New York: Dover, 1973).

'*Fragaria vesca* L.', *GRIN Taxonomy for Plants* (United States Department of Agriculture), http://www.ars-grin.gov/cgi-bin/npgs/html/taxon.pl?264.

Französisches etymologisches Wörterbuch, edited by Walther von Wartburg et al. (Basel: Zbinden et al., 1928–2002).

The French Text of the Ancrene Riwle, edited from British Museum MS. Cotton Vitellius F vii, edited by J. A. Herbet (London: Oxford University Press 1944).

John M. Fyler, *Language and the Declining World in Chaucer, Dante, and Jean de Meun* (Cambridge: Cambridge University Press, 2007).

Geoffroi Gaimar, *L'Estoire des Engleis*, edited by Alexander Bell (Oxford: B. Blackwell, 1960).

Geiriadur Prifysgol Cymru: A Dictionary of the Welsh Language, edited by R. J. Thomas et al. (Caerdydd: Gwasg Prifysgol Cymru, 1950–2002).

Gervais du Bus, *Roman de Fauvel*, edited by Alfred Långfors (Paris, F. Didot et cie, 1914–1919).

Die Gesetze der Angelsachsen, edited by F. Liebermann (Aachen: Scientia, 1960).

William Gillies, 'Scottish Gaelic', in *The Celtic Languages*, edited by Martin J. Ball with William Fife (London and New York: Routledge, 1993).

Glossarium ad scriptores mediae et infimae latinitas, compiled by C. D. Ducange (Paris: C. Osmont, 1733–36).

The Good Wife's Guide: Le Ménagier de Paris, A Medieval Household Book, translated by Gina L. Greco and Christine M. Rose (Ithaca: Cornell University Press, 2009).

Sarah Gordon, *Culinary Comedy in Medieval French Literature* (West Lafayette, Ind.: Purdue University Press, 2007).

Grágás, Hin forna lögbók Islendínga sem nefnist Grágás, edited by J.F. W. Schlegel, Þórður Sveinbjørnsson, and J.-M. Pardessus (Copenhagen: H. H. Thiele, 1829).

Grágás: lagasafn íslenska þjóðveldisins, edited by Gunnar Karlsson, Kristján Sveinsson, and Mörður Árnason (Reykjavik: Mál og menning, 1992).

A Grammar of Basque, compiled by José Ignacio Hualde and Jon Ortiz de Urbina (Berlin and New York: Mouton de Gruyter, 2003).

Grande Dicionario etimológico-prosódico da lingua portugesa, compiled by Francisco da Silveira Bueno (São Paulo: Edição Saraiva, 1963).

Griechisches etymologisches Wörterbuch, edited by Hjalmar Frisk (Heidelberg: C. Winter, 1960–72).

Groot woordenboek der nederlandse taal, compiled by J.H. van Dale ('s-Gravenhage: Martinus Nijhoff, 1976).

Francis Grose, *A Dictionary of the Vulgar Tongue* (London: Hooper and Wigstead, 1785).

Pierre Guiraud, 'De la grive au maquereau: le champ morpho-sémantique des noms de l'animal tacheté', *Le Français Moderne* 34 (1976), 280–90.

Anna Gural-Migdal, 'Représentation utopique et ironie dans *Le Ventre de Paris*', *Cahiers Naturalistes* 74 (2000), 145–61.

Constance B. Hieatt, '"Ore pur parler del array de une graunt mangerye": The Culture of the "Newe Get", circa 1285', in *Acts of Interpretation: The Text in Its Contexts, 700–1600: Essays on Medieval and Renaissance Literature in Honor of E. Talbot Donaldson*, edited by Mary J. Carruthers and Elizabeth D. Kirk (Norman, Oklahoma: Pilgrim, 1982), 219–33.

Constance B. Hieatt and Robin F. Jones, 'Two Anglo-Norman Culinary Collections Edited from British Library Manuscripts Additional 32085 and Royal 12.C.xii', *Speculum* 61 (1986), 859–882.

The historie of Cambria, now called Wales, a part of the most famous yland of Brytaine, written in the Brytish language aboue two hundreth yeares past [attributed to Caradoc of Llancarvan, purportedly translated by Humphrey Llwyd and David Powell] (London: Rafe Newberie and Henrie Denham, 1584).

Richard C. Hoffman, *Fishers' Craft and Lettered Art: Tracts on Fishing from the End of the Middle Ages* (Toronto, Buffalo: University of Toronto Press, 1997).

Randle Holme, *The academy of armory; or, A storehouse of armory and blazon* (Chester: [the author], 1688).

Ricarda Octavia Huch, *Ludolf Ursleu den yngres krönika*, translated by Kerstin Måås (Stockholm: Geber, 1903).

An Icelandic-English Dictionary, compiled by Richard Cleasby, Gudbrand Vigfusson, and William A. Craigie, 2nd ed. (Oxford: Clarendon, 1969).

An Illustrated Gaelic Dictionary, compiled by Edward Dwelly (Herne Bay: E. Dwelly, 1902–11, repr. Edinburgh: Birlinn, 2001).

Indogermanisches etymologisches Wörterbuch, compiled by Julius Pokorny, 5th ed. (Tübingen and Basel: A. Francke, 2005).

Philippe Jousset, 'Une Poétique de la "Nature morte": Sur la pratique descriptive dans *Le Ventre de Paris*', *Cahiers Naturalistes* 44 (1998), 337–50.

James Joyce, *Ulysses: The Corrected Text*, edited by Hans Walter Gabler (London: Penguin, 1986).

Dominique Julien, 'Le "Ventre" de Paris: Pour une pathologie du symbolisme dans l'œuvre d'Émile Zola', *French Forum* 17 (1992), 281–99.

Charles Keith, *The Har'st Rig; and, The Farmer's Ha': Two poems in the Scottish dialect* (Edinburgh,: W. Berry, 1794).

Fergus Kelly, *Early Irish Farming: A Study Based Mainly on the Law-texts of the 7th and 8th Centuries AD* (Dublin: Dublin Institute for Advancd Studies, 1997).

Kathleen E. Kennedy, 'Changes in Society and Language Acquisition: The French Language in England 1215–1480', *English Language Notes* 35 (1998), 1–19.

Die Kildare-Gedichte: Die ältesten mittelenglischen Denkmäler in anglo-irischer Überlieferung, edited by Wilhelm Heuser, Bonner Beiträge zur Anglistik 14 (Bonn: P. Hanstein, 1904).

Nancy Killebrew, '"I Never Died …": The Words, Music, and Influence of Joe Hill', *PBS* http://www.pbs.org/joehill/voices/article.html.

King Arthur's Death: The Middle English Stanzaic Morte Arthur and Alliterative Morte Arthure, edited by Larry Dean Benson (Indianapolis, Bobbs-Merrill, 1974).

Kormáks saga, edited by Einar Ól. Sveinsson, in *Vatnsdæla saga* (Reykjavík: Híð íslenszka fornritafélag, 1939).

Mark Kurlansky, *Cod: A Biography of the Fish that Changed the World* (New York: Walker and Co., 1997).

William Langland, *The Vision of William Concerning Piers Plowman*, edited by William Skeat (London: N. Trübner, 1867–85, 1886).

Monica Lantz and Bengt R. Jonsson, *Emigrantvisor* (Stockholm: LT, 1981).

Larousse Gastronomique (New York: Clarkson Potter, 2001).

Brunetto Latini, *Le Livre du Trésor,* edited by Francis J. Carmody (Berkeley: University of California Press, 1948).

The Laud Troy Book, edited by J. E. Wülfing, *EETS* 121, 122 (London: K. Paul, 1902).

Marc Lescarbot, *Histoire de la Nouvelle France*, edited and translated by W. L. Grant (Toronto: The Champlain Society, 1907–14).

Raphael Levy, *Trésor de la langue des juifs français au moyen âge* (Austin: University of Texas Press, 1964).

Lexique étymologique de l'irlandais ancien, compiled by Joseph Vendryes et al. (Dublin and Paris, Centre National de la Recherche Scientifique, 1959–).

Liber cure cocorum, Copied and edited from the Sloane MS. 1986, edited by Richard Morris (London and Berlin: Asher, 1862).

The Liber de Diversis Medicinis in the Thornton Manuscript, edited by M. S. Ogden, *EETS* 207 (London: Oxford University Press, 1938; rev. reprint 1969).

Anatoly Liberman, *Word Origins ... and How We Know Them* (Oxford: Oxford University Press, 2005).

Bryant Lillywhite, *London Signs: A Reference Book of London Signs from Earliest Times to About the Mid-Nineteenth Century* (London: Allen and Unwin, 1972).

LIV -Lexikon der indogermanischen Verben, compiled by Martin Kümmel and Helmut Rix, 2nd ed. (Wiesbaden: Reichert, 2001).

E. C. Llewellyn, *The Influence of Low Dutch on the English Vocabulary* (Oxford: Oxford University Press, 1936).

Willem Lodewijcksz, *D'eerste boeck, Historie van Indiën, waer inne verhaelt is de avontueren die de Hollandtsche schepen bejeghent zijn ...* (Amsterdam: [s.n.], 1598).

Anthony Lodge, 'Haggis and the Medieval French Connection', in *Essays in Memory of Michael Parkinson and Janine Dakyns*, edited by Christopher Smith (Norwich: School of Modern Languages and European Studies, University of East Anglia, 1996), 7–10.

The Manx Dictionary, compiled by John Kelly (Douglas: Manx Society, 1866).

P. Marchot, 'Notes étymologiques', *Romania* 47 (1921), 207–242.

G. J. Marcus, 'The Greenland Trade Route', *The Economic History Review* 7 (1954), 71–80.

Mediae Latinitatis lexicon minus, compiled by J. F. Niermeyer (Leiden: E. J. Brill, 2001).

Le Menagier de Paris, edited by Georgina E. Brereton and Janet M. Ferrier (Oxford: Clarendon, 1981).

Le Mesnagier de Paris, edited by Georgina E. Brereton and Janet M. Ferrier, and translated by Karin Ueltschi (Paris: Livre de Poche, 1994).

Paul Meyer, 'Le Dit du bon vin', *Romania* 11 (1882), 574–75.

Middle English Dictionary, edited by Robert E. Lewis et al. (Ann Arbor: University of Michigan Press; London: Oxford University Press, 1952–2001).

A. D. Mills, 'Some Late Middle English Fish Names', *Notes and Queries* 11 (1964), 170–71.

Jean-Yves Mollier, 'Émile Zola dans le ventre de la ville: De la réalité à la fiction', *Cahiers Naturalistes* 44 (1998), 263–73.

Bernard J. Muir, *The Exeter Anthology of Old English Poetry*, 2 vols (Exeter: University of Exeter Press 1994).

The Naval Chronicle (London).

Nederlands etymologisch woordenboek, compiled by Jan de Vries and F. de Tollenaere (Leiden: Brill, 1971).

Norrøn Ordbok, compiled by Leiv Heggested, Finn Hødnebø, and Erik Simensen, 4th ed. (Oslo: Det norske samlaget, 1993).

Nouveau recueil de contes, dits, fabliaux, et autres pièces inédites du XIIIe siècle, edited by Achille Jubinal (Paris: É. Pannier, 1839–42).

Colm Ó Baoill, 'Gaelic Ichthyonymy: Studying the Terms Used for Fish in Irish, Scottish Gaelic and Manx', *Zeitschrift für celtische Philologie* 46 (1994), 164–99.

Ordbok öfver svenska språket utgifven af Svenska akademien (Lund: Gleerup, 1898–1999).

The Ordinances of York, in T.F. Tout, *The Place of the Reign of Edward II in English History*, 2nd ed. (Manchester: Manchester, University Press, 1936).

Marijane Osborn, '"Skep" (*Beinenkorb*, **beoleap*) as a Culture-Specific Solution to *Exeter Book* Riddle 17', *ANQ* 18.1 (2005), 7–18.

Overland Monthly (San Francisco).

The Oxford Dictionary of English Etymology, compiled by C.T. Onions (Oxford: Clarendon, 1969).

Oxford English Dictionary, 2nd ed. (London: Oxford University Press, 1989); New Online ed. (Oxford: Oxford University Press, 2012), <http://dictionary.oed.com/>.

Jehan Palsgrave, *L'eclaircissement de la langue française* (Paris: Imprimerie nationale, 1530, repr. 1852, 1969).

The Paris Psalter and the Meters of Boethius, edited by George Philip Krapp (New York: Columbia University Press, 1932).

Jean-François de La Pérouse, *Voyage de La Pérouse autour du monde,* 4 vols (Paris: Imprimerie de la république, 1797).

Philadelphia Weekly Magazine (Philadelphia).

Edgar C. Polomé, 'The Problem of Etymological Dictionaries: The Case of German', *The Journal of Indo-European Studies* 11 (1983), 45–58.

Portugaliae Monumenta Cartographica, edited by Armando Cortesão and Avelino Teixeira da Mota (Lisboa:[s.n.], 1987).

Premier Livre De l'Histoire De La Navigation Avx Indes Orientales, Par Les Hollandois et des choses a eux advenues (Amsterdam: C. Nicolas, 1609).

The principall nauigations, voiages and discoueries of the English nation, edited by Richard Hakluyt (London: George Bishop and Ralph Newberie, 1589).

E.G. Quin, 'Truagh truagh an mhuc [Poor little pig]', *Hermathena* 101 (1965), 27–37.

Michael Quinion, 'Pie in the Sky', in *World Wide Words: Investigating International English from a British Viewpoint* (2001), http://www.quinion.com/words/qa/qa-pie1.htm.

Francois Rabelais, *Pantagruel,* edited by Verdun L. Saulnier (Geneva: Droz, 1967).

——, *Le Quart Livre,* edited by Robert Marichal (Geneva: Droz, 1947).

Hal Rammel, *Nowhere in America: The Big Rock Candy Mountain and Other Comic Utopias* (Urbana: Univ. of Illinois Press, 1990).

Ian Rankin, *Resurrection Men* (London: Orion, 2001).

Reallexikon der germanischen Altertumskunde, edited by Herbert Jankuhn et al., 2nd ed. (Berlin, New York: W. de Gruyter, 1968–2007).

Die 'Regularis Concordia' und ihre altenglische Interlinearversion, edited by Lucia Kornexl (Munich: Fink, 1993).

Laurits Rendboe, *Det gamle shetlandske sprog: George Low's ordliste fra 1774* (Odense: Odense Univrsitetsforlag, 1987).

Dieter Richter, *Schlaraffenland: Geschichte einer populären Phantasie* (Cologne: Diederichs, 1984).

Huw W. Ridgeway, 'William de Valence and his *familiares,* 1247–72', *Historical Research* 48 (1992), 239–57.

Robert d'Orbigny, *Le Conte de Floire et Blanchefleur*, edited and translated into French by Jean-Luc Leclanche (Paris: Honoré Champion, 2003).

Brian K. Roberts, 'The Rediscovery of Fishponds', in *Medieval Fish, Fisheries and Fishponds in England*, edited by Michael Aston, 2 vols, British Archaeological Reports (Oxford: B.A.R., 1988), 1, 9–16.

Callum Roberts, *The Unnatural History of the Sea* (Washington, DC: Island Press, 2007).

William Rothwell, 'A Mis-Judged Author and His Mis-Used Text: Walter de Bibbesworth and His "Tretiz"', *The Modern Language Review* 77 (1982), 282–293.

——, 'Glimpses into our Ignorance of the Anglo-Norman Lexis', in *Medieval French Textual Studies in Memory of T. B. W. Reid*, edited by Ian Short (London: Anglo-Norman Text Society, 1984), 167–79.

——, 'Of Kings and Queens, or Nets and Frogs: Anglo-French Homonymics', *French Studies* 48 (1994), 257–73.

——, 'The Place of *Femina* in Anglo-Norman Studies', *Studia Neophilologica* 70 (1998), 55–82.

Frank-E. Rouvier, 'Datations nouvelles', *Français Modern* 24 (1956), 220–22.

John Row, *The historie of the Kirk of Scotland, M.D.LVIII.–M.DC.XXXVII* (Edinburgh: Maitland Club, 1842).

John Russell, *John Russell's Boke of Nurture*, in *Early English Meals and Manners,* edited by F. J. Furnivall, *EETS* 32 (London: N. Trübner & Co., 1868).

Hans Sachs, *Werke in der Reihenfolge ihrer Entstehung*, edited by Wolfgang F. Michael and Roger A. Crockett, 3 vols (Bern: Lang, 1996).

L.F. Salzman, *English Industries of the Middle Ages* (Oxford: Clarendon, 1923).

George Sand, *Le Meunier d'Angibault* (Brussels: Cans et compagnie, 1845).

William Sayers, 'Diet and Fantasy in Eleventh-Century Ireland: *The Vision of Mac Con Glinne*', *Food and Foodways* 6 (1994), 1–17.

——, 'Some Fishy Etymologies: Eng. *cod,* Norse *þorskr,* Sp. *bacalao,* Du. *kabeljauw*', *NOWELE* 41 (2002), 17–30.

——, '*Exeter Book* Riddle 17 and the L-Rune: British **lester* "vessel, oat-straw hive"?' *ANQ* 19.2 (2006), 4–9.

——, 'The Etymologies of *dog* and *cur*', *The Journal of Indo-European Studies* 36 (2008), 401–10.

——, 'Brewing Ale in Walter of Bibbesworth's 13 c. French Treatise for English Housewives', *Studia Etymologica Cracoviensia* 14 (2009), 255–67.

——, 'An Early Set of Bee-Keeping Words in Anglo-Norman French and Middle English', *ANQ* 22: 2 (2009), 8–13.

——, 'The Genealogy of the Haggis', *Miscelánea* 39 (2009), 103–10.

——, 'Learning French in a Late Thirteenth-Century English Bake-House', *Petits Propos Culinaires* 88 (2009), 35–53.

——, 'Capstan, Windlass and Winch, Hoist, Haul and Tow', Notes & Queries 57 (2010), 465–73.

——, 'Flax and Linen in Walter of Bibbesworth's 13 c. French Treatise for English Housewives', Medieval Clothing and Textiles 6 (2010), 111–26.

——, 'The Etymologies of Some Terms of Disparagement: culprit, get (and brat), gull, job, niggle, prig, vagrant', Notes and Queries 58 (2011), 31–42.

——, 'Challenges Facing English Etymology in the Twenty-First Century, with Illustrations', Studia Neophilologica 84 (2012), 1–25.

——, 'Salmagundi', Notes & Queries 59 (2012), 335–37.

——, 'Brose, Atholl brose, spurtle, and thivel', Scottish Language 31–32 (2012–2013), 59–63.

——, 'Gaulish in French Lexis and Lexicography: The Case of buta "hut, small dwelling"', French Studies Bulletin 34 (2013), 1–3.

——, 'A Source for Dr. Johnson's Self-Referential Entry lexicographer', ANQ 26:1 (2013), 17–19.

——, 'Stew, sty, and steward', Notes & Queries 60.3 (2013), 373–76.

Beverly Scafidel, 'Smollett's Humphry Clinker', Explicator 30 (1972), item 54.

Marie Scarpa, 'Le Ventre de Paris ou "le monde immonde" d'Émile Zola: Lecture ethnocritique', Iris 19 (2000), 45–55.

Karl-Horst Schmidt, 'Zum "Schwein" im Keltischen', in Man and the Animal World: Studies in Archaeozoology, Archaeology, Anthropology and Palaeolinguistics in Memoriam Sándor Bökönyi, edited by Peter Anreiter (Budapest: Archaeolingua Alapítvány, 1998), 713–16.

Christian Schmitt, '"Isti pisces inveniuntur in Mosa": ein Beitrag zur französischen Ichthyonymie', in Studien zur romanischen Wortgeschichte: Festschrift für Heinrich Kuen zum 90. Geburtstag, edited by Gerhard Ernst and Arnulf Stefenelli (Stuttgart: Steiner, 1989), 161–73.

Peter Schrijver, Studies in British Celtic Historical Phonology (Amsterdam and Atlanta: Rodopi, 1995).

Georges de Seyturiers, Manuel administratif, in Paul Benoit, L'Histoire de l'abbaye et de la terre de Saint-Claude, compiled by Abbé de Ferroul-Montgaillard (Lons-le-Saunier: Impr. de F. Gauthier, 1854–55).

R.J. Smith, 'The Swanscombe Legend and the Historiography of Kentish Gavelkind', in Medievalism in the Modern World: Essays in Honour of Leslie J. Workman, edited by Richard Utz and Tom Shippey (Turnhout: Brepols, 1998), 85–103.

Tobias Smollett, The Adventures of Sir Launcelot Greaves (London: J. Coote, 1762),

William Smyth, The Sailor's Word-Book (London: Blacke and Son, 1897).

Snorri Sturluson, Edda: Skáldskaparmál, edited by Anthony Faulkes (London: Viking Society for Northern Research, 1988).

Songs to Fan the Flames of Discontent: The Little Red Songbook (Ypsilanti, Mich.: Industrial Workers of the World, 1995).

The South English Legendary ... from Corpus Christi College Cambridge MS. 145 and British Museum MS. Harley 2277 ..., edited by C. D'Evelyn and A. J. Mill, 3 vols (London: Oxford University Press, 1956–59).

Taillevent, *The Viandier of Taillevent: An Edition of All Extant Manuscripts*, edited by Terence Scully (Ottawa: University of Ottawa Press, 1988).

Alistair Tebbit, 'Household Knights and Military Service under the Direction of Edward II', in *The Reign of Edward II New Perspectives*, edited by Gwilym Dodd and Antony Musson (York: York Medieval Press and Boydell & Brewer, 2006), 76–96.

Rudolf Thurneysen, *A Grammar of Old Irish*, translated by D. A. Binchy and Osborn Bergin (Dublin: Dublin Institute for Advanced Studies, 1946).

Wim Tigges, 'Signs and Solutions: A Semiotic Approach to the Exeter Book Riddles', in *This Noble Craft: Proceedings of the Tenth Research Symposium of the Dutch and Belgian University Teachers of Old and Middle English and Historical Linguistics*, edited by Erik Kooper (Amsterdam: Rodopi, 1991), 59–82.

Trésor de la langue française, edited by Paul Imbs (Paris: Editions du Centre national de la recherche scientifique, 1971–94). *Trésor de la langue française informatisé*, < http://atilf.atilf.fr.>.

Kate E. Tunstall, '"Crânement beau tout de même": Still Life and *Le Ventre de Paris*', French Studies 58 (2004), 177–87.

Thomas Twining, *Recreations and studies of a country clergyman* (London: J. Murray, 1882).

William Twiti, *The Middle English Text of 'The Art of Hunting' by William Twiti, with a Parallel Text of the Anglo-Norman 'L'art de venerie' by William Twiti*, edited by D. Scott-Macnab, Middle English Texts 40 (Heidelberg: Winter, 2009).

Two Fifteenth-Century Cookery-Books, edited by Thomas Austin (London: N. Trübner & Co., 1888).

Richard Unger, *Beer in the Middle Ages and Renaissance* (Philadelphia: University of Pennsylvania Press, 2004).

François Pierre de la Varenne, *Le Cuisinier François* (La Haye: A. Vlacq, 1654).

Variétés historiques et littéraires; recueil de pièces volantes rares et curieuses en prose et en vers, edited by Édouard Fournier (Paris: P. Jannet, 1855–63).

Walter de Bibbesworth, *Le Tretiz*, in *Femina, now first printed from a unique ms. in the library of Trinity college*, edited by William Aldis Wright (Cambridge: Cambridge University Press, 1909).

——, *Le Traité de Walter de Bibbesworth sur la langue française*, edited by A. Owen (Paris: Presses Universitaires de France, 1929).

——, *Le Tretiz*, edited by William Rothwell (Aberystwyth: Anglo-Norman Society, 1990), The Anglo-Norman On-line Hub.

——, *The Treatise of Walter of Bibbesworth*, translated by Andrew Dalby (Devon: Prospect Books, 2012).

William Woys Weaver, 'The Lughnasa Platter: The Celtic Origins of Christmas Frumenty', *Petits Propos Culinaires* 96 (2012), 53–58.

Christian Weise, *The tre yppersta ertz-narrar vti hela werden: Vtur många dåraktige händelser samman sökte, och alle interessenter til bättre eftertän-kiande framställt* (Stockholm: Burchardi, 1697).

Craig Williamson, editor and translator, *A Feast of Creatures: Anglo-Saxon Riddle Songs* (Philadelphia: University of Pennsylvania Press, 1982).

Pauline Wahl Willis, 'Commestibles et commérages dans *Le Ventre de Paris*', *Émile Zola and Naturalism* (*Excavatio*) 14: 1–2 (2001), 63–72.

C.M. Woolgar, *The Great Household in Late Medieval England* (New Haven: Yale University Press, 1999).

The Wordsworth Dictionary of Pub Names, edited by Leslie Dunkling and Gordon Wright (Ware, Hertfordshire: Woodsworth Editions, 1994).

The World Encompassed and Analogous Contemporary Documents Concerning Sir Francis Drake's Circumnavigation of the World, edited by N. M. Penzer (New York: Argonaut Press, 1926).

Wright's Anglo-Saxon and Old English Vocabularies, edited by Richard Paul Wülcker, 2nd ed. (London, Trübner & Co., 1884).

Wynnere and Wastoure, edited by S. Trigg, (London: Early English Text, and New York: Putnam, 1898–1905).

Émile Zola, *Le Ventre de Paris*, in *Œuvres complètes*, edited by Henri Mitterand (Paris: Nouveau Monde, 2002).

——, *The Belly of Paris = Le Ventre de Paris*, translated by Brian Nelson (New York: Oxford University Press, 2007).

——, *The Belly of Paris*, translated by Mark Kurlansky (New York: Modern Library, 2009).

Koldo Zuazo, 'The Basque Country and the Basque Language: An Overview of the External History of the Basque Language', in *Towards a History of the Basque Language*, edited by José Ignacio Hualde, Joseba A. Lakarra, and R. L. Trask (Amsterdam: Benjamins, 1995).

Julian de Zulueta, 'The Basque Whaler', *The Mariner's Mirror* 86 (2000), 261–71.